More

BLACK GRIEF/WHITE GRIEVANCE

"In this soberly eloquent book, Juliet Hooker shows that our common humanity requires all Americans to accept that losses of unjust privileges are not valid grounds for grievance, and that the burdens of unjust losses must not include duties to heroically overcome them. By refusing these wrongful conceptions of loss, we may find more gainful paths for ourselves and others."

—Rogers M. Smith, University of Pennsylvania

"With *Black Grief/White Grievance*, Juliet Hooker examines the two terms of her book's title in all their profound contradictions. Drawing on W.E.B. Du Bois, Claudia Rankine, and many others, she provides the outlines of a racial system built in part on affectual politics, but without ignoring structural racism. By contrasting Black grief and white grievance so coherently and emotionally, by looking at the political weight of racist affect, of white shame and rage, of continuous Black mourning and attempts to transcend it, Hooker makes a serious contribution to the theory of racism. This startling and promising book is not to be missed!"

—Howard Winant, University of California, Santa Barbara

BLACK GRIEF/WHITE GRIEVANCE

Black Grief/ White Grievance

THE POLITICS OF LOSS

JULIET HOOKER

PRINCETON UNIVERSITY PRESS
PRINCETON & OXFORD

Published by Princeton University Press
41 William Street, Princeton, New Jersey 08540
99 Banbury Road, Oxford OX2 6JX

press.princeton.edu

First paperback printing, 2025
Paperback ISBN 978-0-691-24034-7
Cloth ISBN 978-0-691-24303-0
ISBN (e-book) 978-0-691-24302-3

Library of Congress Control Number: 2023937259

British Library Cataloging-in-Publication Data is available

Editorial: Rob Tempio and Chloe Coy
Production Editorial: Karen Carter
Jacket/Cover Design: Heather Hansen
Production: Erin Suydam
Publicity: Kate Hensley and Kathryn Stevens

This book has been composed in Arno

To Chris and Christian, my pandemic bubble buddies

CONTENTS

ACKNOWLEDGMENTS

THE KERNEL OF what would eventually become this book emerged in the summer of 2014, when the Ferguson protests erupted. Feeling the urgency of the historical moment and the need to bring the tools at my disposal as a political theorist to understanding a resurgent moment of Black activism crystallized in the Movement for Black Lives, I organized the panel, "Black Political Thought after Ferguson," at the Western Political Science Association in 2015. That panel, and the conversations that emerged from it, resulted in a journal issue coedited with Barnor Hesse and the creation of the Black Politics-History-Theory Workshop. The workshop provided an invaluable collective space to develop the ideas contained in this book. Completing the book was daunting because the period in which I finished writing the manuscript was marked by the emergence of the Covid-19 pandemic, the racial justice protests of 2020, and the subsequent backlash against them, as well as efforts to undermine the legitimate presidential election results of 2020, all issues that it seemed like a book about political loss needed to address. The challenges we face today are formidable, but my hope is that this book will in some small way contribute to the efforts of the activists who are leading the way. I am inspired by their imagination and commitment and indebted to their labor, as we all are.

I have a deep debt of gratitude to all the people and institutions who supported this book. The initial research and writing began while I was at the University of Texas at Austin, where I received a Faculty Research grant in support of the project in 2016 and 2017. The contours of the book took shape after I moved to Brown University, where the majority of the research and writing have taken place. Brown has been an ideal intellectual community that enriched the project in innumerable ways. Colleagues throughout the university were enthusiastic about the book and provided insightful feedback at various stages. I want to thank the political theory group in political science and other colleagues in the department and throughout the university, in particular Ainsley LeSure, Melvin Rogers, Kevin Quashie, and Tricia Rose. A year of research leave in 2019–20, a Presidential Faculty Research Award, Humanities Research Funds, and a Collaborative Humanities Course Award from the Cogut Institute for the Humanities were instrumental in allowing me to complete this book. The last allowed me to codevelop the course Political Loss and Activism with my colleague and friend Emily Owens, who also read drafts of chapters and had many conversations with me about the ideas in the book. I also benefitted immensely from funny, insightful, passionate conversations about political activism, loss, and Black protest with graduate and undergraduate students in various seminars at Brown. Their enthusiasm renewed my commitment to finishing the book when I needed it most.

A book about loss inevitably has to engage with affect and aesthetics, and I am extremely grateful to the artists who have allowed me to use their work to convey difficult ideas about sacrifice, grief, and mourning better than words could. Thanks to Jonathan Bachman, the Beinecke Rare Books and Manuscript Library at Yale University, Brooks Permissions, Eve Ewing,

Ross Gay, Mike Luckovich, Nate Marshall, and Claudia Rankine for allowing me to reproduce their words and images. Early versions of chapters 1 and 2 were published as "Black Protest/White Grievance: On the Problem of White Political Imaginations *Not* Shaped by Loss," *South Atlantic Quarterly* 116, no. 3 (2017): 483–504; and "Black Lives Matter and the Paradoxes of U.S. Black Politics: From Democratic Sacrifice to Democratic Repair," *Political Theory* 44, no. 4 (2016): 448–69. Thanks to Sage Publishing and Duke University Press for allowing me to reuse portions of those articles.

I was privileged to be able to present drafts of all parts of the book at conferences, workshops, and talks where audience members and fellow participants provided invaluable comments, rigorous feedback, and suggestions for further reading. I have not been able to acknowledge all these contributions individually, but the book was immeasurably enriched thanks to their input. Early drafts of the introduction and portions of chapter 1 were presented at the University Center for Human Values at Princeton University, the University of British Columbia Political Science Department, the New School for Social Research General Seminar, the Center for Global Ethics and Politics at the City University of New York Graduate Center, and the Political Concepts Conference at Brown University. Initial versions of chapter 1 were presented at the first Black Politics-Theory-History Workshop at Northwestern University, the Political Philosophy Workshop at Brown, the Imagination and Social Change Conference at Claremont McKenna College, and the Joint Political Theory Workshop at Duke University and the University of North Carolina. Early versions of chapter 2 were presented at the American Political Science Association, the Western Political Science Association, the University of Washington, and the Rhetoric and Politics of Protest and Direct Action Conference at Northwestern University. Chapter 3 benefitted from feedback from participants in the Philosophy, Social Thought, and Criticism Workshop at Harvard University and the Political Theory Workshop at Yale University. Early drafts of chapter 4 were presented at the American Political Science Association, the Western Political Science Association, the Political Theory Workshop at Georgetown, the University of Chicago Political Theory Workshop, the II Black Politics-History-Theory Workshop at the University of Texas at Austin, the Seeing beyond the Veil Conference at Brown, and the University of Minnesota Political Theory Colloquium. I was also privileged to be able to discuss an early version of the conclusion at the III Black Political Thought and History Workshop, co-organized by Vanderbilt University and Johns Hopkins University. Thanks to all who read, engaged, and provided suggestions in all these venues. You made this a much better book.

Getting a book from the manuscript stage to the final product requires a lot of collective effort, and I appreciate the enthusiasm and care with which Rob Tempio, Chloe Coy, and everyone at Princeton University Press have approached this book. I would also like to thank the anonymous reviewers of the manuscript for their rigorous, detailed, and insightful feedback. Thanks also to Kim Greenwell, who stepped in at the end of the project and provided excellent copyediting that allowed me to finish on time. Writing is often a lonely endeavor made less so by doing it with others. Thanks to all my writing buddies along the way, including the 22 Writing Days in '22 Summer Digital Writing Retreat organized by Sara Angevine, which provided the push I needed to complete final revisions.

This book has benefitted from dialogue and engagement with the work of so many interlocutors, mentors, and friends, but there are three individuals in particular who deserve special thanks. Lawrie Balfour was an early enthusiastic supporter of the book, and she provided keen insights on the introduction in particular that were extremely helpful. Bonnie Honig suggested the book title and was an invaluable sounding board throughout about everything from the role of affect in loss and the relationship between grief and grievance. At a key moment she helped me realize that I was working on two different projects simultaneously, which allowed me to finish this one. Shatema Threadcraft has been a fellow traveler and key interlocutor throughout this project from start to finish. She suggested a chapter reorganization that was essential to clarifying the book's overall argument. She has been there throughout the ups and downs of writing, and her brilliant insights on gender and Black political thought are an inspiration that continues to shape my own work. I also want to acknowledge two towering figures, mentors, and friends who went to join the ancestors while this book was being completed and who are sorely missed, Leith Mullings and Charles Mills. Leith and I were both members of RAIAR, the Anti-racist Research and Action Network of the Americas. Her research on the Movement for Black Lives was central to RAIAR's collective thinking about racist backlash across the Americas, which has shaped my own analysis. Charles's work has always been a touchstone. This book's title is a homage to his *Black Rights/White Wrongs*.

I could not have finished this book (or made it through the Covid-19 pandemic) without the support, laughter, and community of friends and family near and far who sustained me throughout. Jossianna Arroyo, Lizzette Colon and the rest of the Williams '94 zoom crew (Chris Jones, Tina Mahajan, Tanya Nicholson, and Anim Steel), Jay D'Ercola, Kate Gordy, Charlie Hale, Sophia Jordán-Wallace, Megan Ming Francis, Dalizza

Rodriguez, Keisha-Khan Perry, and Sean Theriault, thanks so much for the camaraderie and reminders of all we have to be grateful for. My sister, Thalia Hooker, and our extended Coe family, keep me grounded and have been there since the very beginning.

My deepest gratitude, as always, is to my parents, Thalia Coe and Ray Hooker. These are dark times for democracy in Nicaragua, and my parents' steadfastness and resilience in the face of ongoing assaults on civil society are an inspiration. In them I have always had a model of what it means to work in ways big and small to make the world around you a better place. Finally, to Chris and Christian, thanks for all the joy, love, and shared adventures. You are a light in dark times.

BLACK GRIEF/WHITE GRIEVANCE

INTRODUCTION

What Is Political Loss?

> So many people have reached out to me telling me they're sorry this happened to my family. Well, don't be sorry, 'cause this has been happening to my family for a long time, longer than I can account for. It happened to Emmett Till . . . Philando, Mike Brown, Sandra . . . and I've shed tears for every single one of these people that it's happened to. This is nothing new. I'm not sad. I'm not sorry. I'm angry. And I'm tired. I haven't cried one time. I stopped crying years ago. I am numb. I have been watching police murder people that look like me for years. I'm also a Black history minor. So not only have I been watching it in the 30 years that I've been on this planet, but I've been watching it for years before we were even alive. I'm not sad. I don't want your pity. I want change.
>
> —LETETRA WIDEMAN

> We're not backing down anymore. . . . This is our country.
>
> —JANUARY 6 INSURRECTIONIST

LOSS IS UBIQUITOUS in US politics and society today. Most glaringly, the global Covid-19 pandemic has visited untold losses worldwide. From the horrific death toll, which as of this writing surpasses one million in the United States alone and six million worldwide, to the economic devastation it has wrought, the lives disrupted and upended, the foreclosure of collective occasions to grieve the dead or be with loved ones, and even the smaller, quotidian losses of being forced to dispense with tactile human contact (a handshake, a kiss on the cheek, a hug) because of physical distancing, the losses caused by Covid-19 continue to mount. At the same time, the pandemic and inadequate government responses to it have further exposed existing differential patterns of racialized precarity.[1] From the composition of the not-until-recently-recognized-as-such essential workforce, which is dominated by women of color; to which groups have been disproportionately infected, hospitalized, and killed by the virus (Black, Latinx, and Indigenous peoples),[2] while others (mostly white) protest any government measures to curb the spread, such as mask mandates; to unequal access to vaccines, yawning racial and class disparities in the impact of the pandemic unequivocally demonstrate that we are not in fact "all in this together," as politicians are wont to claim in moments of national crisis.[3] Loss is widespread, but it is by no means evenly distributed. Some losses are also compounded. As the *Washington Post* noted: "Deaths from covid-19 are causing gaps in grief, gaps that are tragically familiar: Black, American Indian and Alaska Native communities suffer a higher bereavement burden given persistent disparities in life expectancy and mortality."[4] At the same time, if the losses that accompany a global pandemic are made political by the disparate effects of state action and inaction and the way existing inequalities exacerbate ostensibly "natural" disasters, other kinds of racialized losses that have indelibly shaped US political development seemingly reached a critical inflection point during the Obama and Trump eras—with grave consequences for US democracy.

Black Grief/White Grievance analyzes the impact of loss on the political imaginations of citizens, as well as the civic practices they develop in response to it.

As the paired epigraphs by Letetra Wideman and one of the thousands of January 6 insurrectionists powerfully illustrate, in the Obama and Trump eras, the two most important forces driving racial politics in the United States have been Black grief and white grievance. Black grief and white grievance are linked because white grievance obscures and supplants Black grief and is often mobilized in response to it. White grievance functions to ensure white priority and inattentiveness to Black loss. It is also the greatest obstacle to the prospect of genuine multiracial democracy in the United States. The ongoing refusal of Donald Trump and his supporters to accept the loss of the 2020 election—which culminated in the attempted insurrection at the US Capitol on January 6, 2021—finally prompted some sectors of the country to begin grappling with this danger. The violent white riot at the US Capitol did not come out of nowhere, however. During Trump's administration long-simmering cries of white victimhood crystallized into a potent politics of white grievance that frames the United States as a white country under siege from threats from within and without at the hands of people of color, such as "ungrateful" and "unpatriotic" Blacks, "criminal" Mexican and Latin American immigrants, "Muslim" terrorists, "violent" refugees, the "kung flu" or "Chinese virus," and so on.[5] Simultaneously, the continued protests for racial justice galvanized by rampant police shootings of Black citizens amid a deadly pandemic that has disproportionately affected people of color, coupled with the key role played by Black activists—particularly Black women—in the electoral defeat of racist right-wing forces in the 2020 election, highlight the continued burdens placed on Black citizens within a white democracy that has never lived up to its egalitarian rhetoric. In the measured words of political scientist Zoltan Hajnal, "America's democracy is racially uneven. Whites are likely to end up on the top as winners, and racial and ethnic minorities are likely to end up on the bottom as losers."[6]

Black Grief/White Grievance takes loss seriously as a key question for political theorists and ordinary citizens. It is centrally concerned with how loss is mobilized politically. How political loss is distributed among citizens is a crucial question for democratic politics, as Danielle Allen has argued.[7] Uneven distributions of the democratic labor of losing, especially along preexisting hierarchies such as race, belie the fundamental tenets of equal citizenship. Yet certain kinds of entrenched structural inequality—such as white supremacy—precisely function to obscure this uneven distribution of democratic labor. Political loss is also not a naturally occurring phenomenon. Rather, our political communities and society have been constituted to produce differential losses and to profit from the losses of nonwhite peoples. As Megan Ming Francis observes, "The current vulnerability of American democracy has much to do with the nation's long history of anti-Black state violence . . . yet, despite the enduring influence of racial violence, scholars of American politics do not usually treat it as a durable threat to democracy." Even in this moment of rising concern about democratic "backsliding" in the United States—a framing that overstates the extent to which equal citizenship had been achieved—there is a tendency to underestimate "the impact of anti-Black violence and its relationship to racial authoritarianism."[8] Being a good democratic citizen entails learning to accept justified political losses. At a time when the racist pathologies of US democracy are painfully apparent, we must therefore ask: Which citizens have historically been expected to develop this crucial civic capacity? Grappling directly with the question of political loss can help us to decide which losses need to be attended to in a democratic political community, so that those who have already historically made the greatest sacrifices do not continue to do so. It can help us think through questions such as: What is the wrong kind of instrumentalization of grief? How should democracies respond to those who refuse to accept legitimate losses? How already disempowered citizens respond to loss, the additional work they have to do to make their losses visible, is a central concern of this book. So, too, is the question of what obligations we have in response to this unequal distribution of democratic labor. At minimum, we have a duty to actively witness and work to redress such losses. One of my central claims is that while Black grief has historically been mobilized by Black activists in service of Black freedom, we must reckon with the loss this entails.

The account of political loss in this book is by no means exhaustive.[9] *Black Grief/White Grievance* is primarily concerned with US racial politics. I draw most closely on the work of African American thinkers and activists, ranging from the post–Civil War era to the contemporary moment, but they are not the only Black thinkers to wrestle with questions of political loss. Indeed, the issue of how loss is mobilized politically has broader global purchase. Nostalgia for past colonial dominance and racial resentment against various "others" is fueling support for racist, far-right political parties in various European countries and played a central role in Brexit, for example.[10] Likewise, in Latin America, we see racist backlash driving support for authoritarianism (most notably illustrated by the far-right administration of Brazilian president Jair Bolsonaro), at the same time as the grieving activism of mothers of those killed by police and state violence (who in countries such as Brazil are primarily

Black) has been the driving force in calls for state accountability.[11] In all these cases, as in the United States, citizens are mobilizing in response to different forms of political loss.

What Is Political Loss?

Political theorists have approached the kinds of experiences I include in the category "loss" by turning to two sets of analogous terms: grief or mourning on the one hand, and harm or injustice on the other hand. Judith Butler, for example, argues that grief can serve as the ground for political solidarity because it is an unavoidable human experience. She stipulates that while there is no "human condition that is universally shared . . . all of us have some notion of what it is to have lost somebody. Loss has made a tenuous 'we' of us all. . . . This means that each of us is constituted politically in part by virtue of the social vulnerability of our bodies."[12] For Butler, grief has political implications and is closely associated with corporeal vulnerability. Yet loss is not simply suffering. Suffering accompanies loss but is not reducible to it. And while grief is one response to loss, it is not the only one. Loss is also not interchangeable with harm or injury. By harm or injury, we generally understand a wrong unjustly inflicted or suffered, which often includes the violation or infringement of a person's rights. As Judith Shklar has argued, this way of thinking about the difference between misfortune and injustice, between random and purposive harm, tends to focus on intent and whether or not rules were broken. Instead, she argues, the focus should be on the political choices made in response to suffering. "It is not the origin of injury, but the possibility of preventing and reducing its costs, that allows us to judge whether there was or was not unjustifiable passivity in the face of disaster.... If the victim's suffering is due to accident or misfortune but could be remedied by public agents, then it is unjust if nothing is done to help."[13] Even Shklar's focus on how victims perceive suffering does not fully capture the experience of loss, however. Injustice or harm is accompanied by, or produces, experiences of loss, but there are elements of loss that exceed these categories. While their applicability in individual cases is often disputed, harm and injustice are legible categories that are adjudicated by answering questions about intent and political efficacy. For example, whether the perpetrators meant to cause harm, and whether there was a dereliction of duty on the part of public officials, and so on. In contrast, there is an ineffable, inarticulable dimension to loss. There are aspects of racialized harm that are difficult to specify and that compound loss. When one is denied a job or a promotion as a result of racism, an injustice has taken place, but there is also the additional burden that comes from knowing that this is not the first nor the last time this will happen in a racist society, that these kinds of harms are happening to others as well, and that many of one's fellow citizens will not acknowledge that an injustice took place. There are costs to trying to make an injustice visible, and there are some harms that can never be fully repaired, and it is these elements that loss captures and is attentive to. Loss encompasses inchoate affective dimensions that exceed categories such as harm or injustice.

In fact, one of the key features of political loss that this book draws attention to is its aesthetic and affective registers. As we seek to name or make visible that which is unrepresentable, aesthetics and affect are ways to try to make the unseen visible and audible.[14] Loss is often described as incapable of being fully articulated in words, and the aesthetic and affective forms that evoke it as producing overwhelming and unspeakable responses. Frederick Douglass, for example, whose considerable rhetorical skills contributed so much to the cause of abolition, described being overcome with emotion long after his escape from slavery upon merely hearing slave spirituals, which "told a tale of woe which was then altogether beyond my feeble comprehension; they were tones loud, long, and deep; they breathed the prayer and complaint of souls boiling over with the bitterest anguish."[15] Similarly, in her theorization of Black visuality as a practice of refusal, Tina Campt describes "images that require the labor of feeling with or through them." It is this "labor of feeling" evoked by aesthetic objects—a labor that requires attention and solidarity as suggested by the phrasing "feeling *with* or through"—that is a key aspect of loss.[16] Indeed, affect and aesthetics play a central role in efforts to mobilize political loss. Harriet Jacobs and Ida B. Wells, two of the key African American theorists of loss analyzed in this book, shift between fact and affect in their rhetorical appeals. Like other Black intellectuals and numerous political movements, from ACT UP to the Movement for Black Lives, Wells and Jacobs move between dispassionate rhetorical modes and more explicitly affective appeals in their attempts to make Black suffering legible. Activists seeking to make loss visible enumerate or quantify the magnitude of loss and tell stories that personalize or humanize it—as in lists of the dead, die-ins, or the AIDS quilt, for instance—and affect and aesthetics are central to both of these strategies. The visual and poetic interludes that precede each chapter in *Black Grief/White Grievance* reflect the centrality of affect and aesthetics to apprehending loss. In this way, the structure of the book itself moves between fact and affect to try to convey the ineffable dimensions of loss.

Loss is therefore more than grief, suffering, harm, or injury, and it has an inchoate, inexpressible quality, but not all losses are necessarily political. The death of a loved one is a loss, but it is not necessarily political. It is political, however, if it is the result of lack of action to alleviate predictable suffering as Shklar suggests, or if the person is a victim of state violence. Losses also become political as a result of civic action to make them visible, as victims seek to have their sense of injustice recognized. Political loss can therefore involve the loss of someone or something. For instance, many of the examples of Black grief analyzed in this book are about the loss of lives (deaths) as a result of white violence. This is not the only kind of loss Black people have suffered, but it is one around which the most visible and consistent political mobilization has occurred. For Indigenous peoples, in contrast, territorial dispossession and denial of self-determination have arguably been more politically salient losses, although loss of life and loss of land are intricately connected in the eliminationist logic of settler colonialism.[17] But political loss also takes other forms. Loss can be anticipatory, as in the case of white grievance. It can be real or perceived, and its political potency does not depend on its veracity. While political loss can therefore take many forms, there are three aspects of the "political" in political loss that I explore in this book: (1) loss that is rendered political as a result of state action/inaction, (2) loss that becomes a site for political mobilization, and (3) losses that democratic citizens—especially more privileged citizens—have an obligation to acknowledge and attend to.

The most obvious form of political loss is defeat in an electoral contest or policy debate. If some but not all types of loss are political, some forms of politics are inevitably about loss. Democracy is one of these. We tend to view democracy primarily in terms of empowerment, but democratic politics requires both exercising power and accepting defeat. In democracies, loss is supposed to be an unavoidable feature of political activity for all citizens. Acceptance of loss is a key civic capacity in a democracy. Hence the subtitle of a recent documentary about Confederate monuments and the Lost Cause aptly describes it as "a story about sore losers."[18] To be a good democratic citizen, one must learn to accept justified political losses. As Allen observes, "democracies inspire in citizens an aspiration to rule and yet require citizens constantly to live with the fact that they do not." Democracies promise citizens "autonomy, freedom, and sovereignty," but these cannot be simultaneously realized for all. "No democratic citizen, adult or child, escapes the necessity of losing at some point in a public decision. . . . An honest account of collective democratic action must begin by acknowledging that communal decisions inevitably benefit some citizens at the expense of others, even when the whole community generally benefits. . . . The hard truth of democracy is that some citizens are always giving things up for others."[19] Political loss is widespread in democracy but is considered legitimate insofar as it is equally distributed. Historically, however, US democracy has never distributed loss equitably.[20] White supremacy assigned to African Americans the pain of losing and reserved for whites the joys of untrammeled political rule, of domination. It was not until after the civil rights victories of the 1960s that the United States ostensibly moved beyond what Allen calls "the two-pronged citizenship of domination and acquiescence."[21] Yet we continue to see different expectations of political loss today that reflect white supremacy's uneven distribution of democratic labor.

Another important sense in which losses are political is whether they are the result of state action or inaction. Individual losses are rendered political by virtue of structural inequalities and systemic disparities that are allowed to persist. For example, while there are still generalized risks to the mother's health associated with childbirth, an individual Black woman's death from complications as a result of maternal mortality is not "natural" but political in light of current racial disparities in health care. Black mothers giving birth in the United States die at three to four times the rate of white mothers.[22] While some of these unequal outcomes can be attributed to economic factors such as disparate access to good medical care, studies have shown that minority patients tend to receive a lower quality of care than nonminorities, even when they have the same types of health insurance and the same ability to pay for health care. Moreover, employment opportunities (which determine health care options in the United States) are also shaped by histories of racial discrimination in the workplace. Current racial disparities in maternal mortality are therefore political losses, even in the absence of direct medical malpractice or negligence. Personal losses become political in part when the context in which they are produced is shaped by collective injustice.

In his analysis of the different "pedagogies of grief" developed by Ralph Emerson and W.E.B. Du Bois in the wake of the death of their sons, Thomas Dumm points to the role of racism in Du Bois's loss in contrast to that of Emerson, who was exempt from this added burden.[23] While both suffered losses (to use my terms), Du Bois's was political, but Emerson's was not:

> So if we are to acknowledge his [Du Bois's] loss, we must try to reckon into the calculus of loss this horrible stain of injustice as part of the experience of Du Bois and not of Emerson. And as democratic theorists, we must try to reckon not only his loss, but his loss as multiplied by the losses of millions of others who one by one have so suffered it directly as its most prominent victims, and indirectly as witnesses who have so far been muted in response to the damage it has done to us, and partially, as our collective inheritance of a culture.[24]

Du Bois's grief has to be understood within a larger context not just of the horrific anti-Black violence that was routine in 1899, but also of ongoing racial health disparities that reflect the institutionalized devaluation of Black life. Du Bois's son died from diphtheria—for which a vaccine had become available in the mid-1890s, leading to precipitous declines in mortality—because he did not have access to adequate medical care in racially segregated Atlanta.[25] While Burghardt was not violently attacked, he was nevertheless killed by racism. His death therefore corresponds to my understanding of political loss.

Losses also *become* political through the process of people mobilizing around them. Simply having suffered a loss does not mean that it will be recognized as such. The category "political loss" does not exist as a preexisting thing outside of or antecedent to politics. Losses become political partly as a result of the efforts of different constituencies (activists, elected officials, artists, academics, etc.) to make them visible and to establish that they require a collective response. Consider, for example, two highly visible examples of loss in recent decades: the September 11, 2001, attacks and the Me Too movement against sexual violence. Many recent texts by political theorists on mourning, grief, and loss take 9/11 as a point of departure because it is seen as an indisputable example of national loss. We immediately recognize the death of a victim of 9/11 as political because it was the result of an attack by foreign actors. In contrast, it required the mobilization of the #metoo movement for the losses women have accrued as a result of sexual violence and sexual harassment to be recognized as more than simply personal, private, individual problems.

Another sense in which losses are "political" is whether they implicate the political community as a whole and require a collective response. Here, I draw on Sheldon Wolin's conception of the political as episodic and instantiated in specific moments when people act together. He takes the political to be "an expression of the idea that a free society composed of diversities can nonetheless enjoy moments of commonality when, through public deliberations, collective power is used to promote or protect the wellbeing of the collectivity."[26] Following Wolin, the political involves collectivity, which means that we have obligations to act with and address the needs of other citizens. As Dumm suggests about Du Bois's loss: "If we hope to take steps in Du Bois' experience of grief, our first step must be to acknowledge how all of us are stained by the specific pain of that which he has experienced and we have witnessed . . . and in doing so *take upon ourselves the stain of racism as our debt,* and hope that it will enable us to acknowledge the indefinitely deeper grief of Du Bois."[27] As Dumm's brief allusion to the duty of democratic citizens to be active witnesses suggests, racism has shaped the experience of loss in ways that democratic theorists must contend with if we are to take the experiences of Black citizens seriously. Some losses are therefore political not only because of the structural disparities that produce them, but also because we have a collective responsibility to attend to them.

The view of racialized political loss sketched thus far departs in important ways from how political theorists have understood the political import of loss. Some political theorists have argued that loss is central to the activity of political theorizing itself. For Peter Euben, "much political theory begins with loss. Loss animates it as an enterprise and forms its problematic." He suggests that loss haunts even utopian political visions, and that thinkers as diverse as the Greek tragedians, Plato, Machiavelli, and Marx can be read as theorists of loss. Of all their accounts of politics, we can ask: Do they present loss "as an aberration in a trajectory of progress or as endemic to 'the human condition'? What rhetorical or poetic devices, what metaphors or prophetic intonations do they use to dramatize the loss they confront and promise to move beyond or redeem? Do they embrace, indulge in, or resist nostalgia, counsel accommodation, endorse revolutionary praxis, or posit some purer realm unsullied by the messiness or undisturbed by the frailty of this world?"[28] Understanding how loss shapes the goals of different thinkers and movements provides a way to assess competing political visions. Loss was an even more central category for Sheldon Wolin, who argued that "loss has a claim upon theory." Drawing on Theodor Adorno, Wolin suggested that, rather than seeing history as a triumphant parade of winners shoving aside the defeated, "what survives of the defeated, the indigestible, the unassimilated, the 'cross-grained,' the 'not wholly obsolete' is what should interest the theorist."[29] Indeed, he repeatedly mourned the loss of local participatory traditions that he argued embodied genuine democratic politics, such that his influential conception of democracy as fleeting and episodic is pervaded by loss and nostalgia. As Lucy Cane has observed, Wolin's "embrace of mournful theory" enabled original insights about the limits of liberal democracy, the threat of corporate power, and ossified elite rule, but it also resulted in "a melancholic relationship with America's democratic past" that tended to gloss over its inegalitarian elements.[30] By mourning an idealized vision of US participatory traditions rooted in local deliberation, Wolin missed other sources of democratic vitality, such as the antiracist, feminist, and queer politics he at times dismissed as impeding solidarity.

If Wolin's "democracy grief" fueled his critique of contemporary democratic politics, others argue that mourning can become immobilizing politically.[31] For Wendy Brown, the "left melancholia" that pervades contemporary accounts of radical pasts has become "a mournful conservative, backward-looking attachment to a feeling, analysis, or relationship that has been rendered thinglike and frozen in the heart of the putative Leftist." The contemporary Left that yearns for past eras of unified movements and class-based politics becomes "a conservative force in history," she argues. The result is that the Right has become revolutionary and radical, while the Left tries to preserve the status quo of the welfare state and civil liberties. This is a Left "more attached to its impossibility" than what it might accomplish.[32] Nostalgic forms of politics that idealize a lost past can lead to political paralysis, and to incomplete understandings of the potential of the present.

In contrast to Brown's critique, the contemporary scholarship on mourning and democracy has celebrated its generative potential. Moving away from canonical views of excessive grief as dangerous to the political community (as in the iconic case of Antigone), these scholars reconceive mourning as a resource that can enrich democratic politics. They view the invisibility of some losses as the locus of mourning's politics and argue that how citizens organize collectively in response to loss has crucial implications for democracy. According to Alexander Keller Hirsch and David McIvor, "Citizens and communities can identify and practice a variety of arts of democratic mourning and, by acting in the face of these bitter experiences, momentarily reclaim and inhabit their birthright as political beings."[33] McIvor and Simon Stow argue for models of democratic mourning that avoid certitude, embrace ambivalence, and reject unitary national narratives. Stow identifies vernacular African American mourning traditions as a necessary countermemory to romantic modes of national public mourning committed to memorializing injuries against the nation and forgetting domestic injustice.[34]

Yet these celebratory accounts do not pay sufficient attention to mourning's costs, especially for those for whom this is a recurring condition.

In contrast, Black political thought, which has also been centrally concerned with loss, offers a distinct account of how loss functions politically that is different in important ways from those above. *Black Grief/White Grievance* draws primarily on the long tradition of thinking about loss in African American political thought, including thinkers as varied as Du Bois, Ida B. Wells, and Harriet Jacobs. Wells, for example, has been described as a "fiercely anti-nostalgic" thinker, and this is an apt description of how Black thinkers in general theorize loss.[35] Black thinkers are not nostalgic for past eras of utopian possibility in the way that Wolin or Brown's left melancholics are. Even African American thinkers who have a more celebratory account of the US founding, such as Frederick Douglass, recognize that the burden of loss is ongoing because the harms of racism have not been repaired.[36] Black thinkers have had to grapple with how to mourn when grief is ubiquitous yet losses are unrecognized by the dominant society. The struggle for Black thinkers and activists has been how to hold on to hope in the face of ongoing grief, not the problematic fixation on loss of Freudian melancholia, nor the overcoming of loss that constitutes successful mourning from a psychoanalytic perspective. As Fred Moten observes, "black mo'nin'" is a third category between mourning and melancholia that disrupts both.[37]

An important strand of Black political thought has resisted reparative approaches to loss that privilege appeals to the state, and insisted instead on the need to attend to how Black life persists even as Black grief is ongoing. Black thinkers have pointed to the ways race works to manage experiences of disempowerment for dominant groups and to obscure the losses of subordinated groups. They suggest that we need to move beyond the false polarity between hope and despair, and learn instead how to practice despairing hope or hopeful despair.[38] The never-ending drumbeat of incidents of police violence and killings of Black citizens is a constant reminder of the disposability of Black life, yet—as Black feminists in particular insist—it is crucial to make space for accounts of ongoing Black life in the context of immeasurable devastation.

Mobilizing Loss: Grief and Grievance

This book takes up two specific responses to political loss: grief and grievance. According to the *Oxford English Dictionary*, grief and grievance have the same etymological origin (from the French term *grever*, to harm). Grief and grievance are both responses to loss, but the most significant difference between them, as the *OED* definition of grievance aptly notes, is that the wrong or hardship that is the ground for grievance can be *real or supposed*.[39] This distinction between "real" and "supposed" harms maps onto the asymmetric attention that Black grief and white grievance have historically been accorded in the United States. Specifically, one of the principal claims of this book is that there has been insufficient space for Black grief because of the imperative to turn to activism to try to remedy racial injustice, even as white grievance has been driven by a refusal to acquiesce to loss, even when those losses are warranted or just. Because Black grief and white grievance are not normatively equivalent, they do not require the same responses. Losses required to dismantle white supremacy have to be accepted, while others (such as some forms of Black grief) need to be witnessed and attempts made to redress them even if they can never be fully repaired. It is never legitimate for the instrumentalization of Black grief to be imposed as a civic demand by the broader public. Nor is it legitimate for white grievance to overshadow or supplant Black grief as has often been the case.

As Wideman observes in her powerful enactment of and invocation of Black witnessing in the epigraph to this chapter, the sacrifices expected of Black citizens and activists for the sake of white democracy are part of a long-standing historical pattern.[40] The protests against police violence led by the Movement for Black Lives continue a long tradition of Black political mobilization catalyzed by Black death as a result of white violence subsequently channeled into public mourning, as was the case with the NAACP's use of lynching photographs to mobilize public outrage against post-Reconstruction-era racial terror in the early twentieth century, or the funeral of Emmett Till as a catalyst for the civil rights movement in the 1950s. In Wideman's words: "this has been happening to my family for a long time, longer than I can account for. . . . I'm also a Black history minor. So not only have I been watching it in the 30 years that I've been on this planet, but I've been watching it for years before we were even alive." For democratic theorists who extol witnessing as a key civic capacity, it is not as a passive bystander activity. Instead, it is an active form of truth telling and listening to the pain of others that might enable agonistic exchange and collective meaning making.[41] Wideman's painful testimony, however, reminds us of the costs of witnessing. As Elizabeth Alexander has observed—and Wideman's invocation of seeing racial violence for years before she was even alive illustrates—racial violence imposes compulsive witnessing on Black citizens.[42] Yet the contemporary scholarship on mourning and democracy has tended to frame Black public grief in a reparative vein that situates it almost solely as a solution to democratic deficits. This has the paradoxical effect of minimizing ongoing and continuing loss. Conceptions of mourning as a democratic resource are an inadequate approach to Black grief. If we are to truly attend to Black grief, we can hold on to witnessing only mournfully and tentatively, without romanticizing it.[43]

Black citizens are called on to repetitively witness for the sake of repairing the wrongs of white democracy, and they are also expected to protest only in the most civil, nondisruptive ways in order for their losses to be legible.[44] Refusals to contain Black rage are said to be counterproductive because they alienate potential white allies. Yet such criticisms are based on a number of mistaken assumptions about the history of Black activism. This is especially true of the dominant official romantic narrative of the civil rights movement in the United States, which emphasizes its commitment to nonviolence and civility rather than its more confrontational tactics. What is often left uninterrogated in critiques of "uncivil" forms of Black protest, moreover, are the very conditions of possibility for the production of "white empathy," which is not the same as political solidarity. To have empathy is to be able to see and identify with the pain or suffering of others. Empathy can therefore remain in the realm of feeling without implying action, and it can also depend on seeing the other as like oneself in some fundamental way. In contrast, political solidarity does not depend on prepolitical bonds and requires taking action to redress injustice.[45] Democratic equality, which is possible only in the context of racial justice, requires much more than white empathy and should not depend on constrained Black political action, which is itself an unjust civic burden.

Moreover, the losses Black grief and white grievance are responding to could not be more different: one is a set of ongoing catastrophes, the other specters of future loss. In contrast to Black grief, contemporary white grievance is animated in large part by prospective losses understood as defeats. It is a form of anticipatory loss.[46] Insofar as whites not only remain the demographic majority within the US polity, but also continue to be the dominant group by all measures (social standing, cultural capital, political [over]representation, economic resources, etc.), the sense of displacement that animates some sectors of US whiteness has been driven by what are at best symbolic nonwhite gains, such as the election of a Black president.[47] In contrast, Black grief is a response to the most extreme material losses, including spectacular and slow death. As a result, white grievance is a nostalgic form of politics that seeks to preserve or return to a (not-yet-actually-past) status quo, while Black grief enacts a politics of transformation oriented to the redistribution of loss.

This contrast between Black grief and white grievance is clear in two instances of political loss that mobilized citizens in highly visible protests during the summer of 2020: the majority-white and often heavily armed antimask protests demanding reopening with no restrictions in the middle of a pandemic, and the nationwide, multiracial, Black-led racial justice protests impelled by the police killings of George Floyd in Minnesota and Breonna Taylor in Kentucky, and the shooting of Jacob Blake in Wisconsin. The antimask protesters were ostensibly motivated by the loss of personal freedom imposed by public health mandates, while racial justice protesters were mourning the, at best, continued indifference to or, at worst, commitment to Black death (manifested in police impunity) of the state and many citizens and were demanding the right to live free of state violence.[48] Racial justice protesters wanted freedom from being killed; antimask protesters were demanding the freedom to have their personal preferences dominate the collective safety of the body politic. Given the racial disparities in infection, hospitalization, and fatality rates from Covid-19, white liberty was expected to trump Black and brown safety. White antimask protesters enacted a conception of freedom as untrammeled liberty, as the ability to dominate others, to behave lawlessly. They demanded a freedom for themselves that was not available to others or depended on the nonfreedom of others.

White grievance is also justified and propelled by phantasmagoric projections of Black violence epitomized by racial justice protests. In Congress, for example, where many GOP elected officials have expressed support for the violent insurrection on January 6, 2021, it was Representative Cori Bush (a prominent Black Lives Matter protest leader in Ferguson, Missouri, elected to represent St. Louis in 2020) who was called a "terrorist" by Marjorie Taylor Greene, the controversial Representative from Georgia and QAnon conspiracy adherent. She accused the Democratic caucus of being "filled with members who supported, cheered on, & funded criminal thugs who riot, burn, loot, attack police, murder, & occupy federal property/ Members who . . . lead a violent mob in neighborhoods, and more."[49] Greene's false depiction of racial justice protesters as violent and criminal is consistent with the narrative of a country under attack that is a central feature of the politics of white grievance fueling right-wing extremism in the United States today.[50] In fact, in contrast to their feelings of aggrieved victimhood, armed white antimask protesters at various state capitals and white insurrectionists at the Capitol received kid-glove treatment compared to the heavy-handed, violent, repressive tactics unleashed on racial justice protesters, echoing a historical pattern of white race riots occurring with impunity and in many cases the outright complicity of state agents.[51]

The anticipatory losses animating white grievance obscure the presently occurring, tangible suffering inflicted on nonwhite populations whose supposed ascendancy is an existential threat.[52] The anticipatory nature of white loss is reflected in the fact that it is not just economically disadvantaged working-class whites who subscribe to white grievance.[53] For instance, a study of indicted January 6 insurrectionists found their demographic profile to be quite different from past right-wing extremists. They are older, many are business owners or hold white-collar jobs, and only a small number (9 percent) were unemployed. "Unlike the stereotypical extremist, many of the alleged participants in the Capitol riot have a lot to lose. They work as CEOs, shop owners, doctors, lawyers, IT specialists, and accountants."[54] The Capitol rioters and others who continue to believe that the 2020 election was stolen subscribe to the potent rhetorical fiction of a new "Lost Cause." Like the one that white southerners deployed so effectively to reverse the racial justice gains of Reconstruction at the end of the nineteenth century, today's "Big Lie" is being used to reverse and prevent any further steps toward multiracial democracy.[55] White grievance is therefore profoundly antidemocratic. If the United States is ever to become a genuine multiracial democracy, it cannot continue to demand sacrifices of some, while allowing others to mourn justified losses they refuse to accept.

White civic capacities and political imaginations have been shaped by the fact that white supremacy has historically insulated them as a group from certain kinds of political loss. For the white majority, therefore, being good democratic citizens will entail learning how to do what has repeatedly been asked of Black citizens: peaceful acceptance of loss. In their case, these legitimate losses are of exclusive access to political power, and privileged social and economic standing. In a democracy, it will always be necessary to manage competing and coexisting losses, as the salience of Black grief and white grievance in contemporary US racial politics illustrates. But in democracies in which racial hierarchy has resulted in unequal distributions of loss—that is, where for some their sense of what citizenship entails is built on the dispossession of others—simply redistributing loss more equally is insufficient. Instead, the meaning of equality needs to be reimagined so that nonwhite loss is not built into what whites perceive to be their baseline entitlement as citizens. Thinking about white grievance in this way proposes a different response to white loss. The usual solution, which follows the classic strategy in public policy on the welfare state and international trade to address backlash, is to "compensate the losers," to argue that with proper policies there need not be losses at all, but can be gains for all.[56] From the perspective of political loss, however, responding to white grievance in this way does nothing to transform zero-sum thinking, nor to develop the key civic capacity of accepting justified losses among those who have historically been exempt from this democratic burden, as I argue in chapter 1.

Black political imaginations have also been narrowed by racism in different ways, such that the challenge in their case is to recognize how the notion of redemptive suffering—the idea that by engaging in exemplary forms of political activism that make Black pain visible, white public opinion will be transformed—has constrained Black politics.[57] Private grief turned public mourning has been a central feature of Black politics because, historically, Black grief has been largely invisibilized. In response to profound losses that are not publicly acknowledged, Black communities have mobilized around spectacular moments of loss when it has been possible to make Black grief legible. One result of this is the difference in public attention to those killed by police violence compared to the "slow deaths" caused by everyday disasters that disproportionally affect communities of color, such as environmental racism.[58] The imperative to channel grief into activism that has been the dominant approach to loss in African American political thought and politics paradoxically constrains Black grief in important ways. It can function to conscript Black grief into the project of repairing white democracy, though important strands in the tradition have refused this aspiration. Instead of conforming to expectations of democratic sacrifice, Black people can enlarge the space for a conception of humanizing, noninstrumental collective Black grief that is not immediately transformed into grievance. Focusing on the more capacious approach to loss developed by Black feminist thinkers centers the question of what Black politics can be if it is not about sacrifice for white democracy.

Political theorists have worried that focusing on political loss will lead either to paralysis (as in critiques of left melancholia) or to what Bonnie Honig calls the lamentation of politics (abandoning the pursuit of power).[59] For Black politics, however, the problem has been a parasitic approach to Black activism as a source of democratic energy and renewal. To the extent that Black grief is approached as a salve for white democracy without addressing justice, it perpetuates expectations of Black sacrifice that constrain Black political agency. As I show in chapter 2, a template for acceptable Black protest based on a romanticized account of the civil rights movement of the 1960s continues to constrain Black activism by reducing it to political martyrdom. Black citizens are asked to make extraordinary sacrifices in an economy of suffering that requires the display of Black pain in order to enable progress toward racial justice. This script of civic exemplarity rests on assumptions that the right kind of activism will generate white solidarity, and it misreads how Black activists understand their political actions. In contrast, chapters 3 and 4 point to a different route for Black politics. Since the affective demand of white grievance is Black/nonwhite submission, redemptive suffering is unlikely to be persuasive. Black people should therefore focus instead on affirming Black life and refusing scripts of sacrifice. Black feminist thinkers, in particular, have developed complex approaches to loss that go beyond the imperative to channel grief into activism. Some, such as Ida B. Wells and Harriet Jacobs, analyzed in chapter 3, seek to balance grief and grievance and are strategic in what they choose to disclose and conceal about Black suffering, while others, such as the grieving maternal activists analyzed in chapter 4, pay attention to the costs of activism and the need to sit with grief in order to make space for Black life in Black politics.

Black Grief/White Grievance is a book about the politics of loss, but it is also about the politics of refusal.[60] Refusal is an important concept for Black politics, and it is a central theme of this book. Each of its four chapters is structured around a political or theoretical gesture of refusal. Chapter 1 traces white refusal and its costs for democracy, chapter 2 argues that Black politics should refuse expectations of political heroism, chapter 3 sketches Black feminist refusal of the imperative to make Black loss public and visible, and chapter 4 calls for grieving activism that refuses to instrumentalize grief and bear the burdens of activism. By refusal, I mean not an abandonment of politics or retreat from the world, but rather a rejection of conceptions of Black politics solely in terms of repair, of instrumental approaches to Black loss that myopically view it as only or predominantly about shoring up white democracy. Taken as a whole, this book is a call to refuse to exchange Black suffering for white identification. Black politics also needs to refuse some of its own dominant scripts, especially those that respond to grief by seeking to transform it into grievance. Refusal in this book is therefore an idiom of political theorizing as well as a means of reorienting Black politics and affirming capacious accounts of Black humanity, which means guarding against the reduction of Black agency to resistance. Finally, *Black Grief/White Grievance* is a call to refuse familiar accounts of democratic politics that focus solely on empowerment and set aside equally central experiences of loss and disempowerment.

The claim that both Blacks and whites need to expand their political imaginations so whites can become better democratic citizens and Blacks can refuse expectations of political heroism might seem contradictory because it simultaneously affirms democratic obligations and rejects liberal democracy as the horizon of possibility for Black politics.[61] But this is an unavoidable tension in a book about how racism has narrowed the political imaginations of both Black and white citizens. While I make a number of claims about the obligations democratic citizens have to each other throughout, this is *not* a book about how democracies can manage the experience of political loss. Instead, it aims to challenge certain familiar ways of thinking about democratic politics and citizenship. Political theorists too often romanticize calls to sacrifice for democracy, without paying sufficient attention to ongoing political loss. *Black Grief/White Grievance* calls attention to the costs of political action and to differential expectations of civic sacrifice. I argue that both Blacks and whites need to learn to sit with loss, for different reasons, and to different ends. Whites need to learn to accept the loss of their political, economic, and social dominance without resorting to grievance, and Blacks need to mourn their losses without acceding to the demand (imposed by majority expectations as well as some strands of their own political tradition) to give meaning to them by mobilizing them in service of projects of democratic repair. My aim here is not to develop a prescriptive account of racial justice activism, but rather to interrogate dominant accounts of democratic politics and suggest alternative conceptions of Black politics that refuse expectations of martyrdom. We can grieve democracy's deficits, but as we do, we must recognize we have never had a genuine multiracial democracy whose demise we can now all mourn. Political loss has been ongoing for some. We can learn from the experiences of those who have historically been the losers in US democracy, but more importantly, we have an obligation to recognize that loss has been unequally distributed, that some citizens have been expected to disproportionately shoulder the fundamental democratic labor of losing from which others have been exempt.

INTERLUDE 1

because white men can't
police their imagination
black people are dying

—CLAUDIA RANKINE, ["BECAUSE WHITE MEN CAN'T"] FROM *CITIZEN: AN AMERICAN LYRIC*

1

White Grievance and Anticipatory Loss

AS SUBSEQUENTLY documented in the pages of *Vanity Fair*, "at 12:11 p.m. on January 5, [2021,] an eight-seat Bombardier Challenger 300 jet took off from Memphis International Airport. A little over an hour and a half and one time zone later, it touched down at Dulles, just outside of Washington, D.C. The following day a seditious horde of Donald Trump supporters [including the private jet passengers], unapologetically encouraged by him, mounted an insurrection to stop the certification of Joe Biden's Electoral College victory."[1] The jet-setting Capitol insurrectionists from Memphis included millionaires with enviable asset portfolios attributable to inherited wealth, including sizable stakes in auto dealerships, financial firms with earnings rivaling those of Wall Street firms, major real estate properties, and registered "plantations" used as hunting clubs. They are members of the "lily white country-club elite" of Memphis, a highly segregated city that is 64 percent Black and 29 percent white, and home of the Lorraine Motel, where the Reverend Martin Luther King Jr. (MLK) was assassinated.[2] They belong to a social set that celebrates the annual Carnival, where they are crowned "queens," "princesses," and "kings," harkening back to "the days when white men ruled and Black people picked cotton."[3] As Democratic congressman Steve Cohen—who represents Memphis thanks to the votes of its majority-Black residents—remarked, the participation of members of the city's wealthy white elite in the Capitol insurrection "goes to show . . . how the Big Lie that Trump put out there didn't just appeal to people who were middle income and [with] lower or lesser education. . . . [It] attracted people that were well educated and have high-income economic status. And I think that was true throughout the country."[4]

The image of wealthy, elite, well-educated white professionals and business owners participating in a violent riot at the US Capitol seeking to overturn the results of a legitimate election is emblematic of how white grievance impedes and undermines multiracial democracy. As Cohen observed, the wealth of the jet-setting Capitol insurrectionists precludes any claim that they were motivated by economic precarity. Instead, the refusal of Trump and his supporters to accept their legitimate loss in the 2020 presidential election is the most recent iteration of a long-standing pattern of white refusal to accept political loss that has been a recurrent feature of US democracy. Indeed, the spate of restrictive voting laws since the 2020 election—enacted in Republican-controlled states and aimed specifically at limiting the ability of nonwhite citizens to impact electoral outcomes—illustrates how white refusal subverts democracy.[5] Because political victories achieved in part by nonwhite votes are by definition illegitimate from the vantage point of white supremacy, if white citizens do lose, the rules of the game must be changed to ensure white dominance. But in a multiracial democracy, sharing political rule is a cost that is supposed to be borne by all citizens. White grievance thus nurtures and sustains antidemocratic commitments to perpetual white political dominance.

While the 2021 Capitol insurrection was an instance of white refusal to accept legitimate political loss, more often than not white grievance is mobilized in response to anticipatory losses.[6] "Anticipatory loss," as I am using it here, is experienced—often quite intensely—despite not having actually come to pass (yet), and despite not necessarily being accurate. Loss can be anticipatory in the sense that it may be experienced as a harm without having yet occurred, and it can also be inaccurate. This combination is particularly virulent. That such losses are neither realized nor realistic matters little to the intensity with which they are feared. Aggressive nationalisms often deploy anticipatory loss rhetoric. The concept of "Lebensraum," for instance, which became a central tenet of Nazi ideology, justified German territorial expansion and annexation of countries in central and eastern Europe and the removal of the so-called inferior races (both Slavs and Jews) that occupied them, on the basis that Germany needed a "living space" in order to "survive."[7] Similarly, white grievance is often mobilized in response to future losses whose purported imminence requires aggressive action in the present. This is clear, for example, in arguments that inhumane, illegal, and violent immigration policies are needed to stem the threat of a Latinx immigrant "invasion" that threatens to overrun and replace Anglo white culture.[8] Ironically, the mobilization of white grievance in response to anticipatory loss reveals that whites are used to dominance but are continually haunted by fear of losing it and being displaced. In response to these fears, white grievance channels racist resentment to reassert white priority.

Despite recurring anxiety that Black rage at ongoing loss will fray the bonds of the body politic, it is in fact white refusal to accept legitimate political loss that is the most profoundly antidemocratic force in US politics.[9] Moreover, white refusal is not new. Writing in 1967, MLK observed that it was "the white American who is even more unprepared" for racial equality than were Black citizens. Even the most liberal white persons, he argued, "proceed from a premise that equality is a loose expression for improvement. White America is not even psychologically organized to close the gap—essentially it seeks to make it less painful and less obvious but in most respects to retain it." Civil rights victories up to that point, even momentous ones such as voting rights, "required neither large monetary nor psychological sacrifice. . . . The real cost lies ahead. The stiffening of white resistance is a recognition of that fact." White America, King argued, had deluded itself into believing that change could be accomplished painlessly, at little to no cost, "at bargain rates."[10] King made an important distinction here. White backlash was a matter not just of unwillingness to share resources, but of an absence of the tools (emotional, affective, cognitive) to envision and practice equality. Even though the costs of racial progress had been minimal up to that point, white resistance was nevertheless fierce.

Yet whiteness is not monolithic. Not all white citizens respond to loss with refusal. King identified different degrees of white resistance in his time. He argued that the white public was divided between "a minority of whites" committed to racial equality, another group just as committed to white supremacy, and a majority of white liberals in the middle discomfited by overt racist violence or too-visible racial discrimination but also unwilling to pay the full cost of justice. The white minority prepared to accept equality was "balanced at the other end of the pole by the unrepentant segregationists who have declared that democracy is not worth having if it involves equality."[11] White refusal today may no longer coalesce in defense of racial segregation as it did in King's time, but we are at another historical moment when some white citizens seem willing to dispense with democracy in order to preserve white dominance. White grievance is not fixed or constant. Yet its historical persistence suggests that it is not a problem that will be solved by demographic change alone.[12] Struggles for racial justice *can* alter white perceptions of racism and enhance support for racial equality, but progress also fuels resistance.[13] As King observed: "Each step forward accents an ever-present tendency to backlash."[14] The election of the first Black president, for example, intensified white backlash, as did the multiracial, Black-led racial justice protests of the summer of 2020.[15]

My analysis of white grievance is thus focused on a particular response to loss among a subset of whites. I use the terms *white* and *whiteness* to designate a political category that emerged at a specific historical point in time (with the development of the modern concept of race and European colonial projects) and that continues to confer certain advantages.[16] More specifically, as Joel Olson argues,

> white citizenship is the enjoyment of racial standing in a democratic polity. . . . It is both a structural location in the racial order and a product of human agency. Individual whites may consciously defend their privileges, reject them, or deny they exist, yet the structure of the racial order makes it difficult for individual whites to "jump out" of their whiteness at any given time. The category does not explain every belief or behavior of every white person but encompasses the structures and social relations that produce white privilege and the ideas that defend it.[17]

While all individual white persons are thus not consciously motivated by a sense of racial grievance, they all benefit from white advantages that they have come to view as normal—which is to say, they don't view them as advantages at all. White citizens are not used to having to give things up for others, even when those losses are legitimate.[18] King, for example, one of the most optimistic Black thinkers on the possibility of white moral transformation, nevertheless observed in 1967:

> As Negroes move forward toward a fundamental alteration of their lives, some bitter white opposition is bound to grow, even within groups that were hospitable to earlier superficial amelioration. Conflicts are unavoidable because a stage has been reached in which the reality of equality will require extensive adjustments in the way of life of some of the white majority. Many of our former supporters will fall by the wayside as the movement presses against financial privilege. Others will withdraw as long-established cultural privileges are threatened.[19]

King's account of how challenges to financial and later cultural privileges lessened white support for the civil rights movement in the 1960s is consistent with the argument in this chapter that both material loss and symbolic loss fuel white grievance.

It is also important to note that while white grievance is central to right-wing politics in the United States today, white refusal traverses the ideological spectrum. Because the current GOP relies so conspicuously on white grievance to mobilize its voters, many of the examples I cite in this chapter involve Republican public figures. But what I am calling white refusal is not limited to the Right. The Left also traffics in white refusal, most notably in the form of appeasement. This is evident in persistent debates about whether the Democratic Party should focus on supposedly more "universal" economic issues and less on so-called "identity politics" in order to appeal to disaffected white voters, and in the way Democratic politicians (white and

Black) often burnish their cross-racial appeal by scolding Black people and demonizing Black youth.[20] Certainly white leftists are generally more willing to recognize the persistence of racism than their right-wing counterparts, but white liberals also resist material redistribution. As a *New York Times* investigative report (that analyzed housing, taxation, and education) on why blue states in which Democrats control all the levers of power nevertheless have some of the highest levels of inequality in the country concluded, "affluent liberals tend to be really good at showing up to the marches and talking about how they love equality . . . but by their actions what they are saying is yes, we believe in these ideals, just not in my backyard."[21] Liberal unwillingness to enact the egalitarian values they profess is a form of white refusal that functions to secure enduring advantage, one that also partakes in white innocence in the form of nostalgia for a time when less was asked of them. The white resistance King described in the 1960s continues to haunt US democracy.[22]

Aside from Black thinkers, however, white refusal has generally not been recognized as the most potent threat to US democracy.[23] In part this is because

> white rage is not about visible violence, but rather it works its way through the courts, the legislatures, and a range of government bureaucracies. It wreaks havoc subtly, almost imperceptibly. Too imperceptibly, certainly, for a nation consistently drawn to the spectacular—to what it can *see*. It's not the [Ku Klux] Klan. White rage doesn't have to wear sheets, burn crosses, or take to the streets. . . . The trigger for white rage, inevitably, is black advancement.[24]

Carol Anderson's account of the opacity of white rage captures the potent affective dimension of white grievance, while simultaneously flagging its quotidian character, the fact that it often works through ordinary legal and institutional mechanisms. This is not to say that white grievance no longer erupts into visible violence. When it does, however, it is often downplayed or whitewashed. Wisconsin senator Ron Johnson's description of the overwhelmingly white Capitol insurrectionists is instructive in this regard: "I knew those were people that love this country, that truly respect law enforcement [and] would never do anything to break a law, and so I wasn't concerned." For Johnson, the patriotism and law-abiding nature of the January 6 insurrectionists was axiomatic even as they were in fact breaking the law. In contrast, he said that had it been "tens of thousands of Black Lives Matter and antifa protesters, I might have been a little concerned."[25] For him and those who share his worldview, rioting, violence, and rage are always the province of Blackness, never whiteness, which is always peaceful and law-abiding. More pointedly, protesting racial injustice (by Blacks or whites) is subversive and threatening, while rioting to uphold white supremacy is not even recognized as violent or criminal.

From the racist backlash to the Obama presidency, to the Capitol insurrection, a decades-long white riot against the prospect of genuine multiracial democracy has been unfolding in the United States in the twenty-first century. Importantly, the defeat of Donald Trump's reelection bid in 2020 did not mark a cessation but rather an acceleration of white refusal, as the claim that the election was stolen has only exacerbated the apocalyptic sense that xenophobic, racist, misogynist, and homophobic policies are needed to preserve a besieged "real America." An important task for democratic theory, therefore, is to identify the kinds of political imaginations and practices wrought by white refusal to accept political loss—in other words, to trace the political constitution of white grievance. What are the constitutive features of white grievance? They include a zero-sum view of politics that mobilizes white victimhood in response to more-often-than-not anticipatory losses and token or incremental nonwhite gains; narratives of white racial innocence; nostalgia for past eras of clear white dominance; a paucity or complete absence of the key democratic capacity to accept legitimate political loss; and apocalyptic conceptions of racial equality as Black rule and white subjugation.

My approach to the problem of white grievance is guided by a number of intertwined arguments about political loss, race, and democracy. How citizens respond to political loss is a crucial question for democratic politics. Yet white supremacy leads to an unequal distribution of loss. Because whites have been dominant historically in the United States, they as a group (to different degrees mediated to a certain extent by social class divisions and ideological or partisan alignments) have therefore not had to accept political loss as much as other citizens. In theory, since the passage of the Voting Rights Act in 1965, white citizens have faced the possibility of sharing political rule with nonwhites in the United States. In practice, however, not only does the representation of nonwhites in the US political establishment still lag behind their proportion of the population, but increases in the number of elected representatives have not led to meaningful power sharing, particularly at the national level. Additionally, voter suppression and other systematic efforts to prevent nonwhites from wielding political power (via gerrymandering, strict voter identification laws, reduced access to voting locations, etc.) continue to result in the systematic political disenfranchisement of nonwhite citizens.[26] White citizens as a group have thus been conditioned to expect white dominance as a key feature of their political identity. As a result, they have by and large developed political imaginations shaped by domination rather than equality and have mobilized discourses of white grievance in response to perceived threats of white displacement.[27]

Furthermore, despite the often-referenced economic anxieties that are said to be driving resurgent white racial resentment, symbolic loss is central to white grievance. In the Obama and Trump eras, symbolic loss has been a crucial a driver of white racial resentment. White grievance is driven by a specific form of racial nostalgia that translates tangible or even token Black gains into occasions of white dislocation and displacement. Resistance to symbolic loss is thus tied to white citizens' continued investment in political dominance and racial hierarchy. This is not to suggest that material and symbolic loss are entirely separate domains.[28] They are difficult to disaggregate in practice, but making an analytical distinction between them is necessary for understanding what drives white grievance. Distinguishing between material and symbolic loss might allow us to consider who can accept which forms of loss. King argued that symbolic losses generate resistance, but that the material losses necessary to bring about a racially just society are even more difficult to accept. Some white citizens may be willing to accept symbolic loss but may balk at material loss. And some may brook neither. Distinguishing between the two might allow us to consider how alternative forms of political imagination compatible with democratic equality could be cultivated among white citizens. What is at stake here is not simply moving beyond white refusal but overcoming impoverished white visions of democracy and freedom. As the poet Claudia Rankine succinctly observes in the interlude that precedes this chapter: "Because white men can't / police their imagination / black people are dying."[29] This is a matter not just of incapacity, however, but of refusal.

Theorizing white refusal as a political and ideological force that is relatively mainstream and structural shows that it would be a mistake to cordon off this political phenomenon as an anomalous or extremist development. Instead, we must contend with the fact that the political imagination of white citizens has been shaped by white supremacy, resulting in a distorted racial political accounting that sees Black gains as white losses—and not simply losses but defeats.[30] As a result, in moments when white dominance is threatened, not only are many white citizens unable or unwilling to recognize Black suffering; they mobilize a sense of white victimhood in response.[31] The challenge of racial justice is thus not only how to make Black (or nonwhite) suffering legible; it is to squarely confront white grievance and refusal to accept loss, real or perceived, material or symbolic. If the so-called liberal democracies of the West are to become truly racially egalitarian, white citizens will need to accept the loss of political dominance. They will have to come to accept being ruled in turn, not only ruling.[32] Black protest and sacrifice cannot save US democracy. Instead, we need to confront white citizens' continued investment in forms of political rule that are not only incompatible with—but indeed directly opposed to—both racial justice and democratic politics.

Theorizing White Refusal

Democratic politics requires that citizens be able to cope with loss. In democracies, which are supposed to ensure the good of all, policy choices are nevertheless routinely made that are more favorable to some groups than others. Danielle Allen argues that "the sacrifices of some citizens are the bedrock of other citizens' lives. Citizens of democracies are often implored to realize that they are in the same boat. . . . Instead . . . [we should] recognize that our fellow citizens *are* the boat, and we in turn the planks for them."[33] As the metaphor of citizens peopling the shared aquatic vessel of democracy illustrates, the operation of democratic politics in practice often involves being stepped on by other citizens, in contrast to democracy's more common portrayal as an experience of empowerment and the conferral of dignity. This feeling of "frustrated sovereignty" or powerlessness is what Allen argues needs to be managed for democratic politics to endure. In her formulation, loss is the central fact of democratic life. "Since sacrifice is ubiquitous in democratic life, and the polity often makes decisions with which one disagrees, all citizens must confront the paradox that they have been promised sovereignty and rarely feel it. Herein lies the single most difficult feature of life in a democracy. Democratic citizens are by definition empowered only in order to be disempowered."[34] Democratic loss is rendered legitimate by the fact that all citizens are supposed to be equally susceptible to experiencing it. Yet, historically, political loss has not been evenly distributed. *Herrenvolk* democracies such as the United States are characterized by political equality among whites and tyranny for nonwhites.[35] What developed was not multiracial democracy but racialized citizenship, where one group was able to exercise political rule, what Allen calls "the work of being sovereign," and another group was assigned "most of the work of accepting the significant losses that kept the polity stable."[36] Authoritarianism, that is, a politics of dominance and submission, is a central feature of white supremacy.[37] If racism is an authoritarian form of rule, then political communities organized on the basis of white supremacy are not simply imperfect democracies; they instill in members of the dominant group the expectation of political rule along with the concomitant disposition to refuse to accept the legitimacy of political losses to nonwhite citizens.

Allen is right to identify acquiescence to legitimate political loss as a necessary civic capacity for *all* democratic citizens, even if I disagree with how she frames peaceful acceptance of political loss by subordinated racial groups as a form of civic virtue (an issue I take up in the following chapter). What I am interested in thinking about here is how we might understand the consequences of what she refers to as "the work of being sovereign" on the civic capacities and political imaginations of members of dominant groups. In other words, if acceptance of loss is necessary for democracy, what happens when a group that is unaccustomed to loss is confronted with it? What kinds of political imaginations and practices of politics are formed by the expectation that one should not have to experience collective political loss? Once the reality of racialized citizenship is taken into account, it is clear that those citizens who need it most have been least conditioned to cultivate the necessary democratic capacity of accepting the experience of frustrated sovereignty.

In effect, the problem is that if politics entails ruling and being ruled in turn, as Aristotle suggested, members of the dominant group in a herrenvolk democracy have been accustomed only to ruling, not to being ruled in turn. In *Politics*, book 1, Aristotle discusses the politics of mastery in both the family household and the *polis*. In the case of the household, he takes up what he considers "natural" hierarchies between masters and slaves and within marital and parental relationships, in order to distinguish these forms of domestic mastery from the kinds of relations established between political equals, between those who rule and are ruled in turn. In the case of the city, it is oligarchs who evince an orientation to domination that contravenes equality, although the poor are also prone to submission. Associating social class with particular political dispositions toward mastery or equality, in book 4, he says of the poor and the wealthy: "We have thus, on the one hand, people who are ignorant how to rule and only know how to obey, as if they were so many slaves, and, on the other hand, people who are ignorant how to obey any sort of authority and only know how to rule as if they were masters of slaves. The result is a state, not of freemen, but only of slaves and masters." Aristotle ascribes the desire for a politics of mastery to oligarchs, who are "both unwilling to obey and ignorant [of] how to obey."[38] Oligarchs (or members of the dominant social class) do not learn how to lose and are in fact committed to staving off loss. Aristotle is clear that the oligarchic commitment to political mastery is about preventing material loss and hoarding social standing; it is a commitment to social and material inequality. His account of how social class shapes orientations to political mastery is helpful for understanding the kinds of political imaginations that are developed by dominant groups in herrenvolk democracies (in which race and class tend to be closely associated) characterized by equality for some and inequality for others.

Indeed, white commitment to political rule results in a zero-sum understanding of politics where gains by subordinated racial others are viewed as losses for the dominant group. As Olson has argued, following W.E.B. Du Bois, white citizenship has historically been a form of racial standing that confers both material and symbolic advantages:

> White citizenship is simultaneously an identity of equality and privilege. The privileges of white citizenship . . . are public, psychological, and material. . . . It does not guarantee that all whites will be successful but it ensures that no white

> citizen will ever be thrown down to the absolute bottom of the social hierarchy. In exchange for this prize, working-class whites acquiesce to the domination of the political and economic system by powerful elites. Whiteness grants working-class whites a special status—not quite rich but *not quite powerless*—that becomes the focus of white citizens' political energy rather than challenges to elite rule.[39]

White dominance narrows the political concerns of the white majority. While all white citizens benefit from the expectation of exclusive access to political power and white priority, the economic advantages of whiteness are not evenly distributed. White supremacy reorients Aristotle's understanding of the relationship between social class and dispositions to political mastery or equality, as white citizens of all social classes (but especially the less economically advantaged) fixate their political energies on preserving their racial standing. White dominance has resulted in a narrow political imagination that constrains the way whites understand citizenship, as asymmetrical access to institutional political power vis-à-vis racial "others." It has also resulted in "a shallow definition of freedom limited to economic opportunity, the absence of government interference in private ventures, and the right to elect public officials. . . . The white citizen's political imagination tends toward a limited notion of equality as well as freedom. . . . [It] is not able to recognize that the advancement of 'whites,' depends on the advancement of those who are not white and that so long as the dark world is degraded whites will be too."[40] In such an understanding of democratic politics as a zero-sum game in which gains by other groups are experienced as losses by the dominant group, white losses become magnified while nonwhite losses are rendered invisible. The result is an unspoken racial syllogism—Black/nonwhite gains equal white losses; Black/nonwhite gains are illegitimate; white loss is therefore never legitimate—whose corollary is that Black loss is both legitimate and illegible.

Narratives of white racial innocence also play a key role in white grievance. We might, for example, wonder how white grievance is plausibly asserted when immigrant children are separated from their families and held in cages at the border to appease nativist fears of racial replacement. To understand how assertions of white vulnerability fuel the disproportionate deployment of state power over racialized others, it is necessary to consider cognitive and affective investments in particular understandings of whiteness. Narratives of white innocence exempt the white majority from complicity in and responsibility for unleashing state power on vulnerable racial others. Charles Mills's concept of "the epistemology of ignorance" is helpful for understanding the construction of narratives of white racial innocence. Mills defines "white ignorance" as "an ignorance, a non-knowing"—in which "white racism and/or white racial domination and their ramifications—plays a crucial causal role."[41] White ignorance results from both: "straightforward racist motivation and more impersonal social-structural causation, which may be operative even if the cognizer in question is not racist." White ignorance is thus not only straightforwardly deployed by racist cognizers; it is also at work indirectly in the case of nonracist cognizers "who may form mistaken beliefs (e.g., that after the abolition of slavery in the United States, blacks generally had opportunities equal to whites) because of the social suppression of the pertinent knowledge, though without prejudice [themselves]. . . . So white ignorance need not always be based on bad faith."[42] White ignorance allows whites to deny the unearned advantages they have accrued as a result of white supremacy. It also enables them to reject the assumption of any responsibility as individuals for its continuation. Beyond potential material loss, part of what movements for racial justice such as the Movement for Black Lives (M4BL) challenge white citizens to do is to confront shameful racist pasts and presents. In such situations, "the privileged stand to lose their *freedom from moral shame*, on the one hand, and *moral pride of place*, on the other, relative to those who are emerging or have become their social equals. In other words, they stand to *lose their sense of moral innocence* . . . in the eyes of the powers-that-be relative to the marginalized."[43] Indeed, one of the reasons symbolic losses are felt so deeply, why they provoke such excessive denial or disavowal, is that they puncture white innocence.[44]

Alongside white commitment to political rule, a zero-sum understanding of politics, and narratives of racial innocence, the pleasures of domination are also a key element of white grievance. If cognitive processes are central to white ignorance, emotion and affect are fundamental to the pleasures that are derived from spectacles of white domination. In particular, they help us understand the desire to punish immigrants, unruly Black protesters, so-called Arab and Muslim terrorists, and Asian citizens scapegoated as responsible for the Covid-19 pandemic, to name some of the most prominent racialized "others" singled out for spectacular deployments of state power and routine displays of disciplinary power in our current historical moment. Johnson's comments about supposedly "law-abiding" white Capitol insurrectionists versus "threatening" Black Lives Matter and antifa protesters, for instance, are not simply an expression of bad faith or white ignorance; they reflect the pleasure derived from simultaneously doling out violence to racial others and care to white equals. This dynamic is likewise reflected in the extreme disparity in police treatment of white rioters and racist mass murderers in contrast to the violent repression of racial justice protesters. As Paula Ioanide has argued in her study of how public feelings rather than facts have shaped the intensification of socioeconomic inequalities, state violence, and punitive control in the post–civil rights era, "emotional rewards and losses play a central role in shaping how and why people invest in racism, nativism, and imperialism in the United States." Analyzing crime, terrorism, welfare, and immigration, she argues that majorities in the United States supported increasingly punitive policies in these arenas

> because they generated the affective rewards of state protection, national security, and global dominance. These shifts enabled people to experience affectively aggressive thrills and enjoyments through their identification with the state's power, allowing them to vicariously feel the pleasures of punishing, policing, and excluding so-called illegal immigrants, suspected terrorists, and supposedly incorrigible criminals. . . . These economies of emotional reward and stigma were overwhelmingly attached to people of color, non-white immigrants, undocumented migrants of color, and/or poor people. They worked because they reified preexisting sensibilities and feelings about race, gender, sexuality, class, and national identity, particularly among dominant white middle- to upper-class constituencies.[45]

While I focus on Black loss in this book, white grievance is mobilized in response to perceived gains by multiple groups that are viewed as threatening white political dominance. It is not just the fear of displacement that fuels white grievance, however, but also the pleasures of domination derived from vicarious (and in some cases direct) enactments of punitive, violent force on already vulnerable groups.[46]

Racial nostalgia is also central to white grievance, particularly nostalgia for an imagined idyllic past in which white dominance was undisputed. Contemporary white nostalgia, aptly encapsulated by the slogan "make America great again," echoes earlier iterations that followed moments of racial progress and change.[47] In a study of segregated neighborhoods in Chicago that became increasingly integrated between 1960 and 1980, for example, white residents framed their feelings of anger, regret, and loss in terms of nostalgia for a "segregated white world" in which "life seemed good, that is, orderly, friendly, safe, and homogeneously white." Nostalgia for this "segregated white world" coincided with "nostalgia for a time when 'white culture' was . . . unquestioningly synonymous with American culture." These white residents of Chicago neighborhoods undergoing racial transitions conjured a now-lost "idyllic [white] world" characterized by "a homogeneous, caring, and tight-knit" white community whose destruction they blamed on "blackness [constructed] as naturally destructive to white communities and property." Despite the role played by other white actors (such as banks, real estate agents, and city officials) in the transformation of their neighborhoods, as well as the fierce resistance they themselves mounted to integration (which manifested in intimidation and sometimes outright violence against Black newcomers), white residents, most of whom fled to all-white suburbs, positioned themselves "as powerless victims of this natural disaster over which they had no control."[48] Nostalgic narratives that conjure a lost, idyllic white world simultaneously obscure white agency—in this example, the choice of white flight rather than integration—and fail to see Black people as fellow victims (in this case of the same predatory institutional forces that resulted in the decline of urban neighborhoods). They also omit the fact that white communities were built on racial segregation that enshrined simultaneous institutional support for white neighborhoods and neglect of Black neighborhoods. Nostalgia for previous historical moments that seem devoid of racial strife are in such cases inseparable from longing for white dominance, since the supposed absence of tension was the result of more overt forms of white supremacy.

Du Bois described how white nostalgia functions in the essay "The White World," in *Dusk of Dawn*, published in 1940. He sketched the views of an imaginary "white friend" who was socially liberal, educated, and until the age of thirty "had not known that he was a white man, or at least he had not realized it. . . . But lately he had come to realize that his whiteness was fraught with tremendous responsibilities. . . . It would seem that colored folks were a threat to the world. They were going to overthrow white folk by sheer weight of numbers, destroy their homes and marry their daughters." The threat of white displacement and Black supremacy that haunted Du Bois's otherwise liberal white friend was fueled by nostalgia for previous eras of unquestioned white dominance. "He had noticed with some disturbed feeling that Negroes in particular were not nearly as agreeable and happy as they used to be. He had not for years been able to get a good, cheap colored cook and the last black yard man asked quite exorbitant wages. . . . He had only last year to join in a neighborhood association to keep a Negro from buying a lot right on the next block!"[49] Du Bois's liberal white friend was committed to white political rule, domestically and internationally: "he could not conceive of a world where white people did not rule colored people."[50] Such commitment to white domination, Du Bois argued, showed that "the democracy which the white world seeks to defend does not exist." But white Americans could not admit this to themselves because their commitment to white rule was the result not only of consciously held principles, but also of "conditioned reflexes, of long followed habits, customs and folkways; of subconscious trains of reasoning and unconscious nervous reflexes."[51] The attitudes, opinions, and feelings of Du Bois's liberal white friend illustrate the unconscious level at which affective attachment to white dominance operates for many white persons. The lack of recognition of themselves as "white" or as just as enmeshed in and committed to "identity politics" as nonwhites, in turn, enables a mistaken belief that they are committed to color blindness.[52] Ironically, many white citizens are nostalgic for (and attached to) white dominance, and simultaneously committed to minimizing the impact of white supremacy. In other words, they mourn past eras of untrammeled white rule, while also downplaying the impact of racism on the lives of nonwhites and on the formation of the political community as a whole.

The fact that the loss of white dominance is legitimate has not made it easier to accept, partly because white citizens have not historically been required to develop the key democratic capacity of peaceful acquiescence to loss. As a result, gains by nonwhites are experienced as instances of loss, even when they redress long-standing racial injustices and inequalities. As recurrent racist backlash following racial justice gains demonstrates, whites have historically not been good losers. Many respond with white grievance instead. Ostensibly, the acceptance of the end of white political dominance occurred in the United States with the end of racial segregation and belated legal enforcement of Black electoral participation via the Voting Rights Act of 1965. But these civil rights victories, momentous as they were, did not fundamentally transform the character of the racial state nor white expectations of political dominance.[53] As Zoltan Hajnal's analysis of minority representation has shown, in the United States, race is the most important attribute that predicts who is able to win policy debates and have meaningful political representation: "American democracy [continually] gives more weight to the views and votes of White Americans than to the views and votes of racial and ethnic minorities. Race—more than class, and more than any other demographic characteristic—determines who wins and who loses in American democracy."[54] The result is that whites as a group have been theoretically confronted with the possibility of sharing political rule with nonwhites but have rarely had to experience it in practice.

Additionally, even when less economically advantaged white citizens are unable to actively exercise political rule, racial standing has provided other ways to avoid feeling "powerless." Extrapolating from African American experiences of political loss, Allen suggests that all "democratic citizens have a special need for symbols and the world of fantasy." Because loss is central to democracy, she argues, democratic citizens are able to experience the autonomy, freedom, and sovereignty that democracy promises "fully, in reality, only in their symbol worlds. The manipulation of ideal symbols . . . gives a democratic citizen psychological access to political power."[55] For dominant groups in herrenvolk democracies, the gap between expectation and reality is much narrower. As Hajnal shows, white political preferences are still much more likely to prevail in US democracy, even after the ostensible end of officially sanctioned second-class citizenship for nonwhites. The expectation of white political dominance is one of the symbolic rewards of whiteness, one that is especially important for those who are economically disadvantaged. White citizens have been conditioned to expect continued white dominance as a key feature of their political identity. The expectation of that dominance explains the wrenching loss that many white citizens experienced at the election of the first and only Black president in US history. Until then, the president's whiteness was symbolic reassurance that political power also remained white.

White unwillingness to accept even legitimate political loss also manifests itself in the expectation that policy debates should be oriented toward white interests and needs, that politics should center the concerns of whites as a group, that is, white priority. Consider the rejoinder "All Lives Matter" in response to the "Black Lives Matter" protests against disproportionate police killings of Black citizens. This counterslogan perfectly captures the absurd outcome that an attempt to redress a specific injustice generated feelings of exclusion in some white citizens. Clearly, if all lives already mattered equally, it would not be necessary to assert that Black lives *also* matter. The rejoinder "all lives matter" is a way of reasserting white priority. Yet the conflation between whiteness and political rule also manifests itself in a complex distortion of national historical narratives: at the same time as some white citizens long to reassert a supposedly waning dominance, they simultaneously refuse to acknowledge the contemporary implications of said dominance. Nostalgia for unchallenged eras of white dominance is accompanied by a reflexive desire to relegate racism to the distant past in order to deny the existence of nonwhite subordination in the present and preserve white innocence. The public remembrance and reverence for symbols of the Confederacy in many states in the US South in the name of supposedly nonracist appeals to "tradition" illustrate this dynamic. On the one hand, Confederate emblems are said to be innocuous symbols, but on the other hand, they have been built and most fiercely defended in precisely those eras when white supremacy was being challenged.

The impact of white grievance on contemporary racial politics is profound. When white vulnerability (real or perceived) is politicized, it results in moments of existential crisis for whiteness, with extremely dangerous consequences for the never-fully-realized project of US democracy. Together, the different aspects of white refusal—a zero-sum view of politics that mobilizes white victimhood in response to (more-often-than-not anticipatory, symbolic, or incremental) nonwhite gains; narratives of white racial innocence; nostalgia for past eras of clear white dominance; apocalyptic conceptions of racial equality as Black rule and white subjection; and unwillingness to accept legitimate political loss—remain some of the principal obstacles to the US becoming a full democracy.

The Obama Presidency and "the Phantom of Black Supremacy"

The election of the country's only nonwhite president in 2008 was widely hailed as evidence that the United States had finally become the vaunted postracial society some claim it has supposedly always aspired to be. But the public euphoria that greeted the election of a Black president quickly gave way, during his two terms in office, to an era of heightened white racial resentment and outright racist backlash. This spiral of white backlash culminated in the election of Donald Trump, the chief propagator of the racist "birther" conspiracy theory, whose administration openly embraced white nationalism. Obama's election was therefore clearly neither the result of, nor a catalyst for, a radical transformation in US racial attitudes to reject racism.[56] It did, however, represent the apotheosis—and ensured the collapse—of the "racial liberal consensus" that had dominated US politics since the 1970s. The terms of this tacit compact were that overt bigotry was verboten yet attempts to dismantle institutional or structural racism were also not to be pursued too vigorously. Obama's presidency made the contradictions in the racial status quo impossible to ignore. This was partly because his election did nothing to alter the "dire political iconography" of police violence and militarized repression to which Black Lives Matter protests would later respond. But it was also because "his very presence in office, his blackness in the whitest of houses, was a daily affront to those who still prefer to see the United States as a white man's country. . . . For people on the racial Right, the Obama presidency was essentially intolerable from day one, and 'massive resistance' was again the order of the day."[57] In other words, Obama's election became the occasion for a virulent intensification of white grievance that manifested itself in a resurgence of the kind of overt racism that the country had supposedly moved past in the 1960s.

That the perceived loss Obama's election represented resulted in white backlash should not have been surprising, as, historically, progress toward racial equality in the United States has been followed by the retrenchment and reconsolidation of white supremacy. As King observed, white resistance has been a recurrent reaction to racial progress in the United States. Emancipation and Reconstruction were followed by the consolidation of Jim Crow racial segregation, official adherence to white supremacy, racial terror, political disenfranchisement, and xenophobia in the late nineteenth and early twentieth centuries. Likewise, the civil rights victories of the 1960s were followed by the retrenchment of the welfare state (which was justified by racially coded appeals) and the concomitant rise of mass incarceration that continued to ensure material racial inequality despite the absence of mandated racial segregation. Historically, then, most white citizens have not shown the kind of peaceful acquiescence to loss that Allen argues is necessary for democratic stability. Yet emancipation and the civil rights victories of the 1960s were widescale transformations in the US racial order, whereas the election of a single Black officeholder, albeit to the highest political office in the land, did not alter the disproportionate mass incarceration rates of Black and Latinx citizens, the existing income and wealth disparities between whites and nonwhites exacerbated by the 2008 financial crisis (and later the Covid-19 pandemic), the continued deportation and harassment of undocumented immigrants, or the continued confinement of poor nonwhite citizens to "the carceral spaces of the prison and the ghetto."[58] Yet the election of a Black president, as symbolic a gain as this was for nonwhites, was experienced by some sectors of US whiteness as a moment of existential crisis, when expectations of white priority were upended and white dominance was threatened. The racist reaction to Obama's election was initially exemplified by the rise of the Tea Party and its calls to "take our country back." During the Trump era, this evolved into a panoply of white grievances ranging from open embrace of white nationalism to demands that white supremacist views not be condemned (i.e., so-called cancel culture panics).[59]

To understand why the election of a Black president was experienced by a significant portion of white citizens as a moment of existential crisis—despite the fact that Obama campaigned and governed as a mainstream Democratic politician committed to racial reconciliation and to transcending race—it is instructive to recall the fears of a "black emperor" elicited by the enfranchisement of African Americans following the abolition of slavery almost a century and a half ago. Frederick Douglass, the brilliant Black thinker, orator, and fugitive ex–slave, mocked such fears of "black supremacy," which fancifully imagined that were the United States to allow its Black inhabitants to cease being treated as chattel, "the republic . . . [would] give place to a vast American empire under the sway of a jet black emperor who shall have a snow white empress—a court of all shades and colors—and a code of laws considerately enacted to protect the unfortunate whites from insults offered by the insolent and dominant blacks!"[60] If the mere prospect of the end of enslavement and subsequent Black enfranchisement conjured "the phantom of black supremacy" and miscegenation for white observers in the nineteenth century, we can see how the election of a Black president in the twenty-first century would lead some white citizens to once again be haunted by this persistent fear of Black rule. Through the lens of white commitment to political rule, Black equality can be imagined only as the specter of Black domination.

Indeed, apocalyptic narratives of white loss that transform anticipatory losses into foregone defeats are a key feature of resurgent white grievance in the United States.[61] As the compounded losses that some sectors of whiteness see themselves as having suffered since 2008 reveal, in their dystopian vision racial equality can only be conceived as nonwhite rule and white subjugation. Obama's presidency was characterized not only by his two electoral victories, but also by the emergence of a highly visible and energized Black protest movement. The protests that erupted in Ferguson, Missouri, in 2014, and the subsequent disproportionate police repression of citizen protesters, marked an important inflection point in US racial politics. It signaled an era of more radical Black demands, when pragmatic forms of Black politics that followed the civil rights victories of the 1960s, which were principally aimed at descriptive representation, have been replaced by a vocal protest movement seeking to dismantle some of the key pillars of contemporary white supremacy: mass incarceration, violent policing, a biased criminal punishment (not "justice") system, and the pervasive criminalization of Black life.[62] This shift from reform to abolition is reflected in the Movement for Black Lives' call to defund the police and invest in Black communities instead.[63] Not only has this level of sustained Black protest not been seen in the United States since the 1960s; Black Lives Matter protests are taking place in the era of social media, when Black suffering and Black losses can be amplified and broadcast in a way that makes them viscerally accessible via the continuous loop of viral videos showing police killing unarmed Blacks. While it is undoubtedly true that the visual evidence of police violence has been disputed and the actions of Black victims prior to and during encounters with the police have been endlessly dissected, Black Lives Matter protesters refuse to adopt frames of Black respectability to couch their assertion that Black life is disposable in the United States. Their critique is also leveled directly at representatives of the state, some of them Black officeholders: from the police, prosecutors, district attorneys, and the entire criminal punishment apparatus, to elected officials such as mayors and governors.[64]

There was thus an important paradox in the racial politics of the Obama presidency: the losses fueling rising white grievance were anticipatory or at best symbolic. There was a palpable rise in feelings of white grievance among some sectors of US whiteness because of symbolic nonwhite gains. But even these gains were rather tenuous. Indeed, the difficulty of grappling with current perceptions of white loss is that, in the post–civil rights era, dominant forms of Black politics, constrained by neoliberalism and political pragmatism, were predominantly oriented toward palatable forms of liberal reform. Resurgent white grievance has thus been driven by symbolic Black gains—such as the Obama presidency—that functioned to support the status quo of, at best, incremental change toward racial equality, accompanied by the retrenchment or slow erosion of the significant civil rights victories of the 1960s. While racial justice activists have once again begun to make transformative demands, it remains to be seen whether the other side of the racial liberal consensus—the refusal to tackle deep institutional, structural racism—can indeed be overcome. White grievance is therefore predicated on anticipatory loss, while it is simultaneously deployed precisely to forestall the apocalyptic outcome of shared rule imagined as white subjugation.

Material and Symbolic Loss

If the post–civil rights era has not been a period of rapidly expanding Black/nonwhite gains, if it has rather been characterized by, at best, incremental and tenuous advancement, what are the losses driving resurgent white grievance?[65] The usual explanation for contemporary white grievance is that it is primarily driven by working-class whites who feel left behind economically and alienated from the political process. But a large proportion of the working class—whether defined by income or education level—is nonwhite. And the white working-class voters who appear to be most motivated by a sense of white grievance are, in fact, still economically better off than most nonwhites.[66] Most centrally, contrary to all that has been written about so-called economic anxiety, white grievance is *not* solely or primarily a working-class phenomenon. For instance, of the factors that drove support for Trump in 2016—in a campaign characterized by racist rhetoric that explicitly sought to mobilize white racial resentment—economic anxiety was not the most salient consideration. Instead, racist resentment, anti-immigrant sentiment, and sexism were the primary motivation of many of his supporters.[67] Additionally, the largely middle- and upper-class composition of the white insurrectionists who stormed the US Capitol on January 6, not to mention the plethora of elected officials who were prepared to toss out the legitimately cast votes of their fellow citizens (particularly in majority-Black or multiracial cities and states), directly contradicts the idea that white grievance is fueled mainly or solely by economic anxiety. White grievance is also not confined to a single geographic region; it spans liberal and conservative states, as well as rural and suburban communities.[68] White grievance therefore cannot be understood solely in economic terms.[69]

This is not to say that the white working class has not suffered significant material losses in recent decades, but so too have nonwhites.[70] Yet the shared losses of the white working class and the nonwhite working and middle classes are obscured. The United States today is a society defined by growing economic inequality, where the differences between the top 1 percent and the rest are stark. In economic terms, it could be argued that only the 1 percent is winning and everyone else is losing. Whites and nonwhites are suffering from these economic trends, yet many of the former have wrongly attributed their declining economic prospects to competition from nonwhite workers, especially migrants. In fact, on average, working-class whites still have higher incomes than working-class Black and Latinx workers. Indeed, the structural economic changes that are now limiting the prospects of middle- and working-class whites began to affect African Americans in the 1970s. Moreover, Latinx and Black households disproportionately suffered the brunt of the economic losses of the 2008 financial crisis and ensuing recession, as well as the Covid-19 pandemic.[71] Material loss is not a phenomenon confined to the white working class; nonwhites also experience it. In fact, nonwhite communities suffer *steep* material losses, both in terms of lower employment rates and in the form of police violence and the death and economic depredation that accompany the carceral state, to name a few. Yet it is middle- and working-class whites who have supposedly been politically galvanized by declining economic opportunities and economic insecurity. White grievance is not fueled simply by those experiencing economic displacement, however. Indeed, "it is often the more privileged rather than the most dispossessed who drive the authoritarian revolt, and . . . their aggression is not directed against the causes of material suffering, but is always already linked to certain marginalized groups."[72] Whites are not the only group experiencing economic losses, nor are these losses the result of Black/nonwhite gains. Rather, the loss that working-class whites are feeling is the erosion of white priority, especially in symbolic realms.

If democratic empowerment is only ever fully realized via symbols (as Allen contends), this helps explain the significance of symbolic loss. In her account of the drivers of contemporary neo-authoritarianism, Eva von Redecker argues that "propertized oppression" not only has operated in modern societies through institutional arrangements that "explicitly guarantee property-like control to oppressors; it also structures social relations through internalized norms." Modern liberal capitalist societies, she argues, "have relied on in-built entitlements to group-based oppression . . . [that] historically took on a form analogous to property." Slavery and patriarchal marriage were two paradigmatic cases of dominion ("legally sanctioned, institutionalized control over living human beings"), but after their legal elimination, the "embodied dispositions and corresponding cultural schemas" they fomented live on in the form of "phantom possession," which intensifies in the face of resistance.[73] Phantom possession shields the dominant subject from the loss of the object of dominion (itself an autonomous subject); it also allows the fantasy that a "sphere in which unaccountable sovereignty can be enacted" is still readily available. She argues that "Phantom possession provides social protection on a symbolic level, thereby compensating and coopting parts of the laboring classes. It wields the archliberal promise not of equal freedom before the law, but of unlimited freedom after it, if only in that small, bounded domain that one can call one's own and does not fully possess anyhow, and if only in the stunted form of authoritarian freedom."[74] Phantom possession, in von Redecker's view, compensates for contemporary dispossession even as it is itself the assertion of an entitlement to appropriation and a symbolic shoring up of the sovereign status ascribed to whiteness and maleness.

Von Redecker's account of phantom possession is helpful for thinking about the complex ways that gender and symbolic loss factor into white grievance. White grievance is gendered and sexualized in particular ways, as dominant white imaginaries are intersectional; in addition to being white supremacist, they are also patriarchal and heteronormative.[75] Trump supporters, for example, express misogynistic and homophobic fears about gains by women and lesbian, gay, bisexual, transgender, and queer (LGBTQ+) citizens.[76] And in 2022, the panic against the supposed teaching of critical race theory in public schools has been followed by a spate of antigay and antitrans state legislation, including bills on school policies (such as those that ban discussions of sexual orientation or all-gender restrooms), bans on gender-affirming medical care, and bans on trans youth in sports.[77]

Feminist theorists have argued that the disposition to enact unaccountable sovereignty that is central to traditional conceptions of masculinity fuels a vision of politics as violent domination. For Kate Manne, "some hitherto dominant social actors, e.g., disappointed white men, will punch down fairly indiscriminately—for example, to nonwhites and immigrants, as well as white women—when they develop withdrawal symptoms or a deprivation mind-set vis-à-vis women's social and emotional labor."[78] She emphasizes how perceived white male losses of women's attention, care, and concern are central to fueling misogyny, of both the routine and spectacularly violent varieties. Bonnie Honig, meanwhile, calls attention to the key role of feminization in Trumpism, which she defines as "a kind of male entitlement for which it feels like freedom to just be able to say what you think and grab what you want." She argues that feminization is a strategy of domination applied to a series of subordinated "others":

> Feminization is the complex array of discourses and practices that reproduce, secure, and advance hierarchical divisions of sexuality, gender, race, ability, indigeneity, ethnicity, lineage, and class that make the world legible, hospitable, and accessible to some more than others. Feminization is a device of disorientation and a practice of desensitization. It works at a sensorial level by demeaning and degrading whole swaths of populations, outlooks, and behaviors, demanding their submission, compliance, or silence, and exhorting others to join the circle of bullying.[79]

Honig's and Manne's analyses of feminization and the logic of misogyny allow us to see that one of the ways in which anticipatory loss is assuaged in white grievance is by enacting cruel forms of domination—such as migrant family separation or militarized and violent policing—over feminized groups, such as immigrants, queer and trans youth, Black people, and so on. The gendering of white dominance also means that white women get to enact their belonging by participating in the pleasures of domination over feminized racial others (as they did in prior historical eras via, for example, lynching spectatorship).[80]

Paying attention to the role of dispositions to embodied entitlement and the pleasures of domination in white grievance is helpful for understanding what is fueling white refusal in a context of incremental or largely symbolic Black/nonwhite gains and shared material losses (across racial groups) by the economically less advantaged. Material and symbolic loss are connected, but it is important to make a conceptual distinction between them. That is because symbolic loss is crucial to understanding why white grievance has become a galvanizing political force in an era of rights retrenchment and tenuous (at best) economic advances for nonwhites. One of the key claims of this chapter is that in the Obama and Trump eras white grievance has been being driven in important ways by symbolic loss.

There are two senses in which I am using the term symbolic loss here. One refers to loss in the realm of symbolic (especially cultural) representation. This, for example, is what sparked outrage at the *New York Times*' 1619 project, for centering slavery and the contributions of Black Americans to US history. Part of what Trump's white supporters get from his rhetoric is symbolic recognition that assuages such feelings of cultural displacement. They feel empowered by his unequivocal embrace of white nativism and his populist, xenophobic, and racist appeals targeting Latinx immigrants, Muslims, and Black Lives Matter protesters. His racist rhetoric and policies are reassurance that white priority not only is legitimate, but also remains the central organizing principle of US politics and society. Symbolic loss also refers to the work of white racist fantasy, in which "seeing whitely" leads to the projection of white desires and actions onto racialized others. Judith Butler's analysis of the use of video evidence in the Rodney King trial draws attention to "the inverted projections of white paranoia" that led jurors to view evidence of King being brutally beaten and construe it instead as a scene in which he was the one threatening violence, "whose agency is phantasmatically implied."[81] In this sense, symbolic loss also refers to the anticipatory losses constructed by white paranoia, whereby desires for domination and erasure are projected onto racial others. This kind of racist fantasy is partly what is at work (in addition to bad faith) in claims that Black racial justice protesters are necessarily violent threats to white property even as it is the police who mete out disproportionate violence. This kind of racist projection is what allows televangelist Pat Robertson to claim that critical race theory teaches that white people are racist "and therefore the people of color have to rise up and overtake their oppressors and then—having gotten the 'whip handle,' if I can use that term—then to instruct their white neighbors how to behave."[82] White grievance is an expression of continued expectations of political, economic, and social dominance, even (or especially) as those forms of dominance are imagined to be threatened by menacing nonwhites ready to enact revenge. Material losses are not the only or main driver of contemporary white grievance; rather, it is symbolic losses that increasingly seem to propel white rage.[83]

Consider, for example, the US Treasury Department's decision to add a Black woman to a US treasury bill for the first time, which would seem like an improbable instance of white loss. Yet it is precisely this kind of symbolic loss that elicits outbursts of white grievance.[84] The decision to replace Andrew Jackson with Harriet Tubman—the fugitive slave, abolitionist, and advocate of women's suffrage—which was approved during the Obama presidency and delayed by the Trump administration, was opposed by conservatives, who argued that it represented a dislocation of white men from their central role in US history. They viewed the decision as emblematic of an axiom of the politics of white grievance that women, racial minorities, and LGBTQ+ citizens are the recipients of special, unearned "gifts" from a state that is committed to perpetual loss for white males.[85] The opposition to Tubman's inclusion on US currency perfectly captures white grievance's contorted racial math, in which tenuous or purely symbolic Black/nonwhite gains are experienced as magnified white losses. In fact, many Black commentators viewed the decision to replace Jackson with Tubman as exemplary of the kind of token symbolic gestures that have characterized racial politics in the post–civil rights era. From their perspective Tubman's addition was an example of symbolic representation without institutional transformation. Black critics questioned the meaning of such a gesture when Black people continue being killed by agents of the same state that sanctioned the institution of slavery that Tubman valiantly fought against. They noted the irony of a woman who had been bought and sold as property being depicted on US currency, when ex-slaves and their descendants have never been compensated for their forced unpaid labor. For many Black observers, making Tubman one of the faces of US currency was thus hardly a gain; it was a ruse of power. Yet these instances of symbolic representation are often met with the same kind of outrage by aggrieved whites as if they heralded significant structural change.

Contemporary white grievance is therefore propelled not by economic decline per se, but by both material and symbolic loss. This is not to suggest that these two dimensions of loss are discontinuous from each other, but rather that it is possible to distinguish between them for analytical purposes.[86] Moreover, distinguishing between material and symbolic loss is important because it has normative implications for how we assess different forms of white grievance. For example, whether white material losses raise issues of fairness in a democratic polity depends on how they are framed and understood. They are a more legitimate grievance if they are framed as part of a larger problem of rising socioeconomic inequality that is also affecting nonwhites. If what is being mourned is relative white economic advantage over nonwhites, however, then such claims are normatively suspect. As we shall see, symbolic losses tend to be even more normatively problematic, because they flow directly from political commitments to, and affective investments in, white priority that are incompatible with racial egalitarianism. More generally, racial justice and democratic politics precisely require that whites learn to accept loss, both material and symbolic. To illustrate this, I turn to two emblematic instances of white symbolic loss that show that white citizens have rarely been "good" losers.

Losing Whiteness

As MLK despairingly predicted in the wake of the civil rights victories of the 1960s, white resistance would become fiercer and more entrenched as whites were required to accept not just symbolic but also material loss. The symbolic and the material are inextricably intertwined in the politics of white grievance. I turn to two prominent recent examples of white refusal to consider if and when white loss is ever accepted: (1) the backlash to Black Lives Matter protests *against* violent policing, and (2) right-wing protests against the removal of symbols honoring the Confederacy. What losses, we might ask, are incurred when police violence is denounced or when symbols honoring racists are removed? Why do some white citizens experience these as losses?

The hashtag #BlackLivesMatter was intended as a call to action. It emerged after seventeen-year-old Trayvon Martin was "posthumously placed on trial for his own murder and the killer, George Zimmerman, was not held accountable for the crime he committed." Asserting that Black lives matter "is an ideological and political intervention in a world where Black lives are systematically and intentionally targeted for demise."[87] Instead, what some white people have heard is that when Black lives matter, white lives *don't* matter, as the counterslogan "All lives matter" reveals. This reaction to a movement created to bring attention to the disproportionate violence faced by Black people shows how white grievance supplants and erases Black grief. It also shows that white grievance is often mobilized in response to perceived symbolic loss. The decentering of whiteness implied by saying #BlackLivesMatter could only be taken only as a devaluation of white lives by those who believe that politics should always center the concerns of whites as a group. But the Movement for Black Lives' critique of violent policing and their abolitionist demands could benefit all citizens; indeed, their activism has already been the impetus for the election of progressive district attorneys who promise to deemphasize punitive carceral policies, to increase scrutiny of police impunity codified in union contracts, and to reconsider the allocation of local budget priorities that deemphasize social services in favor of police funding.[88] The M4BL could thus benefit *all* citizens.

At the same time, the reaction to the symbolic loss of authority experienced by the police in the wake of Black Lives Matter protests has had profound negative *material* consequences for Black people, such as doubling down on carceral policies that disproportionately impact Black communities. The material impacts of the backlash to racial justice protests are also evident in legislative efforts to make it a hate crime to target police officers, to criminally punish protest participation, and to grant immunity to those who injure racial justice protesters. Blue Lives Matter legislation, which was proposed in various states and enacted in Louisiana, equates the risks that police officers face because of their chosen occupation with discrimination based on stigmatized identities such as race, gender, sexual orientation, and religion.[89] Blue Lives Matter laws conflate critiques of use of excessive force by police officers and the militarization of law enforcement with "hatred" of the police. This, in turn, functions to transform the police, who routinely go unpunished for killing unarmed citizens, into the supposed victims. Likewise, since 2016, punitive antiprotest legislation that limits the right to peaceful protest and penalizes protesters with serious crimes carrying lengthy sentences for vaguely defined offenses have also been proposed and even enacted in many US states.[90] Recently enacted antiprotest bills that penalize damage to property (and to monuments in particular) also include provisions that confer immunity on those who injure racial justice protesters. An antiprotest law, HB 1/SB 484, enacted in Florida in 2021, for example, "could encourage violence against protesters, by creating a new affirmative defense in civil lawsuits for personal injury, death, or property damage, such that a defendant could avoid liability by establishing that the injury, death, or damage they committed 'arose from' conduct by someone 'acting in furtherance of a riot.'" In the racial calculus of the wave of antiprotest legislation that followed Black Lives Matter protests, racial justice protests are always already "riots," and the protection of property is paramount while the lives of protesters are disposable.[91] In contrast, instances of majority-white rioting, such as the January 6 insurrection, are often not recognized as riots, as the reactions of those who have bristled at the use of the term to describe the assault on the Capitol reveal.

The M4BL challenged the unquestioned deference to state authority and the hagiography of the police that became de rigueur in the United States after 9/11, and this symbolic loss mobilized fears of antipolice violence that materialized in Blue Lives Matter and antiprotest legislation that displaces the source of violence, obscures the Black dead, and renders those who dare to protest even more vulnerable to state and counterprotester violence. Blue Lives Matter and antiprotest legislation as a response to the symbolic displacement of Black Lives Matter has clear material consequences for the politics of race, policing, and anti-Black violence. It disregards Black grief and furthers the continued disposability that the cry "Black Lives Matter" was meant to highlight and counter.

If antiprotest legislation shows that some white citizens are unwilling to accept the symbolic challenge to white priority that antiracist protests enact, an even more pointed instance of the unjust racial calculus required for the acceptance of white loss is the debate about the removal of Confederate symbols. Confederate iconography involves tangible objects—flags (which are emblazoned on all manner of objects, from license plates to t-shirts to official seals), place names (of parks, streets, highways, and schools), statues, and monuments—that have both material and symbolic effects, such as the demarcation of public spaces as white-only or enforcing and taking pleasure in Black loss.[92] But their removal is an instance of symbolic loss because removing racist monuments will not immediately alter structural elements of white supremacy, such as economic disparities between whites and nonwhites, democratic deficits (such as limiting the voting power of nonwhites), anti-Black and other forms of racist violence, and so on. Yet, until very recently, the widespread removal of confederate symbols from shared public spaces seemed extremely unlikely. Demands for their removal had resulted in decades of inertia and stalemate. Some confederate monuments were the subject of protracted struggles to remove or contextualize them, involving lengthy local city council deliberations, statewide legislation, and extended legal proceedings. In a sign of how contentious some of these struggles over confederate monument removal became, opposition to the removal of the Robert E. Lee monument in Charlottesville, Virginia, inspired the deadly "Unite the Right" rally in 2017. Indeed, widespread confederate monument removal did not become possible until two highly visible instances of white violence and Black death: the mass murder of nine innocent Black citizens in a church in Charleston by an avowed white supremacist shooter in 2015, and the killings of George Floyd and Breonna Taylor in 2020, which sparked massive national and global protests against racism.

The Charleston massacre at Emanuel African Methodist Episcopal Church (a historic institution associated with various Black freedom struggles, including the failed slave revolt led by Denmark Vesey in 1822) was an instance of horrific Black loss. Its victims, who ranged in age from twenty-six to eighty-seven years old—Sharonda Coleman-Singleton, Cynthia Hurd, Susie Jackson, Ethel Lance, DePayne Middleton-Doctor, Clementa Pinckney, Tywanza Sanders, Daniel Simmons, and Myra Thompson, because we must say their names—had gathered for a prayer service. This was one of the rare instances where the innocence of the Black victims could not be questioned and where the racist motivations of the shooter were also incontrovertibly established.[93] Following a familiar pattern that has also been replicated in high-profile cases of police killings of Black people that have sparked subsequent protests, the relatives of the Black dead were asked to express immediate forgiveness to ensure democratic stability. They and the rest of the Black community were expected to peacefully accept their deadly losses. At the same time, because the shooter was photographed displaying various racist symbols (including the Confederate battle flag), the debate over the removal of Confederate iconography was immediately reignited. Many who had in the past opposed demands to remove the Confederate battle flag now joined calls to remove it from the South Carolina statehouse. One conservative commentator, for example, argued that the Confederate flag "represents something more than visceral racial hatred" and bemoaned how "today's 'racial activists' are keen to cast the Civil War as a simple contest of Good-versus-Evil." He nevertheless also explicitly invoked the idea that white symbolic loss might in this instance be necessary given the immeasurable Black losses of the Charleston massacre: "If reducing the visibility of these symbols would offer relief to those genuinely hurt, and would remove an object of contention keeping persons of different races from cooperating to advance *true* racial justice, that is something supporters of Confederate symbols should be able to do."[94] The about-face on the removal of the Confederate flag in South Carolina following the Charleston massacre is instructive regarding the lack of equivalence between Black and white loss. Horrific and undeniable Black losses were required to render a minor symbolic white loss (the removal of the Confederate flag) palatable.[95] To put it starkly, nine innocent Black citizens had to die to enable peaceful white acquiescence to an instance of symbolic loss.[96] This is not a sustainable balance sheet of loss.

Since the protests sparked by the killings of George Floyd and Breonna Taylor in the summer of 2020, numerous Confederate monuments have been removed, schools and buildings have been renamed, and the display of the Confederate battle flag was prohibited or abandoned by many organizations, including the Mississippi legislature (which removed it from its state flag), NASCAR, and the US Army. Since May 2020, over one hundred racist monuments have been removed (or are slated to be removed) in states across the United States, most of them confederate statues.[97] Contemporary monument removal has, in some cases, been legal and officially sanctioned (although often following defacement of the monument by protesters), but in many cases, removals have been spontaneous and have involved deliberately breaking laws prohibiting removal.

The removal of racist monuments has itself become fodder for white grievance, and attempts to impede it illustrate how resistance to white symbolic loss can have important material consequences for Black people and racial justice activists. Florida's 2021 antiprotest law, HB 1/SB 484, for example, "creates a new 3rd degree felony offense, punishable by up to 5 years in prison, for anyone who 'willfully and maliciously defaces, injures, or otherwise damages by any means' statues, flags, paintings, displays, or other 'memorials' and the value of the damage is more than $200. As 'deface' is not defined, protesters who apply paint or graffiti to a monument in the course of a peaceful protest could face up to 5 years in prison."[98] Laws such as this one aim to prevent the transformation of confederate monuments through graffiti, art installations, or spontaneous removal into sites of antiracist reflection, democratic action, and Black joy, however temporarily.

For some, then, the response to the 2020 racial justice protests has been continued refusal to accept even symbolic white loss. For instance, spray painting "white lives matter" on a monument to tennis legend Arthur Ashe in Richmond (which was installed in 1996 amid great controversy as a counterweight to the five Confederate statues that used to line the city's famous

Monument Avenue), was justified as a tit-for-tat response to the defacement of Confederate monuments. The rationale for vandalizing Ashe's statue illustrates how white grievance works to displace or obscure Black grief: "You put it on our statues, I'll put it on yours. . . . Why is it okay to spray paint on this statue 'black lives matter,' but not 'white lives matter'? What's the difference? . . . They all matter. Everybody matters, right?"[99] This assertion of equivalence willfully ignores the difference between monuments to supporters of white supremacy and the monument honoring Ashe, a trailblazing athlete who integrated a predominantly white sport, not to mention the larger antiracist public memory deficit in Richmond (a majority-Black city whose landscape was dominated by confederate statues) that his statue was meant to address.

Today's resurgent white grievance echoes the white backlash that followed previous moments of racial progress in US history. Viewed through this lens, even symbolic losses such as the removal of racist monuments and demands for fair treatment by Black/nonwhite citizens continue to be experienced by some white citizens as deeply unfair erosions of white priority. From racial justice protests to Confederate monument removal, important sectors of US whiteness are experiencing the current era as a period of repeated symbolic losses that signal the end of unquestioned white dominance. The irony is that fears of "black supremacy" and white subjection are surfacing in response to tenuous or at best token Black and nonwhite gains, coupled with real and deadly material losses. Even as Black protests have led to a certain amount of peaceful white acquiescence to symbolic loss, there is still an unequal economy of suffering at work, as momentum for racist monument removal has come only from moments when Black suffering is hypervisible. The removal of statues made of stone should not require sacrifices of blood by Black people, as protesters have noted. Amid the graffiti covering the Robert E. Lee statue in Richmond in 2020 following the protests in that city, four words on the granite base stood out: "How much more blood?" Flags and statues have been removed, but Black people are still dying. As (some) whites mourn lost statues and lost causes, Blacks mourn their dead.

Whither White Refusal?

After the massive racial justice protests of the summer of 2020 and the Capitol insurrection of January 2021, the fundamental question of contemporary US racial politics is whether aggrieved whites can learn to acquiesce to legitimate political loss. The gravest threat to US democracy today is not Black radicalism but white grievance—indeed, if anything it is Black citizens who continue to bear the brunt of democratic sacrifice. There have been instances, historically and contemporarily, in which white citizens have been able to meet the requirements of racial justice without resorting to refusal. In 1951, for example, a white reader wrote a letter to Paul Robeson's newspaper, *Freedom,* which was reprinted under the headline "'I Lose Too,' Says White Reader." The letter writer from Los Angeles, California, explained that they were motivated to write by the fact that too often discussions about racism focused on the effects of white supremacy on Black people, without paying sufficient attention to its impact on whites, who as a result did not realize why *they* should also struggle to eliminate "this horrible monster." White supremacy, the letter writer observed, distorted the civic capacities of whites by encouraging them to nurture racial hatred and to embrace dishonesty ("cheating") as business acumen. "How many times have we heard it said that the person who cheats is smart and the one who is cheated is a sucker?" In addition to making them bad citizens, racism led whites to accept authoritarian and violent state institutions for the sake of protecting white priority: "Third, we let the police attack, jail, frame, and kill the minority people, so that more and more the police and the people who run the courts are saying they are the law. If you do say anything, you are hit on the head or shot for resisting arrest." In contrast to today's aggrieved whites who cannot see that demands to stop violent policing and rethink punitive approaches to public order by the M4BL would in fact benefit all members of the political community, this midcentury white reader argued that whites also stood to benefit from antiracist struggles. The letter writer concluded by asking Black "and other minority people . . . please keep fighting and let me and my people cooperate with you. For we all have so much to gain in this fight."[100] Like Robeson's midcentury white reader, not all white citizens today partake of the politics of white grievance; some choose to be racial renegades. Yet the obstacles to dismantling white supremacy remain profound, and aggrieved whiteness that prevents white citizens from seeing progress toward racial justice as anything but a loss for them is one of the key impediments.

Racial politics in the United States today thus seems headed for an intractable impasse. On the one hand, there is a highly visible Black-led protest movement galvanized by ongoing police violence, while, on the other hand, there is a large cross section of whites mobilized by a deeply felt sense of grievance and racial resentment. This does not bode well for the possibility of strides toward racial justice in the immediate future. According to legal scholar Derrick Bell, historically, Black gains in the United States have been achieved when they converged with white self-interest.[101] In the current economic context of declining opportunities for the 99 percent and rising inequality, it is difficult to see white majorities being able to view Black or nonwhite gains as anything other than special rights that detract from their own prospects.[102] Interest convergence in an era of white grievance driven by deeply felt symbolic losses seems highly unlikely.

It is therefore instructive to turn to an earlier era of fierce white backlash in US history to think about the problem of white moral and political imaginations shaped by dominance (and the fear of losing it) rather than equality. During the post-Reconstruction era, white supremacy was unquestioned, but there was nevertheless widespread white violence and racial terror fueled by the backlash against fleeting Reconstruction-era Black gains. Then, as now, the racial math was both simple and complex. Blacks were no longer enslaved, but they were also still unfree. Whites were politically, socially, and economically dominant, yet they were so determined to forestall racial equality that their dominance had to be symbolically and materially reaffirmed in the ritualized public spectacle of lynching. The dead Black body was then, as it is now, the terrain on which white fears of loss of political rule, social standing, and economic dominance were contested.

Reflecting in 1894 on the monstrous violence that dashed his Reconstruction-era hopes that the United States would become a genuine multiracial democracy in the essay "Why Is the Negro Lynched?," Frederick Douglass described the US body politic as "disfigured" by the "ghastly horrors" of lynching. United States democracy, he argued, was being rendered monstrous by the accumulating bodies of Black dead produced by the unchecked racial violence of the time. "There is nothing in the history of savages to surpass the blood-chilling horrors and fiendish excesses perpetrated against the coloured people of this country, by the so-called enlightened and Christian people of the South . . . [who] gloat over and prey upon dead bodies."[103] It was not only Black lynching victims, but also the US body politic, that was being mutilated by white violence. Reveling in the pleasures of domination, white mobs were rendered monstrous by their own actions. For Douglass, the unchecked racial violence of the post-Reconstruction era was directly connected to slavery, which had warped the civic capacities of whites by accustoming them to economic and political mastery and to a thorough disregard for Black life. White participants in southern lynch mobs had been "brought up in the exercise of irresponsible power."[104] White southerners could engage in such violence because they held Black people in disregard. They "care no more for the Negro's rights to live than they care for his rights to liberty, or his right to the ballot or any other right."[105] Douglass's critique was not confined to the South, however, as the North was also guilty of engaging in less violent forms of racial domination. "You kill their bodies, we kill their souls," he wrote.[106] It is haunting to read Douglass's century-old condemnation today, when police violence continues to *kill our bodies*, while the tacit (and at times explicit) acquiescence to Black death by many white citizens motivated by racialized fears of crime continues to *kill our souls*. To extend Douglass's insight, if white humanity is diminished by indifference to Black loss, Black citizens are doubly burdened by the seemingly unceasing repetition of the following cycle: dead Black body, protest, indictment or (more likely) nonindictment, eventual nonconviction, killer walks free. As Black citizens continue to be killed, those who remain are forced to bear witness to the dead. This too is a continued assault on our souls.

In an apt lesson for how we should approach the problem of contemporary white grievance, Douglass concluded that the solution to lynching and racial terror was not to frame it as an issue of Black struggle. Instead, what was required was change on the part of white citizens.[107] Douglass forcefully rejected the framing of anti-Black violence as a "Negro problem." This formula, he argued, "lays the fault at the door of the Negro and removes it from the door of the white man, shields the guilty and blames the innocent, makes the Negro responsible, when it should so make the nation."[108] Douglass rejects the tendency to conceive white violence as a problem for Black people to solve. His refusal can be understood as a recognition of the fact that the gravest threat to US democracy is white refusal, as this chapter has argued. Can white citizens learn to accept legitimate political loss? In 1894, Douglass argued that the solution to lynching was to "let the white people of the North and South conquer their prejudices. . . . Let them give up the idea that they can be free while making the Negro a slave. Let them give up the idea that to degrade the coloured man is to elevate the white man. . . . They are not required to do much. They are only required to undo the evil they have done."[109] In other words, whites must learn to accept political loss. As Douglass observed, democracy requires that all groups give up expectations of political dominance. The resurgent white nationalism and nostalgia for prior eras of nonwhite subordination that mark our current moment are a result of aggrieved whites' inability to accept the loss of unearned privilege and unjustified advantage. The often-symbolic white losses being mourned are not the kind of losses that Black or Indigenous people have had to bear or that the children separated from their families and held in cages at the border have been subjected to—not least because these are losses of forms of power and privilege nonwhites have never collectively had access to. Aggrieved white citizens cannot expect their nonwhite fellow citizens to mourn the loss of white priority or share their nostalgia for prior eras of unquestioned white dominance. If they are to be good democratic citizens, whites must reshape their political imaginations and learn to accept legitimate political loss without resorting to white grievance. United States democracy depends on it.

INTERLUDE 2

Taking a stand in Baton Rouge. World Press Photo Awards 2017—Jonathan Bachman, Thomson Reuters.

2

Black Protest and Democratic Sacrifice

SINCE AUGUST 2014, when the protests sparked by the killing of Michael Brown in Ferguson, Missouri, were met with disproportionate police repression against citizen protesters, Black life remains disposable in the United States (and globally).[1] The list of unarmed Black persons—men, women, and children, queer, straight, trans, from New York City, to Baltimore, to St. Louis, to Chicago, to Texas—killed by violent, predominantly white police officers only continues to grow. From Eric Garner to Akai Gurley to Tamir Rice to Aiyana Stanley-Jones to Rekia Boyd to Sandra Bland to John Crawford to Laquan MacDonald . . . there is no discernible end to the tragic parade of the unarmed Black dead.[2] Perhaps the only difference is that now some of us, their fellow citizens, though certainly not all, make a point of saying their names and asserting that "Black lives matter." This chapter tries to make sense of the complex response to contemporary protests against police violence. In particular, I'm interested in condemnations of those who have taken to the streets to protest the routine killing, with near-total impunity, of Black persons across the United States by representatives of the state for minor, if not imagined, offenses, and the ensuing debate about how to understand protesters' actions.[3] In a clear example of the racialized politics of solidarity, protesters and their critics have viewed the same events through very different lenses.[4] This was exemplified by the dueling Twitter hashtags that arose in the wake of the protests over the killing of Freddie Gray in Baltimore in 2015. Where some saw unlawful "riots," others participated in justified "uprisings." These dueling frames raise deeper questions about the forms of politics that Black citizens, who are experiencing a defining moment of racial terror in the United States in the twenty-first century, can and should pursue.

What are the costs of enacting "appropriate" democratic politics in the face of systematic racial violence? The events of Ferguson, Missouri showed two central facts about US democracy: "the absence of reciprocity where Blacks are concerned and the disposability of Black lives," as Melvin Rogers has observed. In contrast to expectations that all citizens are susceptible to political loss, which serves to temper the disempowerment that accompanies the experience of losing that is a central feature of democratic life, "the death of Brown, like so many before him, proves this logic to be a lie where Black folks are concerned. They are perpetually losers in American democracy."[5] In democracies, sacrifice is supposed to be equally distributed, as are care and concern for the losses suffered by fellow citizens. The absence of reciprocity thus calls into question not only the notion of US democracy (democracy for whom?), but also the kinds of democratic obligations that can be fairly placed on Black citizens as a result.[6] When other citizens and state institutions betray a pervasive lack of concern for Black suffering, which in turn makes it impossible for those wrongs to be redressed, is it fair to ask Blacks to make further sacrifices on behalf of the polity?

Taking as its starting point the status of Blacks as perpetual losers in US democracy, this chapter explores whether the display of exemplary citizenship by Black people in the face of such unequal bargains constitutes an unjust form of democratic suffering. We might disagree with the designation of citizens' actions in Ferguson and Baltimore as "riots," or we might think that riots can be justified as legitimate forms of political action if they meet certain conditions.[7] But whether or not we adopt either of these positions, if expectations of undue democratic sacrifice are unjust, riots might be inadequate but necessary forms of democratic repair for Black citizens in the face of racial terror. The limits of liberal democracy's ability as an institution to deal with certain types of injustice—particularly systematic racial violence that is (implicitly or explicitly) sanctioned by other citizens and carried out by the state—raise key questions about our expectations of Black citizens. In particular, they force us to confront the inability to accept Black anger as a legitimate response to racial terror and violence.

If anger at injustice is politically productive and even necessary, we need to contemplate, paraphrasing Audre Lorde, the "uses of [Black] anger" in order to make sense of events like the Baltimore uprising and so-called disruptive actions by Black Lives Matter (BLM) protesters.[8] In this regard, it is instructive that even those Black thinkers most associated with nonviolence and love (supposing we take these to be the antithetical political emotions to anger) such as James Baldwin and Martin Luther King Jr. do not simply dismiss Black anger as self-destructive. In his last published text, written after the Watts uprising in 1965 while he was living and organizing in struggling Black neighborhoods in Chicago, King describes an encounter with "a group of youngsters [in Watts] who said to us joyously, 'We won.' We asked them: 'How can you say you won when thirty-four Negroes are dead, your community is destroyed, and whites are using the riot as an excuse for inaction?' Their answer: 'We won because we made them pay attention to us.'" King rejects this assessment of rioting, which he describes as "self-defeating," but he adds that "the amazing thing about the ghetto is that so few Negroes have rioted." In his view, refraining from rioting is a triumph of hope against despair amid hopeless conditions. King observed that "being a Negro in America means trying to smile when you want to cry."[9] Or rather, as James Baldwin declared, it means trying to smile when you want to scream. "To be a Negro in this country and to be relatively conscious, is to be in a rage almost all of the time."[10] King and Baldwin, both of whom explicitly turn to love as a more productive political emotion than anger, nevertheless also refrain from blanket condemnations of Black anger. King, for example, refused to accept the framing of Black anger as the cause of white backlash: "riots are not the causes of white resistance, they are the consequences of it."[11] African American thinkers have thus offered complex and nuanced accounts of rioting and anger, but some have also endorsed or accepted sacrificial accounts of the role of Black dissent in white democracy that have problematic implications for Black politics.

In particular, I focus here on Danielle Allen's meditations on democratic sacrifice derived from her reading of Ralph Ellison's tragic account of the constrained space for Black political action in the context of white supremacy. The transmutation of Black sacrifice into political exemplarity has profound consequences for how we conceive Black political praxis. In one reading, for example, the radical disregard for and antipathy to Black life revealed by negative responses to the Black Lives Matter protests is not indicative of a crisis of US democracy but rather is politics as usual in the racial state.[12] If this is the case, we are forced to consider not only whether (echoing James Baldwin) inclusion is worth "the price of the ticket,"[13] but if there is also a conceptual trap in historical narratives of Black politics that recast peaceful acquiescence to loss as a form of democratic exemplarity in the face of political losses that are seemingly not repairable within the constraints of traditional liberal politics, including norms of "civility." Such romantic narratives of racial progress and reconciliation make it plausible to suggest, as some have done, that a civil rights icon such as Martin Luther King Jr. would be "appalled" by the Black Lives Matter protests, or to demand immediate Black forgiveness after horrific losses such as the massacre in Charleston, South Carolina, at the hands of an avowed white supremacist shooter.[14]

Expanding our understanding of legitimate Black political action is necessary in order to free Black politics from the expectation that it should be about repairing white democracy, as well as to overcome the unequal distribution of democratic labor that situates Black suffering as political martyrdom. This might seem like a hyperbolic assertion after massive racial justice protests in the summer of 2020 following the killings of George Floyd and Breonna Taylor led to a national reckoning with white supremacy. Yet we need only look at the lack of protection for minority voting rights despite the key role played by Black organizers and voting rights activists in the 2020 elections, and at the reactions to the guilty verdict in the trial of the officer who killed George Floyd, to realize that the political labor of Black citizens continues to be predominantly framed in terms of sacrifice.

Black (and other nonwhite) voters continue to face formidable obstacles to full participation in US democracy, at the same time as they are also the backbone of US democracy in certain ways. Despite systematic disenfranchisement and blatant voter suppression targeted at minority voters via restrictive voter ID laws, purging of voter rolls, and so on, Black women continue to be some of the country's most engaged and reliable voters. They have also been at the forefront of efforts to counter these undemocratic minority voter suppression measures. They have created grassroots voter registration and mobilization organizations such as *Black Voters Matter* and *Fair Fight Action*—which was founded by Stacey Abrams following her own close loss in Georgia's gubernatorial race in 2018, in which voter suppression was a major factor—that have been credited with playing a major role in increasing turnout in the pivotal 2020 elections. Abrams's crucial activism was captured in a *Vogue* profile entitled "Can Stacey Abrams Save American Democracy?"[15] Even more pointedly, Michael Luckovich, the acclaimed editorial cartoonist of the *Atlanta Journal-Constitution*, sketched an image of the late civil rights leader and congressional representative John Lewis as "The Bridge" over which a line of black stick figures march to the voting booth (see figure 2.1).[16] These depictions of Lewis and Abrams reveal the continued understanding of Black citizens as the heroic bearers—on "the bridges called their backs"—of the civic burden of saving US democracy from itself.[17] Yet, despite their Sisyphean labors on behalf of US democracy, the alarm bells being sounded by Black activists about ongoing, systematic efforts to strip people of color of political power continue to go unheeded.[18]

Even more egregious examples of how Black loss is understood only in terms of political activism, and of how that activism is itself consistently framed as democratic martyrdom, are the statements issued by local and national politicians in reaction to the guilty verdict—a rarity—against the white police

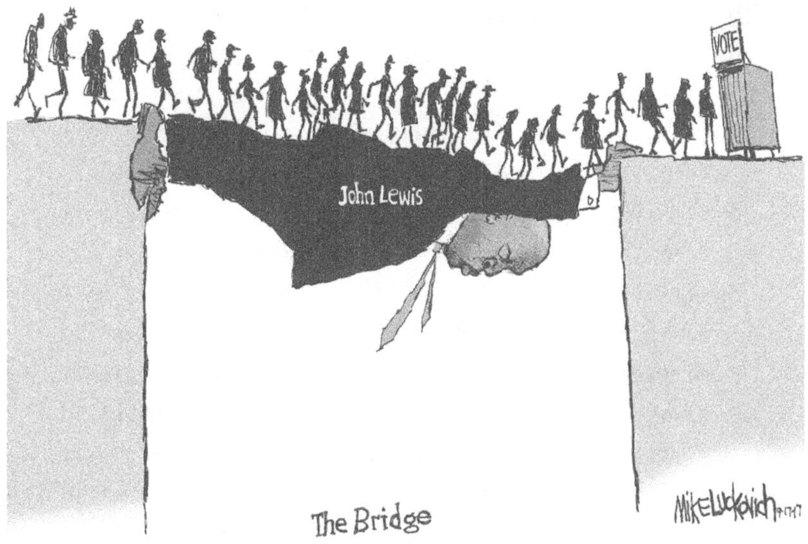

FIGURE 2.1. John Lewis as "The Bridge," 2020. Mike Luckovich—*Atlanta Journal-Constitution.*

officer who knelt on George Floyd's neck for nine agonizing minutes. "George Floyd came to Minneapolis to better his life. But ultimately his life will have bettered our city," tweeted Minneapolis mayor Jacob Frey.[19] In similarly tone-deaf fashion, House Speaker Nancy Pelosi initially stated (to wide condemnation and disbelief): "Thank you, George Floyd, for sacrificing your life for justice, for being there to call out to your mom."[20] It should not, but does, require saying that Floyd was not an activist. He was not a willing political martyr in the cause of US racial progress. He was a Black man killed because "a police officer pressing his knee into a Black man's neck until he dies . . . [is] the logical result of policing in America. When a police officer brutalizes a Black person, he is doing what he sees as his job."[21] George Floyd's death was not an exemplary democratic sacrifice.

That it has been framed as such is emblematic of the forced political labor white democracy continues to extract from Black citizens.

In fact, the Chauvin trial perfectly illustrates the unceasing work Black people must undertake to receive any kind of redress in white democracy, how they must turn their grief into grievance. Achieving this rare guilty verdict in a white police officer's killing of a Black person required extraordinary effort and activism. This included the crucial video evidence recorded by witnesses, some of them children, all of whom refused to look away and were traumatized by their inability to save Floyd. They were then required to relive their grief and publicly share their trauma on the witness stand in order to counteract the defense's attempt to frame them as angry Black people and therefore unreliable witnesses. There were also the massive protests across the country during a global pandemic, in which protesters had to risk their health in order to generate the public pressure that led to Chauvin being charged and tried at all. There was the eloquence of Floyd's family. There was the successful prosecution of the case, which was in large part the result of a Black attorney general who brought in private lawyers to try the case, rather than the regular district attorneys who work closely with the police. There were the fellow police officers willing to testify against one of their own; a local community defiant and mobilized despite a violent and militarized response to their constitutionally protected protests; the constant presence of the community outside the courthouse during the trial reminding all involved of how much was at stake. How to begin to reckon with these democratic debts?[22]

In this chapter, I challenge the transmutation of undue democratic sacrifice by subordinated racial groups into democratic exemplarity via an interrogation of the unwarranted assumptions of liberal democratic progress and perfectibility that undergird it. In particular, the chapter contests three key theoretical and historical assumptions of the conceptualization of Black politics as democratic sacrifice. One problematic historical assumption is the reduction of a long history of Black activism to a specific, sanitized version of the civil rights movement of the 1960s that then sets the terms for what are considered legitimate forms of Black politics. A second theoretical misunderstanding is a mistaken account of white moral psychology that overstates the efficacy of peaceful acquiescence to loss on the part of subordinated groups in bringing about transformations in the ethical orientations of dominant groups. Third, framing nonviolent protest as acquiescence or sacrifice obviates the self-understanding of Black activists (both in the 1960s and today) who see themselves as engaging in acts of defiance.

To consider how Black activism might productively refuse these dominant scripts, I turn to other strands of Black political thought that refuse these constraints on Black politics. Since the earliest moments of the tradition, Black political thought has grappled with the problem that the struggle for Black life and freedom often requires acting outside the strictly legal, beginning with those fugitive slaves who gained their freedom by committing the crime of "stealing" themselves. As a result, Black thinkers tend to have a more capacious account of dissent than, for example, the sharp distinctions between civil and uncivil disobedience found in liberal philosophical defenses of legitimate forms of protest.[23] Strands of Black political thought that map a politics of refusal enable us to conceive and enact more radical democratic subjectivities. Black feminist accounts of refusal, in particular, point away from democratic sacrifice and toward other forms of politics that Black people might productively enact in the face of racial terror.[24]

This emphasis on Black political imagination reflects the fact that this is not a book about how democracies can manage the experience of political loss. My concern is not primarily with repairing (white) democracy. Instead, *Black Grief/White Grievance* argues for an expansion of the political imaginations of both Blacks and whites. In this instance, that means thinking past the paradoxes of Black politics produced by the problematic reification of democratic sacrifice as the paradigmatic example of Black political excellence and civic virtue.

From Democratic Loss to Black Sacrifice

Danielle Allen has argued that democratic politics is characterized by loss and that, as a result, one of the central tasks facing democracies is the challenge of managing the experience of loss.[25] Drawing on the Aristotelian formulation of politics as the practice of ruling and being ruled in turn, Allen suggests that democracy imbues citizens with the desire to be sovereigns, but their experience is more often one of frustrated agency. Because citizens have conflicting preferences, all policy decisions inevitably generate winners and losers; citizens thus have to learn to reconcile themselves to the experience of losing. This creates a challenge for democracies, because they "inspire in citizens an aspiration to rule and yet require citizens constantly to live with the fact that they do not. Democracies must find methods to help citizens deal with the conflict between their politically inspired desires for total agency and the frustrating reality of their experience."[26] According to democratic theory, the losses experienced by citizens are justified because they befall them arbitrarily; that is, all can win or lose a given public policy debate, and there are no systematic winners and losers. Historically, of course, this has not been the case, and some groups of citizens have disproportionately borne the burden of loss. Allen's analysis of the problem of democratic loss thus quickly pivots into a discussion of the virtues of democratic sacrifice—of citizens who cope with the experience of loss in an exemplary fashion—because citizens who sacrifice by being good losers are key to democratic stability. The paradigmatic example she offers of such exemplary citizenship are African Americans who responded to racial terror during the civil rights–era struggles of the 1960s with nonviolence. This is hardly coincidental. While this is certainly not her intent, Allen's account of African Americans' peaceful acquiescence to loss as an act of exemplary citizenship does not directly challenge the disproportionate distribution of loss that she points to as a breeding ground for distrust.[27] In a racial polity, nonwhite loss is perpetual. In such a context, peaceful acceptance of loss by subordinated groups cannot be lauded only as political maturity. Instead, it is important to recognize how this might morph into something more akin to a demand for resignation.[28]

Allen derives her notion of acceptance of democratic loss as a political virtue from the dispute between Hannah Arendt and Ralph Ellison over school desegregation battles in the 1960s. In her controversial essay "Reflections on Little Rock," Arendt objected to federally ordered desegregation for three main reasons: it turned a social matter into a political one, it violated states' rights, and it asked children to take on political activities that were the purview of adults.[29] As commentators at the time and since have noted, Arendt's commitment to an idiosyncratic distinction between the social and the political led her to misunderstand the actions of the Black parents who sent their children to the front lines of school desegregation battles in the South; it also prevented her from recognizing that state-sanctioned educational disparities were a political issue (as it was one of the key means by which white supremacy was maintained).[30] In Arendt's view, the Black parents who allowed their children to desegregate previously all-white schools had failed to protect their offspring. They exposed them to interpersonal rejection for the sake of social climbing: "My first question was: what would I do were I a Negro mother? The answer: under no circumstances would I expose my child to conditions which made it appear as though it wanted to push its way into a group where it was not wanted. . . . If I were a Negro mother in the South, I would feel that the Supreme Court ruling, unwillingly but unavoidably, has put my child into a more humiliating position than it had been in before."[31]

In his critique of Arendt, Ellison rightly observed that her reading of the motivations of the Black parents was an act of profound misrecognition. She misunderstood their actions, viewing them as motivated by material self-interest, and completely failed to see the day-to-day sacrifice and heroism that survival under Jim Crow demanded of all African Americans.[32] Not only were Black parents not asking their children to take up burdens that they themselves were unwilling to bear, Ellison argued; they viewed such sacrifices as necessary lessons in survival within a hostile world. Arendt and Ellison's disagreement about how to interpret the actions of Black parents who allowed their children to take on the burden of school desegregation reflects the dilemma of what Lisa Tessman has called the "burdened virtues" required of politically resistant selves, one of which is courage. Because political resistance can require the adoption of traits disconnected from and even detrimental to the resister's own flourishing, it has a self-sacrificial character.[33]

Resistance and the adoption of burdened virtues is necessary, but it entails costs to those who perform this kind of political labor. Ellison, much more so than Arendt, was attuned to these losses, and to their inescapability for African Americans living under white supremacy.

In his response to Arendt's essay, Ellison formulated a notion of African American sacrifice as a public act on behalf of the common good, and also as a duty to the self.[34] According to Ellison, Arendt's critique of the Black parents and of the NAACP for putting Black children on the front lines of desegregation battles failed to recognize the political heroism of ordinary African Americans. She did not understand that the peaceful endurance of racial violence was a form of civic sacrifice. African Americans in the South, Ellison argued, "learned about violence in a very tough school. They have known for a long time that they can take a lot of head-whipping and survive and go on working toward their own goals. We learned about forbearance and forgiveness in that same school, and about hope too. So today we sacrifice, as we sacrificed yesterday, the pleasure of personal retaliation in the interest of the common good."[35] Here, Ellison presents sacrifice as a strategy for surviving white violence as well as a gift to the political community as a whole. He argues that African Americans have a special duty to sacrifice the need for revenge: "while still pressing for their freedom, they have the obligation to themselves of giving up some of their need for revenge."[36] For Ellison, African American sacrifice is a dual obligation. African Americans learned to meet racial terror with nonviolence in order to preserve their own lives within an arbitrary system in which responding in kind to any insult or harm could lead to sudden death. But peaceful acquiescence also exposed the reality of white violence to other whites who might be persuaded to support the cause of racial justice. For African Americans confronted with ever-present and senseless violence, Ellison suggested, "personal courage had either to take another form or be negated, become meaningless. Often the individual's personal courage had to be held in check, since not only could his exaction of satisfaction from the white man lead to the destruction of other innocent Negroes, his self-evaluation could be called into question by the smallest things and the most inconsequential gesture could become imbued with power over life or death."[37] Yet exercising such restraint was difficult. Meeting racial terror with nonviolence, Ellison argued, "places a big moral strain upon the individual, and it requires self-confidence, self-consciousness, self-mastery, insight and compassion."[38] In sum, Ellison described African American political heroism both as a public sacrifice on behalf of the polity, and as an ethical duty to the self. The relative weight of these motivations is of crucial importance in evaluating the fairness of (Black) democratic sacrifice, however, as external and internal obligations have different ethical import.

Drawing on Ellison, Allen suggests that democratic sacrifice is an obligation shared equally by all citizens. She argues that sacrifice is both a central political virtue and an enabling condition of democracy: "of all the rituals of democracy, sacrifice is preeminent. No democratic citizen, adult or child, escapes the necessity of losing out at some point in a public decision." Because public policy decisions will rarely benefit all citizens equally, those citizens "who benefit less than others from particular political decisions, but nonetheless accede to those decisions, preserve the stability of political institutions. Their sacrifice makes collective democratic action possible. . . . The hard truth of democracy is that some citizens are always giving things up for others."[39] For such sacrifices to be legitimate, however, they must be evenly distributed among citizens. Allen is clear that, historically, US democracy has dealt with the inevitable fact of loss in politics by unevenly distributing the burden of sacrifice. In the US polity, the "paradoxical fact that most democratic citizens are, at the end of the day, relatively powerless sovereigns" was resolved via "the two-pronged citizenship of domination and acquiescence," which assigned "to one group all the work of being sovereign [whites], and to another group [Blacks] most of the work of accepting the significant losses that kept the polity stable."[40] The political loss endemic to democracy, in other words, has historically been managed via white supremacy, insulating white citizens from loss and the experience of disempowerment (at least vis-à-vis subordinated racial others). Allen recognizes that this approach to managing the problem of political loss is "a breeding ground of distrust." She suggests in response that democratic sacrifice, in order to be legitimate, must meet the following preconditions: it must be made voluntarily, it must be equally shared (i.e., it cannot routinely be expected of the same group of citizens), and it needs to be honored by those citizens who are its beneficiaries.[41]

Ellison's and Allen's identification of African Americans' nonviolent response to racial terror, and of struggle against systematic racial subordination within the parameters of the rule of law and the norms of liberal politics, as a heroic form of democratic sacrifice is compelling in many ways. On this reading, undue democratic suffering is transformed into democratic exemplarity. But what are the dangers of this understanding of democratic loss and political virtue for those that have been the paradigmatic "losers" in US democracy, who have already disproportionately shouldered the burden of democratic sacrifice? What is the price of such acquiescence for the struggle to achieve racial justice? Is this a self-defeating form of political heroism? One of the questions raised by the notion of Black sacrifice as political exemplarity is its implied ranking of competing political goods. In other words, in Allen and Ellison's vision, democratic citizenship demands of racially subordinated groups that they pursue political projects aimed at making the entire political community more just and free, but it is important to consider whether fulfilling such obligations could come at the expense of their own interests and claims to justice. Moreover, at what point does it become unjust or indeed un-democratic to expect citizens to continue to peacefully acquiesce to repeated political losses?

In his essay on the Ferguson protests, for example, Steven Johnston places them within a tradition of "democratic politics as forceful, militant resistance." He argues that violence can be "democratically contributive. . . . Citizens who have no official outlet for redress of grievances need to be self-reliant."[42] At the end of the essay, however, Johnston lauds the Ferguson protesters in a way that makes a political virtue of their vulnerability, thereby drawing attention away from the question of whether it is fair to ask some citizens to make such unequal sacrifices. "These citizens were badly outgunned and held their ground. In the face of a Frankensteinian police force . . . they didn't flinch." Johnston ends his essay with a call for equal vulnerability, but the problem is precisely that all citizens are not called on to make themselves equally vulnerable. In the case of subordinated groups facing racial terror and violence, understanding their losses as democratic exemplarity can also become a demand for extraordinary sacrifices from precisely those citizens least positioned to make such "gifts." In other words, are there any limits to the democratic suffering that this notion of political virtue demands of already-subordinated groups in a polity? What are the limits of expectations of Black sacrifice for the sake of white democracy? Does asymmetric democratic vulnerability not become political martyrdom at some point?

The key question is whether other citizens have been expected to display the kinds of democratic sacrifices for which Black citizens have been lauded. We can assess whether the burden of sacrifice is still unequally distributed by considering how the traditional winners in US democracy have coped with loss. As I argued in chapter 1, white citizens have generally *not* been good losers. The civil rights victories of the 1960s that resulted in the end of legally enforced segregation in the South, for example, did constitute a moment of political loss for white citizens committed to a racial polity in which they had exclusive access to political power and privileged social and economic standing. And the reaction to this loss was fierce white backlash. As MLK observed, the uprisings of the 1960s were a reaction to white resistance, not the other way around. White grievance fueled successful efforts to hollow out the legal rights recently gained by Black activists and to forestall further progress toward racial justice. As King argued, "the white backlash is nothing new. . . . It was caused neither by the cry of Black Power nor by the unfortunate recent wave of riots in our cities. The white backlash of today . . . is an expression of the same vacillations, the same search for rationalizations, the same lack of commitment that have always characterized white America on the question of race."[43] Historically, victories in the struggle for racial equality have been followed by eras of deep and sustained racist backlash, in which Blacks and other minorities have borne the brunt of racial terror, violence, and xenophobia.[44]

This dynamic is certainly evident in the climate of white racial resentment that quickly followed the postracial euphoria occasioned by the election of Barack Obama in 2008. Today, a narrow white political imagination that views citizenship as racial standing, freedom as the absence of state intervention, and equality as privileged opportunities for advancement,[45] functions to legitimize contemporary efforts to suppress nonwhite voter participation, the rejection of mask mandates and gun control as impingements on personal liberty, and criticisms of enhanced unemployment benefits as disincentives to work. This limited political imagination is also why demands that whites renounce racism are viewed by some as an infringement of their personal freedom and a devaluing of their status as citizens, because an expanded sphere of (white) individual liberty not afforded to other citizens has been a consistent feature of US democracy.[46] In such a context, the democratic sacrifices of members of subordinated groups, rather than being honored, might instead be resented by members of the dominant group, who might also ironically develop a sense of white victimhood when that democratic labor is withdrawn.

What if, then, Arendt was right (albeit for reasons different from those she articulated) and Ellison was wrong about the advisability of sacrifice and the burden of political heroism? In her essays on school desegregation, Arendt explained that her critique was prompted by one of the widely circulated photographs of adolescent African American girls facing abuse by racist mobs as they tried to integrate all-white public schools: "The girl, obviously, was asked to be a hero."[47] Arendt's critique centered on the fact that it was children, not adults, who were being asked to display political courage. But perhaps we should broaden her criticism to the expectation that it is those who have been the victims of racism that should do the work of democratic repair, that they should make further sacrifices on behalf of the polity. The question is how to square democracy's commitment to equally distributing the burdens of citizenship with the fact that racially subordinated groups are asked to bear primary responsibility for the work of racial justice. Moreover, it is also important to consider whether the underlying historical and theoretical assumptions on which the notion of Black sacrifice as political exemplarity is based hold up under further scrutiny. I argue that they do not.

Peaceful Acquiescence or Black Defiance?

One of the most common critiques of the Black Lives Matter protests, by white and (some) Black commentators alike, has been its failure to emulate the political exemplarity of the civil rights movement of the 1960s.[48] Contemporary Black Lives Matter protesters have been critiqued for failing to follow the disciplined adherence to nonviolence now attributed to earlier antiracist struggles; for not embodying Black respectability; for not adopting a visible hierarchical leadership structure; for not formulating clear policy goals; and so on.[49] On this reading, white public opinion has not become uniformly mobilized in support of the Black Lives Matter protests against police violence because of the failures of the protesters to make visible to a white audience the reality of an unjust criminal justice system via the willing sacrifice of their innocent, nonresisting bodies to racial violence.[50] As media scholar Sarah Jackson has argued, however, it is precisely the framing of current protest in contrast to a nostalgic and sanitized collective memory of the civil rights movement that "has bound representation of today's [Black] activism from the start."[51]

These criticisms of contemporary Black activism reflect three key historical and theoretical assumptions about how antiracist change has occurred in the United States and on which the notion of Black politics as democratic sacrifice depends, all of which turn out to be mistaken upon further examination. They are (1) a romantic narrative of the civil rights movement of the 1960s that results in a teleological account of racial progress and the perfectibility of US democracy, (2) a claim about the effect on political solidarity of meeting racial terror with nonviolence and peaceful acquiescence derived from a mistaken understanding of the moral psychology of "the white citizen,"[52] and (3) a theoretical gloss on nonviolent protest as sacrifice that does not correspond with the way participants in Black protest movements themselves understand and intend their own actions as defiance or resistance. The notion that peaceful acquiescence to democratic loss is the best frame for understanding the sacrifices demanded of Black citizens not only unfairly places the burden of responsibility for repairing racial wrongs on those who are already most harmed by racism; it also rests on misguided assumptions about how to achieve racial justice that might actually prevent the dismantling of white supremacy in the long run.

One assumption underlying conceptions of Black politics oriented to democratic sacrifice is historical, and reflects a specific liberal understanding of both racism and US democracy. According to what we might call the perfectibility of US democracy thesis, political relations among citizens are constantly moving in a more egalitarian direction, and gradual progress toward racial justice is therefore inevitable and natural. President Obama symbolically invoked this idea in his second inauguration, when he swore the oath of office on MLK's Bible and described his election as a step in the country's gradual but inexorable progress toward racial equality and the creation of a more perfect union. This teleological conception of US race relations is especially evident in what Brandon Terry has persuasively characterized as the romantic narrative of the civil rights movement that predominates in public memory. As Terry observes, it is important for political theorists to be clear about what is at stake philosophically in the versions of history they choose to adopt. The relationship between historiography and philosophy remains underexamined but is in fact crucial because the particular understandings of historical events adopted by political theorists implicitly shape the supposedly abstract arguments they develop. Terry suggests that political theorists need to pay more attention to how the particular historical narratives they adopt serve specific philosophical ends.[53]

This is especially true of the civil rights movement of the 1960s. The romantic narrative that dominates the historiography of this moment of victorious Black protest reinforces a distorted view of both US racism and Black politics. Because romance as a genre involves the idea of movement toward a telos or goal (in this case, unity), Terry argues that to emplot the civil rights movement in this way is to portray it as the culmination of the country's inevitable march toward racial equality, a reading of US history that in turn renders racism as epiphenomenal to US democracy. Terry argues that the romantic narrative of the civil rights movement tends to downplay the more radical aspects of the movement, and to erase the fact that there was significant disagreement among Black activists and intellectuals at the time about how best to pursue racial justice, the efficacy of nonviolence, the primacy of issues of political and legal inclusion versus economic redistribution, and so on.[54] This narrow conception of the civil rights movement functions to foreclose other (possibly more radical) forms of Black politics and preemptively delegitimizes them. It results in the assumption that nonviolent protest aimed at inclusion into the existing legal and political order is the most effective political strategy that Black citizens can and should pursue.[55] Black political action that does not follow the script of the romantic narrative of the civil rights movement, with its implicit expectation of democratic sacrifice, then comes to be viewed as both illegitimate and ineffective. Moreover, the romantic narrative of the civil rights movement shifts attention away from Black loss to the idea that Black politics should be oriented toward the goal of democratic repair rather than racial justice. Ellison's point that racial terror in the South taught African Americans to survive violence and keep working toward their own goals—which meant that they also learned about "hope"—illustrates how the racial perfectibility of US democracy thesis can require that those who have already suffered the greatest political losses reconcile themselves to further sacrifice.

A second problematic claim underlying the notion of Black politics as democratic sacrifice is a theoretical account of white moral psychology that positions exemplary forms of political activism by racialized minorities as the most effective means of inducing positive ethical transformations in members of the dominant racial group. Peaceful acquiescence to racial terror is viewed as an exemplary act of citizenship because of the assumed capacity of this act of democratic sacrifice to sway the moral orientations of members of the dominant racial group—who, upon observing such naked displays of violence, will be shamed into renouncing racial injustice. Allen, for example, argues that "those who agree, in the face of violence and domination, cast aggressive acts into the starkest relief by allowing them to expend their full force. Those who are agreeable in this way show up violent citizens for what they are, and force witnesses to the spectacle to make a choice about whether to embrace or disavow the violence."[56] According to this notion of Black political excellence as peaceful acquiescence to democratic loss, there are "fundamentally healthy elements of the citizenship of subordination—the ability to agree, to sacrifice, to bear burdens in order to force contradictions in the citizenship of the dominated, until this citizenship caves in upon the rottenness of its inherent ills."[57] But, of course, it is not a given that dominant groups will be shamed into renouncing racial power. Indeed, as Karuna Mantena argues regarding MLK's appeal to the conscience of the "decent majority" of the US public, King's posture "was not premised on an empirical assessment of white opinion. It was an interpolation, a constructive act. The decent majority, the majority of liberal opinion, was a public that King brought into being through the rhetorical framing of the civil rights movement."[58] Yet judging democratic sacrifice by racially subordinated groups to be a "healthy" political strategy depends on this claim about the effect of meeting racial terror with nonviolence on white moral psychology.

In my view, there is a general tendency in democratic theory to overstate the ability of protest and dissent to induce shame and thereby produce a moral reorientation among members of dominant groups. The point here is not only to challenge the calculus that deems the costs of democratic sacrifice acceptable, but also to highlight how the work of nonviolent suffering is misunderstood. Mantena, for example, argues that the kind of white moral transformation that King hoped nonviolence would provoke was an active process of self-evaluation activated by shaming, not the passive emotion of pity:

> Pity is an externalizing impulse. In pity one is moved by scenes of oppression without necessarily feeling implicated in them. Moreover, when people are made objects of pity, it diminishes their agency just as it empowers those who pity. The latter become potential saviors, whose benevolence can be withdrawn at any moment. Shaming, by contrast, works by directing attention inward. It forces observers to reckon with their own place in the racial order. In the context of

> protest, nonviolent suffering was not aimed at presenting the black body as abject and in pain, generating pity. Instead it staged black dignity—in the wake of brutality—to turn the viewers' gaze back upon themselves and their complicity in perpetuating injustice.[59]

I take Mantena's point that, for King, white moral transformation was prospective; that is, he was trying to call a "decent" white public into being that would feel ashamed at racial oppression and recognize Black humanity. But we still have to contend with the fact that the effects of spectacles of Black suffering on the white public are complex (as is the impact of all political or aesthetic acts), and this must alter our assessment of democratic sacrifice. As Brandon Terry has argued, King believed that civil disobedience as an aesthetic act would produce different responses in the white public from what rioting would produce; rather than inducing fear, it would produce something like sublime awe.[60] But it is precisely this reaction that is contestable, because even the most nonviolent examples of Black civil disobedience have been equated by their critics with acts of terror or racial hatred.[61] The dilemma for Black politics is that eliciting democratic witnessing from the white public is always highly uncertain and comes at enormous cost that should be reckoned with.[62]

Yet dominant accounts of how the civil rights victories of the 1960s were achieved rely on false assumptions about how racialized solidarity works.[63] According to the dominant romantic historical narrative of the civil rights movement, well-behaved, respectable, middle-class protesters engaged in the "right" kind of political activism and were thus able to incite solidarity with Black suffering among white observers.[64] This account elides the fact that observers might—and frequently do—read the same event in radically different ways. Writing about the use of video evidence in the trial of the police officers who beat Rodney King, Judith Butler observes:

> In the Simi Valley courtroom, what many took to be incontrovertible evidence *against* the police was presented instead to establish police vulnerability, that is, to support the contention that Rodney King was endangering the police. Later, a juror reported that she believed that Rodney King was in "total control" of the situation. How was this feat of interpretation achieved? That it was achieved is not the consequence of ignoring the video, but, rather, of reproducing the video within a racially saturated field of visibility. If racism pervades white perception, structuring what can and cannot appear within the horizon of white perception, then to what extent does it interpret in advance "visual evidence"? And how, then, does such "evidence" have to be read, and read publicly, *against* the racist disposition of the visible which will prepare and achieve its own inverted perceptions under the rubric of "what is seen"?[65]

Indeed, race has historically impeded the recognition that fellow citizens who are racial others deserve the same care, concern, and respect, or even that the harms they suffer merit the same attention. To put it bluntly, the problem with the bet that Black suffering will catalyze shame by highlighting white violence is that even civil Black activism is often perceived as violent and dangerous. Indeed, despite the fact that the civil rights movement reintroduced the idea of civil disobedience under the banner of nonviolence in the 1960s, for white Americans "violence, not nonviolence, had become the watchword of the decade," and they viewed Black protests as inherently violent.[66]

Arendt's "Reflections on Little Rock" exemplifies the varied ways in which the public at the time responded to nonviolent Black protest. It shows that some observers of Black acquiescence to racial violence saw it not as heroic, but as motivated by self-interest rather than as a sacrifice on behalf of the common good. Indeed, Arendt literally misread what she was seeing. As Kathryn Gines has shown, the photograph on which Arendt based her critique of Black parents and the NAACP did not in fact depict a young Black girl forced to face a racist white mob alone. Instead, Dorothy Counts was accompanied both by a Black friend of the family (who Arendt assumed was white, despite the fact that he was identified as Black in the accompanying article) and by her father (see figure 2.2).[67]

Arendt's response to contemporaneous critiques of "Reflections on Little Rock" also exemplifies why democratic sacrifice might be a self-defeating form of Black political activism, since it demands so much of Black citizens in exchange for the uncertain prospect of white solidarity. In "A Reply to Critics," Arendt reveals another way that white citizens might react to being forced to confront the reality of their own racial advantages: rather than experiencing shame, they could respond with resentment and defensiveness. Indeed, one of Arendt's counterarguments to her critics was that federal intervention to enforce school integration had produced a sense of grievance among southern whites: "The series of events in the South that followed the court rulings . . . impresses one with a sense of futility and needless embitterment."[68] Likewise, in the preface to the version of "Reflections" that was finally published, Arendt includes a telling explanation of her personal history as a Jewish European

FIGURE 2.2. Dorothy Counts, fifteen, the first Black student to attend Harding High School in Charlotte, North Carolina, accosted by a shouting white mob of students following school on September 5, 1957. AP Photo/Douglas Martin/*Charlotte Observer*.

immigrant to the Unites States, which she suggested should absolve her of any possible charges of racism:

> I should like to remind the reader that I am writing as an outsider. I have never lived in the South and have even avoided occasional trips to Southern states because they would have brought me into a situation that I personally found unbearable. Like most people of European origin I have difficulty in understanding, let alone sharing, the common prejudices of Americans in this area. . . . I should like to make it clear that as a Jew I take my sympathy for the cause

> of the Negroes as for all the oppressed or underprivileged peoples for granted and should appreciate it if the reader did likewise.[69]

There is, of course, a terrible irony in Arendt's recourse to the familiar trope of European moral superiority to the United States on the question of racism only a decade after the Holocaust. But precisely because she viewed herself as someone whose ethical judgments could not possibly be distorted by racist preconceptions (as a victim of anti-Semitism herself), Arendt could disavow the demand for identification with Black suffering that nonviolence was supposed to evoke. The common assumption that Black sacrifice will induce shame among white citizens, which will in turn produce a reorientation to racial justice, is thus predicated on a particular account of how white moral orientations are transformed that does not fully grapple with the effects of racialized solidarity.[70] Black acquiescence has costs even if it can induce white moral awakenings. This is one of the dilemmas facing Black politics.

Moreover, even if Black sacrifice did produce changes in white moral orientations in the 1960s, the varied response to the current Black Lives Matter protests suggests that shaming whites into solidarity with Black suffering may be far more difficult today, when (false) claims that the United States had become a postracial society have been superseded by open racist backlash and resurgent white grievance manifested in high degrees of white racial resentment against racialized minorities. As a result, the bar for proving the continued existence of structural (or even individual-level) anti-Black racism is extremely high. This dynamic is evident in the dissection of the pasts of unarmed Black victims of police violence, even children (as in the cases of Aiyana Stanley-Jones and Tamir Rice), for evidence of criminality in order to claim that they were not innocent and were thus mainly or partly responsible for their own deaths. The problem is that if white solidarity requires Black innocence, then the goalposts for racial justice continually shift because every specific instance of injustice becomes a discussion of whether or not a particular Black victim was "deserving," which displaces the focus away from questions of racial injustice, democratic suffering, and Black loss. There are thus important questions that need to be asked about the model of Black politics as democratic sacrifice. For example, what kind of economy of suffering requires protesters or victims of police violence to suffer more in order to merit care and concern on the part of their fellow citizens, when their lives are already shaped by violence and other forms of racial oppression?[71]

Finally, the characterization of Black activism as peaceful acquiescence to loss is also called into question by the different way in which participants in protest movements understand their own actions.[72] The iconic photograph of Dorothy Counts's confrontation with a racist mob referenced by Arendt in "Reflections" illustrates this dynamic whereby ostensible moments of Black sacrifice were in fact intended and experienced by the subjects in question as instances of Black defiance. Counts's reading of the event was a far cry from what Arendt (and perhaps many of the white observers who were moved by the image) assumed. She later claimed to have felt not fear, but pity. She explained: "*if you look at the picture the right way, you see what I see*. What I see is that all of those people are behind me. They did not have the courage to get up in my face."[73] What those who subscribe to the romantic narrative of the civil rights movement also miss is that, rather than seeing themselves as passive victims, African American protesters in the 1960s viewed themselves as engaged in defiant resistance.

At the same time, it is also possible that peaceful acquiescence to violence, rather than being read as sacrifice, could be interpreted as Black submission, and that this is the price of white acquiescence to steps toward racial equality, which suggests a much different account of the impact of these gestures on white moral orientations. In a counterintuitive reading of the "hands up, don't shoot" gesture that became a rallying cry for protesters after the killing of Michael Brown, for example, art historian Dora Apel argues that there is a racialized visual economy that shapes how images of Black protest are read:

> The submissive hands up gesture of black protesters facing a militarized police force is meant to appeal to liberal sympathies by showing that they are "respectful" and law-abiding, suggesting the opposite of "uppity." [In the 1960s] . . . images of blacks offering no resistance to police violence were selected by white editors because it was easier to gain white liberal sympathy by visually defining racism as excessive acts of brutality, from which moderate and liberal whites could distance themselves, while at the same time their racial anxiety could be quelled by the picturing of black nonresistance.

Some of this certainly seems to be at work in Arendt's reading of the Counts photograph, which she interpreted as depicting Black humiliation and self-abasement for the sake of material advancement. Apel suggests that there might be a similar dynamic at work in the visual record of Ferguson, where "photos of the militarized police facing black protesters who are nonresistant perform reassuring symbolic work that manages white anxieties about race." In her view, such images have the effect of "normalizing black passivity and even subtly promoting ongoing black humiliation."[74] As was the case with Dorothy Counts, however, there is also a more complicated reading of the "hands up/don't shoot" gesture of current protests against police violence. Protesters may have intended the gesture not as deference, but as defiance. Particularly when coupled with chants such as "who do you serve? who do you protect?," which were delivered as indictments of police officers that fail to protect Black citizens, the gesture could also be read as combining deference and defiance at the same time.[75] In other words, the problem for theoretical accounts of Black activism as democratic sacrifice is that there is a complicated politics of reception and performance at work in moments of racial strife: a gesture that ostensibly bespeaks submission (and that could be read as peaceful acquiescence) might in fact be intended as a challenge to a democratic order that continues to expect some groups to disproportionately bear the burden of loss.[76]

The key theoretical and historical assumptions underlying understandings of Black protest as democratic sacrifice are therefore mistaken, but this framing has very real and concrete political consequences. Critics of the Black Lives Matter protests who have applauded the disproportionate police response to the protests regard the assertion of the right to protest by Black citizens as an illegitimate deployment of violence, as an unjustified challenge to norms of civility that supposedly already prevail in the polity. If the affective price of white acquiescence to demands for racial justice is (imagined) Black submission, this might explain why so many white observers not only fail to empathize with the Black Lives Matter protests, but actively laud police violence against Black citizens, as illustrated by legislation protecting those who injure protesters and the support for white vigilantes such as Kyle Rittenhouse who kill protesters. In the tragic political trap created by the transmutation of Black sacrifice into democratic exemplarity, there is very little room for Black persons to express outrage at injustice, or to enact a politics of defiance of their expected status as peaceful democratic losers.

Rioting and Black Refusal

How then might we move beyond notions of democratic sacrifice to begin to conceive forms of Black activism that are more appropriate for a context defined by racial terror, state depredation of poor Black communities, mass incarceration, racial profiling, excessive use of force by the police, disparities in sentencing, and lack of accountability of law enforcement? The disproportionate state repression of Black Lives Matter protesters exercising their constitutional rights from Ferguson to Baltimore to Portland to Kenosha was possible because by virtue of being Black (or in the case of non-Black participants, being associated with a racialized demand), protestors were already viewed as criminals or soon-to-be criminals undeserving of the normal protections of citizens. In a carceral society, the dynamic that governs interactions between the police or other representatives of the state and "criminals" inevitably bleeds over into other encounters between the state and "law-abiding" citizens. Democracies defined by the deployment of moral panics around crime to manage dispensable populations are uneven democracies, where large populations have only marginal access to the rights of citizenship, and where the standing of those who do is defined precisely in light of the denial of such rights to others.[77] One of the effects of the Black Lives Matter protests is that they have, to a certain extent, rendered continued willful white ignorance about the dehumanization of Black life more difficult to sustain.[78] Disregard for Black life antecedes fatal encounters with the police. It has its origins in the development of urban ghettos as a specific aim and consequence of state policy,[79] and in the criminalization of entire communities in order to make them subject to predatory looting by corrupt iterations of the state.[80] A conception of acceptable Black politics that emphasizes further sacrifice in the form of peaceful acquiescence to democratic loss seems both inadequate and counterproductive in such a context.

In fact, the failure of the victories of the civil rights movement to eliminate structural disparities in wealth and the criminal justice system raise important questions about the limited ability of liberal democracy to truly address racial justice. Descriptive Black political representation, for example, has not transformed the racialized character of the state, just as the presence of Black police officers does not prevent violence toward Black citizens. White supremacy produces a racial state that exceeds mere demography or phenotype.[81] In Ferguson, for example, there was a white political structure and administrative apparatus ruling over a predominantly Black citizenry; this has changed since the protests, but the election of more Black officeholders or infusion of more Black police officers will not solve the economic shortfalls that led it and other municipalities to criminalize the daily lives of their poorest citizens in order to fund their operations. Moreover, democratic responsiveness and accountability are elusive for poor Black citizens. Even in those instances in which they mobilize and appear to win concessions from the state and secure public goods in the short term, they tend to lose in the long term. For Black citizens, civic participation often comes at too great a cost.[82] But if Blacks are condemned to be perpetual losers in US democracy, how can democratic theory account for this specific form of racialized political loss? And how do we conceive forms of Black politics that do not prioritize democratic repair over racial justice?

If formulations of Black politics as democratic sacrifice create a trap whereby any deviation from submission, respectability, and nonviolence serves to render Black grievances illegitimate, perhaps we should instead consider instances of "rioting" as a form of democratic redress for Black citizens, even if, in and of themselves, riots cannot transform the prevailing racial order. These instances of violence, which are often viewed as self-destructive, might be productive for Black citizens because they allow for the expression of Black anger and pain, which is otherwise precluded by expectations of Black sacrifice and forgiveness. In order to move past critiques of disruptive protest that reify the demonization of Black anger and set a high bar for Black activism that does not lend itself to the frame of political martyrdom, we need to accept Black anger as a legitimate response to injustice. While scholars of social movements have recognized anger as a political affect with mobilizing effects, philosophical views of anger are more mixed.[83] Martha Nussbaum, for example, acknowledges that anger can be productive, that it may be necessary for self-respect, to respond appropriately to wrongdoing, and to combat injustice; nevertheless, she argues that it is normatively problematic because it always includes the idea of retribution.[84] In her view, anger is a problem in the political realm because it makes punishment or criminal law retributivism the focus of redress, a perspective that resonates with some of the arguments of contemporary prison and police abolitionists. Yet her focus on forgiveness as the alternative to anger, absent attention to the specific dynamics of Black anger, would seem to compound the problems of democratic sacrifice analyzed here. Indeed, historically (dating back to fears of rebellion by enslaved people), Black anger has been seen as threatening and equated with violence. These cultural prescriptions against Black anger have far-reaching consequences.

According to Davin Phoenix, there is a "racial anger gap" in US politics that is the result of "stark divides in the senses of expectation and entitlement that black and white Americans are socialized to draw from the political system, as well as the legitimacy that the polity ascribes to the grievances articulated by these respective groups." Black and other nonwhite Americans, he argues, are more likely to respond to political loss with resignation than anger.[85] As the previous chapter showed, if white rage is often whitewashed and not recognized as such, Black anger is equally misunderstood to be pervasive and senseless.

Black "rioting" is a case in point. Designating an event as a riot instead of a protest or an uprising has the effect of depoliticizing and trivializing it. As Dilip Gaonkar has argued, rioting is a recurring form of political activity globally, but "within the liberal democratic imaginary, riots have no redeeming social value," a view consistent with "a deep and abiding anticrowd strain [that] animates Western political thought."[86] Yet riots recur, and the fact that they do tells us something about the lack of legitimacy and the unfairness of the political orders in which they take place. For example, the events in Baltimore in 2015 echoed those of 1968, over whose meaning there was a similar tug of war. For many outside onlookers, the violence in the wake of Freddie Gray's killing was self-destructive behavior that placed added burdens on the local community (by making necessary goods inaccessible, for example), and using the term *uprising* was an attempt to endow with political meaning random violence directed at "innocent" targets such as retail establishments. Participants, however, framed the events differently. In their view, so-called rioting performed a certain kind of civic work. It provided an outlet for responses to the losses generated by white supremacy that participants were otherwise precluded from expressing in public, visible ways. As one participant in the 1968 uprising explained, "I felt at that point people had such grief and sense of loss and anger that they had to express it somehow."[87] It is important to note here that this account of rioting centers the implications and effects for participants and their communities; it is not contingent on how their actions might be interpreted by the broader (white) public. Likewise, critiques of rioting that focus only on the taking or destruction of property, situate property—rather than the injustice that prompted mobilization in the first place—as the most important loss. They also set aside the potential anticapitalist dimensions of rioting or looting, particularly in the context of long-standing racial expropriation (without reparations) of Black labor and Black wealth, the latter at times via white rioting as in, for example, the Tulsa race massacre and looting of "Black Wall Street" in 1921. As Jonathan Havercroft has argued, "looting could be justified if the rioters use it to redress an economic injustice."[88] Rioting, then, need not be seen simply as senseless, self-destructive violence.

This is not intended as a normative defense of rioting per se, however, although a number of those have been put forward recently by political theorists and philosophers. Havercroft, for example, argues that while it would require a higher threshold of justification than would other forms of political resistance, it is possible to formulate a "just riot theory" that would allow us to distinguish between, for instance, riots after sporting events and those protesting police murders of unarmed citizens.[89] Avia Pasternak, meanwhile, argues that political rioting is morally defensible even in democratic societies when it is the only means for oppressed citizens to secure important political goals, when it has a reasonable chance of success, and when it is properly constrained so that the harm inflicted on the state and on fellow citizens is proportionate.[90] More broadly, Candice Delmas and José Medina have defended the legitimacy of uncivil disobedience, including rioting. Delmas argues that we have a moral duty to resist injustice, and that we should expand our understanding of principled lawbreaking to include uncivil acts of dissent that do not meet the standard criteria of civil disobedience because they are covert or anonymous, evade punishment, involve violence, or are offensive or disrespectful.[91] Medina refutes the idea of a clear-cut distinction between civil and uncivil disobedience that can be drawn a priori, arguing that we should think of civil and uncivil protests as being in a continuum; he defends a confrontational view of protest that does not rule out in principle any form of engagement that protest may take.[92] Black rioting meets most, if not all, the criteria set out in these normative defenses of rioting and uncivil disobedience. Yet, historically, Black citizens have also more often than not been the *victims* of rioting and political violence, and this means that we need to consider how to incorporate concerns regarding vulnerability into accounts of uncivil disobedience that expand the repertoire of political resistance.[93]

The claim I am making here is therefore more limited. It is that riots, for lack of a better term, might constitute a form of democratic redress for African Americans. This is not because they are a solution to structural problems and institutionalized injustices, but because they allow Black citizens to express their pain and make their losses visible to each other. This is especially important in a racial order that allows little room for Black anger or responses other than peaceful acquiescence to compounding loss.[94] Congresswoman Maxine Waters recognized this in 1992 when she refused to condemn those among her constituents who took to the streets of Los Angeles to protest, sometimes violently, the acquittal of the white police officers that had brutally beaten Rodney King. She described the events as an insurrection rather than a riot and pointedly refused "to tell people to go inside, to be peaceful, that they have to accept the verdict. . . . I accept the responsibility of asking people not to endanger their lives. I am not asking people not to be angry. . . . I am angry and I have a right to that anger and the people out there have a right to that anger."[95] Waters's refusal to condemn violent Black dissent draws our attention to the fact that Black politics has been uniquely constrained by expectations of democratic civility.

If rioting can be seen as a form of democratic redress for Black citizens, it is important to be clear about what is meant by redress in this context. I use the term "redress" rather than "repair" here to signal my critique of the dynamic whereby Black politics is viewed primarily in terms of its potential to solve the problems of white democracy.[96] My understanding of how rioting could function as redress corresponds to Margaret Urban Walker's argument that what is powerfully at stake in reparations claims is moral vulnerability. She argues that for the victims of wrongdoing, this means having the standing to call wrongdoers to account and to have their claims heard and affirmed by the broader community. In the absence of legal accountability, I am arguing that rioting can be a means of asserting that sense of moral standing. As she observes: "It is obvious in many cases that what has been lost can never be returned or compensated. No one knows this better than the victims."[97] Rioting is an assertion of this demand. It is what the young people in Watts meant when they told MLK "we won."

There are resources in Black political thought that can allow us to develop an account of more radical Black political subjectivities along these lines that move beyond democratic sacrifice. In the 1960s, for example, Black Power intellectuals defended both Black anger and rioting.[98] Black feminist accounts of radical refusal also point the way to forms of politics that Black people might productively enact in the face of racial terror beyond democratic sacrifice. Black women's radical practices of intimacy and sabotage in the context of segregation and incarceration in the early twentieth century offer an expanded account of Black politics.[99] In this sense, they act as an antidote to narrow, romanticized accounts of legible Black protest. As historian Sarah Haley explains: "Sabotage is not about success or triumph against systematic violence and dispossession. Instead it is about the practice of life, living, disruption, rupture, and imagined futures; it is about the development of epistemologies of justice and collectivity."[100] Black women's practices of radical refusal can serve as "blueprints to freedom" for contemporary Black politics in order to avoid the strategic dead ends produced by the enshrinement of a romantic narrative of the civil rights movement as an exemplary moment when racial progress was achieved via political activism that fully acquiesced to liberal democratic norms.[101] Yet it could be argued that a politics centered on refusal has democratic costs, because it is a turning away from the collective power required to transform institutions. In the case of Black politics, however, the problem has not been a lack of investment in democracy so much as the subordination of Black freedom to the parasitic shoring-up of white democracy. In this sense, refusal becomes an essential check on expectations of unreciprocated democratic labor. It is also a reminder to look beyond the state.

Black feminist refusal recognizes the fact that law is *not* the opposite of violence, rather that it is deeply imbricated with it.[102] As Angela Davis has argued, because the law can and does act to reproduce injustice and inequality, Black liberation must entail "ways of contesting the absolute authority of the law."[103] One of the ways in which the violence of the law functions is that its own inaugural violence is obscured, while subsequent responses to injustice that transgress the legally permissible or the norms of civility are rendered hypervisible.[104] This dynamic is captured in an interview with Davis in prison in 1972 when she was asked whether she approved of violence. As Davis walks the Swedish interviewer through the reality of violent, racist policing of Black people in California at the time and the Sixteenth Street Baptist Church bombing by the Ku Klux Klan in her hometown of Birmingham, Alabama, in 1963, she exposes the false premise of the question.[105] To focus on the "explosions" of Black rage that are reactions to everyday injustice is to assert the law's racial innocence, to look away from the routine, everyday violence that structures Black life. If the law is often the source of racist violence and one of its principal instruments and regulating idioms, the question for Black politics becomes: How do you engage a state that is trying to kill you (or is at best indifferent to whether you live or die)? This question goes beyond a defense of resistance to unjust laws, to the more profound issue of how and if to appeal to the law, given that the law is a source of violence and is incapable of fully redressing the harms that it both produces and functions to obscure. Already in 1967, for example, MLK observed that the great legislative and legal victories of the civil rights movement had become dead letters, at the same time that the passage "of the law itself is treated as the reality of the reform." One year later, the same activists who had successfully fought for the passage of the historic Voting Rights Act of 1965 "were leading marchers in the suburbs of Chicago amid a rain of rocks and bottles, amid burning automobiles, to the thunder of jeering thousands, many of them waving Nazi flags."[106] Legal victories achieved at great cost and requiring enormous sacrifice were simultaneously greeted as if racial justice had been achieved and were also almost immediately hollowed out by fierce white backlash.

Reflecting the lessons learned from the backlash to the limited gains achieved by even the most legible—per the criteria of liberal democracy—forms of Black activism, the contemporary Movement for Black Lives is committed to envisioning a world in which Black people can thrive, not to upholding the legitimacy of the law or repairing US democracy per se. As legal scholar Amna Akbar observes, the M4BL "has largely refrained from fighting to strengthen preexisting rights or demanding legal recognition of new ones. The focus is not on . . . restoring criminal justice to some imaginary constitutional or pre-raced status quo." While remaining skeptical about the possibilities of legal reform, the M4BL has not rejected the law altogether. Its approach, however, "is rooted in a decarceral agenda rooted in an abolitionist imagination. Instead of striving to improve the police and criminal law, the Vision [of the M4BL] focuses on reducing its large social and fiscal footprint, and shifting resources—and therefore modes of governance—elsewhere."[107] The Movement for Black Lives—with its emphasis on intersectional leadership and centering those who have been marginalized in previous Black freedom struggles; Black love and self- and communal care; Black feminist-informed politics and movement structure; rejection of the politics of respectability; critique of racial capitalism; and demand for police abolition and investment in Black communities instead—appears to have incorporated some of the lessons of Black feminist refusal.[108] The insistence that "*all* Black lives matter" by Black Lives Matter protesters, for example, is indicative of a more radical critique of the carceral state that rejects the distinction between law-abiding, middle-class Black citizens and always-already criminalized Black "thugs" in urban ghettos. Demands for prison and police abolition and the rejection of a state oriented toward punishment rather than care recognizes that Black politics must actively resist the simultaneous criminalization of and disinvestment in Black lives. At the same time, at great personal cost, Black Lives Matter protesters have continued to demand accountability for Black death and state violence.

The seemingly endless litany of dead Black victims needing to be named, mourned, and remembered—Jamar Clark, Samuel Dubose, Sandra Bland, Walter Scott, Natasha McKenna, Bettie Jones, Laquan McDonald, and on and on and on—coupled with the backlash to the Black Lives Matter protests and the fervent embrace of Trumpism and white nationalism, makes it difficult, if not impossible, to engage in naive exercises of democratic hope in the United States at this moment. But this is an ongoing crisis. Black citizens have been exemplary democratic citizens while also knowing that they were (and still are) expected to be the losers in US democracy. Particularly where racial justice is concerned, there has been a very unequal distribution of the burden of dissent. The multiracial protests of 2020 following the killing of George Floyd and Breonna Taylor seemed to portend a moment when that shared obligation was taken up by a wider group of citizens. But the backlash that followed—exemplified in diminishing public support for BLM, increased funding for policing, and the panic surrounding the supposed teaching of critical race theory in schools—shows that this is an ongoing struggle. Recognizing this entails rethinking our notions of political obligation. *Instead of asking how Black people should protest so that their grievances can be heard, we need to ask: what do we owe Black citizens?* Answering this question means considering more than just what our obligations are to Black protesters (though this chapter has taken up that question), but also what we owe to Black people in their full humanity. This would involve taking seriously Kevin Quashie's exhortation to think about Blackness as about more than just resistance, to consider the interiority and full humanity of Black people.[109] In 1968, shortly after King's assassination and the uprisings that followed, *Esquire* magazine interviewed James Baldwin and asked:

> ESQ: How can we get the black people to cool it?
> JAMES BALDWIN: It is not for us to cool it.
> ESQ: But aren't you the ones who are getting hurt the most?
> JAMES BALDWIN: No, we are only the ones who are dying fastest. . . .
> [ESQ] So that when we come to you with the question, How do we cool it? All we're asking is that same old question, What does the Negro want?
> [JAMES BALDWIN] Yes. You're asking me to help you save it.
> [ESQ] Save ourselves?
> [JAMES BALDWIN] Yes. But you have to do that.[110]

Baldwin engages in various forms of refusal in this exchange: a refusal to disavow Black anger, a refusal to frame Black dissent in terms of how to save US democracy, and a refusal to absolve white citizens of the obligation to resist white supremacy. If white backlash is not new, as King observed, neither is Black refusal. But it has been overshadowed by Black sacrifice.

The backlash against the Black Lives Matter protests is a signal that we should rethink the notion of Black sacrifice as political exemplarity. Black feminist thought on refusal can help us imagine alternative forms of Black politics that do not fit easily within the bounds of liberal democracy. Envisioning different democratic futures requires ceasing to expect Black citizens to be political heroes. Taking seriously the idea of riots as a form of democratic repair for Black citizens means recognizing that responsibility for racial justice does not lie primarily with those who have already suffered the lion's share of the losses inflicted by racism. In the wake of Ferguson, Baltimore, Charleston, and the numerous other instances where it has become necessary to affirm that Black lives matter, even in death, Black politics must move beyond peaceful acquiescence to loss. Democratic sacrifice is no longer enough.

INTERLUDE 3

A Small Needful Fact

Is that Eric Garner worked
for some time for the Parks and Rec.
Horticultural Department, which means,
perhaps, that with his very large hands,
perhaps, in all likelihood,
he put gently into the earth
some plants which, most likely,
some of them, in all likelihood,
continue to grow, continue
to do what such plants do, like house
and feed small and necessary creatures,
like being pleasant to touch and smell,
like converting sunlight
into food, like making it easier
for us to breathe.

—"A SMALL NEEDFUL FACT" BY ROSS GAY (ORIGINALLY PUBLISHED THROUGH SPLIT THIS ROCK'S "THE QUARRY: A SOCIAL JUSTICE POETRY DATABASE")

3

Representing Loss between Fact and Affect

DESCRIBING THE CHALLENGE of telling a story of rape and incest from the point of view of a Black girl child victim or would-be-victims in a way that "justified the public exposure of a privacy," Nobel laureate Toni Morrison described *The Bluest Eye* as a "(failed) attempt to shape a silence while breaking it."[1] As Morrison's observation illustrates, Black intellectuals and artists have continually wrestled with the question of how to craft their depictions of Black life in a way that honors the disclosure of Black suffering. Making loss visible, which is required in order for it to be seen and recognized as political, has costs. It poses important ethical and strategic dilemmas. On the one hand, some losses are unrepresentable.[2] On the other hand, there is the question of which representational strategies—enumerating or quantifying loss (e.g., gathering statistics on its magnitude) or telling stories that personalize or humanize it—are most likely to impel the public to see and feel the loss in question.[3] W.E.B. Du Bois understood this as a question about what kind of Black rhetorical appeals would induce moral transformations in white audiences. The horrific lynching of Sam

Hose in 1899 shook Du Bois's faith in the ability of detached scientific data alone to move white hearts and minds, and this led him to experiment with rhetorical modes and literary genres more conducive to imagination and feeling.[4] Confronted with horrific racist violence firsthand, he became less convinced that facts alone could alter white affective investments in Black suffering.[5] Like Morrison and Du Bois, Harriet Jacobs and Ida B. Wells also grappled with the dilemma of what to conceal or disclose about Black suffering in order to make Black loss visible.[6] Structured in part by the different gendered constraints they faced as Black women, both authors move between sentimental and unsentimental modes of writing, between fact and affect, in order to account not just for Black pain, but also for Black life. They attend to both grief and grievance and in the process show (in contemporary parlance) that Black lives matter. At a historical moment when we are bombarded with viral videos of Black people dying, which are shared in the name of demanding democratic witnessing of Black pain to elicit racial redress, Jacobs and Wells remind us of the ethical dilemmas that attend to representations of (Black) suffering. Their work is deeply relevant to our contemporary moment because it reminds us that it is possible to balance grief and grievance in accounts of loss. Wells and Jacobs show us how to tell stories of Black life, not just Black pain, or Black death.

Jacobs and Wells are exemplary theorists of loss. They formulated capacious accounts of Black loss that reckon with democracy and freedom's costs, balancing grief and grievance in service of making space for Black life amid ongoing Black death.[7] In their texts, they seek to create the conditions for Black life as they tell stories of ongoing loss. They document Black grieving and in so doing show that paying attention to loss and sitting with grief are key to fostering the conditions for Black life. Instead of dwelling in or on Black suffering to elicit white sympathy in the pivot from grief to activism, they provide a more capacious account of Black grief that insists on paying attention to Black life-in-community and balancing grief and grievance.

Jacobs and Wells lived in different eras and wrote under different circumstances but faced similar challenges as Black women intellectuals. Jacobs [1813–97], the fugitive slave, author, and activist on behalf of freedpersons, and Wells [1862–1931], the journalist, tireless antilynching crusader, proponent of women's suffrage, anti–racial segregation activist, and cofounder of pioneering African American institutions, made use of different literary genres. Jacobs's slave narrative, *Incidents in the Life of a Slave Girl*, the first authored by a woman in the United States, was published in 1861 prior to the Civil War and abolition.[8] In contrast, Wells was part of a generation that came of age after emancipation, and she had a prolific career as a journalist.[9] As Black women concerned with slavery and racist violence and hoping to persuade white audiences to embrace the cause of racial justice, Wells and Jacobs turned to literary genres with which their readers were already familiar—the slave narrative, sentimental fiction, and journalism—and adapted them to fit their needs. Their choices about what to disclose and conceal about Black loss were shaped by the shared constraints on different rhetorical modes of expression they faced as Black women, and the conventions of the respective literary genres from which they borrowed and which they transformed.

Because they wrote in such different literary genres, it might be tempting to read them as following diametrically opposed approaches to representing loss: Jacobs as trafficking primarily in affect, and Wells as wedded solely to fact. Wells's use of statistical data and focus on documenting the hidden record of white violence could be read as exemplary of "unsentimental writing," while Jacobs's slave narrative was famously influenced by sentimental fiction.[10] But the work of both Jacobs and Wells blurs genre distinctions and partakes of both sentimental and unsentimental elements. Wells, for instance, might be viewed as emblematic of accounts of loss that foreground Black death at the expense of Black life and that pivot too quickly from grief to activism. Yet her writings show an attempt to balance grief and grievance that never completely displaces Black loss. Even in those texts where Wells is at her most sociological and dispassionate, she takes care to tell the stories of the Black dead, as well as the living who survive the violence. In Jacobs's case, it might also be tempting to focus on the excessive affect conventional to the sentimental fiction that influenced her narrative. Yet Jacobs was also strategic about what she chose to reveal and conceal about Black loss. Her narrative highlights Black women's quotidian struggle for survival and refuses to offer up their pained bodies for white consumption. Despite adhering to some of the genre conventions of sentimental fiction, Jacobs does not afford her readers easy affective identifications; she is wary of the "satisfactions of sympathy," of the way her white readers might derive pleasure from their own emotional response to the suffering of enslaved women.[11] Like Wells, she forces them to contend with white violence and complicity. Wells and Jacobs thus exemplify a capacious account of Black grief that points to what Christina Sharpe calls "the important work of sitting (together) in the pain and sorrow of death as a way of marking, remembering, and celebrating a life. . . . While the wake produces Black death and trauma . . . we, Black people . . . still produce in, into, and through the wake an insistence on existing: we insist Black being into the wake."[12]

Not only did Wells and Jacobs draw on both fact and affect in their rhetorical appeals; the distinctions between the slave narrative, sentimental fiction, and journalism were not so clear-cut in the nineteenth century. The slave narrative, sentimental fiction, and journalism ostensibly have very different genre expectations. Journalism is supposed to be characterized by the dispassionate presentation of facts, while the slave narrative was expected to be suffused with feeling, and sentimental fiction was ostensibly concerned with the supposedly apolitical subjects of romance, family, and domesticity. As a journalist, Wells might therefore be seen as participating in a masculine, unsentimental genre focused on overtly political thematic subject matter, in her case, documenting the hidden record of white violence.[13] In contrast, slave narratives were a form of autobiography aimed at moral suasion that relied heavily on sensational depictions of violence, and Jacobs's text could thus be seen as concerned primarily with the feminine subjects of family and the private sphere.[14] But journalistic writing during this era was itself "drenched in the yellow ink of sensationalized reporting tactics," and Wells's own antilynching writings "were calculated to shock readers."[15] Sentimental literature, meanwhile, was also a complex genre.[16] Its subject matter exceeded the stereotypical focus on romantic relationships and tender feelings. Sentimental novels were a space where gender inequality and hierarchies in the domestic realm could be explored, and where questions of political membership and the nature of civic association were translated into the grammar of the domestic and familial.[17] When wielded by Black women, sentimental writing drew attention to the racialized and gendered inequalities in the family and domestic sphere often overlooked by the focus on the civic and economic harms of racism.[18]

Yet Black women navigating traditional gender expectations and genre conventions had to walk a difficult tightrope. Wells and Jacobs faced different risks than their male counterparts as they moved between *logos* and *pathos* to represent Black suffering. They faced heightened constraints because of both gender and genre. On the one hand, because epistemic injustice shapes the ways raced and gendered testimony is received and interpreted, Black women could not rely on the facts alone to make the case for Black freedom and racial justice.[19] But, on the other hand, they had to guard against the way appeals to emotion have been gendered and used to delegitimize women's standing in the masculine public sphere. As Hazel Carby observes, Black women have a relationship to affect different from that of white women. During the nineteenth century, white abolitionist and antislavery narratives relied on depictions of the pained female Black body and of enslaved men and women as passive victims to elicit the sympathy of white readers.[20] Surviving the ordeal of slavery also marked enslaved women as both insufficiently feminine and morally inferior. At the same time, women in the nineteenth century were expected to write in a sentimental vein, and racism further constrained the self-presentation of Black women. The prevailing ideal of womanhood at the time hindered middle-class Black women from expressing certain emotions in public, especially anger. Sentimental and unsentimental rhetorical modes thus presented different challenges and constraints for Wells and Jacobs. They shifted between the two modes as they sought to confront Black loss head-on while simultaneously placing limits on the disclosure of Black suffering in order to elicit potential white identification.

My aim in tracing how Wells and Jacobs move between fact and affect, grief and grievance, is not to single out any one strategy as the only useful approach to representing Black loss. Multiple approaches are present in the work of individual thinkers, and in African American political thought as a whole. Instrumental accounts of Black loss to propel mobilization for racial justice have been dominant, however, while capacious accounts of Black grief have been less prominent. In contrast, Wells and Jacobs balance grief and grievance in their depictions of loss. They show us how to make Black loss visible while also *feeling* loss. Wells and Jacobs make clear that while the turn to activism in the wake of otherwise unbearable loss has generated important resources for Black politics, noninstrumental accounts of Black grief are equally essential to a politics that seeks to center Black life. Their accounts of Black loss are filled with "small, needful facts," to paraphrase the poem that serves as an interlude to this chapter. In it, Ross Gay unearths Eric Garner's use of his large hands to plant flowers that New Yorkers continue to enjoy, giving us an image of his life beyond the viral one of his death. In the same way, Wells and Jacobs memorialize mundane facts of Black life, not only to humanize Black loss in order to propel grievance, but to remind us to attend to Black people in their full humanity, to pay attention to the lives beyond the violence, to the fact that Eric Garner also gently planted flowers.

Harriet Jacobs on Slavery's Facts, "No Fiction"

If Wells is viewed as having produced an eminently unsentimental, data-driven response to racist violence in the post-Reconstruction era, Harriet Jacobs's depiction of Black life in slavery and fugitivity has instead usually been read as overly sentimental and overabundant in affect. This reading of Jacobs's *Incidents in the Life of a Slave Girl* results from the text's incorporation of formal elements of sentimental fiction, and from its focus on the specific forms of unfreedom faced by enslaved women, such as maternal dispossession, coerced reproduction, and pervasive sexual violence. *Incidents* is a complex text, however. While the conventions of sentimental fiction opened greater space for affect in Jacobs's narrative, it does not descend into mawkishness. There are elements of both the sentimental and the unsentimental in *Incidents*.[21]

Jacobs simultaneously condemns white moral failure while foregrounding the quiet heroic struggle to preserve quotidian Black life constantly threatened in and by slavery. In contrast to male slave narratives, she centers the denial of sexual autonomy, the destruction of family ties, and thwarted maternity as the central harms of slavery.[22] While Wells's accounts of lynching and white race riots tend to focus on the most extreme public acts of white violence, Jacobs focuses on intimate, quiet losses that are (in some instances) the result of more indirect violence, such as the denial of shared mourning. Jacobs gives a nuanced account of Black grief in *Incidents*. She confronts loss and sorrow directly and does not offer easy answers or pat resolutions to her readers. In this way, the text is more akin to unsentimental writing than one might expect.[23] In fact, in contrast to male slave narratives, which often presented a much more seamless passage from slavery to freedom, there are no easy, clear-cut victories in *Incidents*. Even as Jacobs triumphs over her oppressors, these are gradual, painstakingly won, ambivalent gains that exemplify a different conception of Black politics. Instead of the spectacular, public, physical, singular act of frontal confrontation, Jacobs practices a more quotidian, underground politics of Black resistance that relies on concealment, conspiracy, and solidarity. Even from a confined space of captive freedom, she participates in a community of freedom-bestowing, care-providing people who are a mix of enslaved and free.

Like Wells, Jacobs went to great pains to align her text with fact rather than affect, even as her assertion in the very first lines of the preface that *Incidents* was not fiction was delivered in a form that would have been familiar to readers of sentimental novels. She writes: "Reader, be assured this narrative is *no fiction*. I am aware that some of my adventures may seem incredible; but they are, nevertheless, strictly true. I have not exaggerated the wrongs inflicted by Slavery; on the contrary, my descriptions fall far short of the *facts*."[24] Jacobs's claim that her narrative was a factual, not fictional, account of slavery is particularly relevant considering Harriet Beecher Stowe's offer to include *Incidents* in *The Key to Uncle Tom's Cabin*, Stowe's reply to criticisms that the portrayal of slavery in her best-selling novel, the paradigmatic sentimental antislavery text, was exaggerated. Had Jacobs consented, she would have been placing her facts in service of Stowe's fiction. Jacobs rejected Stowe's offer, as she wanted the story of her life to appear "entirely by itself which would do more good and it needed *no romance* but if she wanted some *facts* for her book that I would be most happy to give her some."[25] Jacobs's refusal points to a desire to distinguish between her narrative and the sentimental abolitionist fiction produced by white writers. Like other enslaved people, she faced the challenge of telling her own story rather than having it told for her or subsumed into white abolitionist narratives. In her exchange with Stowe, she navigates this dilemma via the distinction between fact and affect: her life story, which still fell short of fully detailing the facts of slavery, "needed no romance."[26]

At the same time, however, Jacobs was highly aware of the risks of "breaking the silence." She anticipates Morrison's concern with how to tell the stories of Black women's suffering ethically. Jacobs rejects sympathy for her individual suffering and marks the cost of revealing her losses:

> I have not written my experiences in order to attract attention to myself; on the contrary, it would have been more pleasant to me to have been silent about my own history. Neither do I care to excite sympathy for my own suffering. But I do earnestly desire to arouse the women of the North to a realizing sense of the condition of two millions of women at the South, still in bondage, suffering what I suffered, and most of them far worse. I want to add my testimony to that of abler pens to convince the people of the Free States what Slavery really is.[27]

Jacobs thus co-initiates a tradition—which continues to this day in viral videos of lethal police encounters—of Black witnessing that seeks to show the reality of racism to a white audience via the exposure of Black pain. Like Douglass in "What to the Slave Is the Fourth of July?," Jacobs performs humility (e.g., her reference to "abler pens"), even as she asserts her understanding, based on firsthand knowledge, of the (gendered) harms of enslavement, and weaves her testimony to slavery's facts. As a nineteenth-century Black woman writing about sex, she was keenly aware of the costs of such visibility: exposure was itself a loss.[28] But if silence was not an option, Jacobs sought to shape the terms on which Black women's suffering was revealed. Her use of *pathos* sought to compel action, not simply to allow white readers the "satisfactions of sympathy." Such gratification could be "narcissistic (the heightened self-regard of displaying how compassionate one's feelings are), moral (the displacement of guilt in that if I feel bad, I must be good, even if I'm not doing anything), or sensual (the pleasures of intensity, the excitement of sharing feelings)."[29] In exchange for making the private public, Jacobs demanded that white readers examine their own racism.

While Jacobs's choices about what to disclose and what to conceal about Black women's suffering were undoubtedly shaped by concerns about how to evade the stigma of sexual promiscuity, their effect is a deeply ethical engagement with the issue of how Black pain is consumed that is later articulated by Morrison and Black feminist scholars.[30] Even as Jacobs foregrounds sexual autonomy as central to freedom for Black women, her critique of slavery does not rely on graphic depictions of the pained and violated Black female body for its emotional impact, as male slave narratives and abolitionist texts and images often did.[31] Jacobs was more "frank" and "blunt" in raising the question of women's sexual agency than was the norm in sentimental fiction and in slave narratives. At the same time, she chose to focus on Black women's quotidian survival—and attempts to forge life and maintain family in the face of ongoing loss—rather than on scenes of spectacular violence (sexual or otherwise) against enslaved women.

This attention to both grief and grievance is evident throughout *Incidents*, especially in Jacobs's depiction of Black maternity. As Black feminist interpreters of the text have argued, *Incidents* was a pioneering text in revealing the fraught politics of Black motherhood during slavery. The imperative to preserve family ties has multifaceted effects in *Incidents*. It constrains Jacobs's fugitivity, as her escape initially occurs within the space of plantation slavery, not beyond it, so that she can remain close to her children in the South.[32] But close family ties are also what keep her and other enslaved people in *Incidents* from succumbing to grief, and they are ultimately what enable whatever "interstitial inhabitations of freedom" she and they eventually achieve, as

Jasmine Syedullah argues.[33] Jacobs's exploration of the complexity of Black motherhood under slavery anticipates what Jennifer Nash has called the dual political work of Black motherhood, which is posited as a site of loss "constituted by grief and . . . made visible (only) because of its proximity to death," but also as a generative, life-affirming source of redemption.[34] In our current moment, Nash argues, Black mothers are often represented as "symbols of trauma and injury, of pain that can be mobilized for 'legitimate' political ends and social change."[35] In contrast, Black feminist theory seeks to reimagine Black maternity: "If black motherhood is imagined as a death-world, black feminist theory has become squarely invested in reimagining and amplifying the potential, power, and possibility of black motherhood."[36] As a result of this contestation over how to understand Black mothering, Nash argues, "in this cultural moment . . . black motherhood is . . . a powerful and densely loaded site of political meaning."[37] The same was true of the pre–Civil War era, in which Jacobs published *Incidents*.

Jacobs's text anticipates this simultaneous political work of Black motherhood as a site of trauma and injury and a life-affirming generative site of political meaning. Spending six years and eleven months "in prison" in "the loophole of retreat"—a crawl space under the roof of her grandmother's attic that was only nine feet by seven feet wide, and three feet high at its highest point—is as paradigmatic an example of heroic sacrificial Black maternity as one can imagine. Being confined within it was necessary because Jacobs had a collective understanding of freedom centered on the Black family.[38] The loophole of retreat was a site not just of imprisonment, but also of psychological trench warfare. For example, the letters Jacobs wrote to Dr. Flint from within it, which were purportedly sent from the North, led him on a fruitless wild-goose chase. Her rebellion in a space of confinement points to the insurrectionary potential of domesticity. At other moments in the text, however, Jacobs unflinchingly shines a light on the fact that Black maternity under slavery was inescapably accompanied by loss.

Incidents is a veritable litany of Black maternal grief.[39] It is a central theme in the text. For instance, Jacobs recounts the superimposed and accumulated losses of two generations of enslaved Black women, who remain unnamed (like many lynching victims in a subsequent era). In a tragic deathbed scene, a "young slave girl" and her (also unnamed) mother were mocked by their female enslaver as the daughter lay dying after giving birth to a "child nearly white." In response to the mockery of the white woman, whose husband was the rapist, "the girl's mother said, 'The baby is dead, thank God; and I hope my poor child will soon be in heaven too.'"[40] Enslaved mothers grieved the loss of their children, but death was also a release from the horrors of slavery.[41] Jacobs ends the chapter by juxtaposing cold, unfeeling white maternity and grieving, overburdened Black maternity: "Seven children called her [the white mistress] mother. The poor black woman had but one child, whose eyes she saw closing in death, while she thanked God for taking her away from the greater bitterness of life."[42] This is the last sentence in the chapter. Jacobs provides no further details about the lives of these enslaved women, mother and daughter. We know nothing about whatever joy or solace they may have found in the midst of loss, or the textures of the lives they might have been able to steal away apart from the enslavers' power. In this instance, the life before the violence is not reanimated in Jacobs's text other than in the love between mother and child and in Black maternal grief. Instead, the focus of the chapter is on white violence, and specifically the cruelty of white women, as Jacobs aims to show that "from others than the master persecution also comes in such cases."[43] Jacobs uses any potential tears her white female readers might shed for "the poor black woman" to direct their gaze to white women's (and their own) complicity.

In contrast to the unnamed enslaved mothers described in this chapter, there are other moments in *Incidents* where Jacobs offers richly textured accounts of Black grief that center Black life, Black family, and Black community. This is particularly true of the chapter entitled "Aunt Nancy," the only chapter title throughout *Incidents* to include a proper name rather than a second- or third-person description of its subject, such as, for example, "Childhood," "A Perilous Passage in the Slave Girl's Life," and "Important Era in my Brother's Life."[44] In "Aunt Nancy," Jacobs tells the story of the life and death of that beloved relative, her mother's sister, and of her family's sorrow. The chapter moves back and forth between describing the various ways in which the family fought for the right to mourn their dead, something that enslaved people were routinely denied, and detailing a litany of suffering and losses (both material and spiritual) inflicted by white cruelty.[45] Through the story of her aunt's life and death, Jacobs directly connects the forced reproductive labor that Black women were made to perform in caring for white children with the breakdown of their bodies and the impossibility of caring for their own children. Aunt Nancy, whose real name was Betty, was allowed to marry an enslaved man, Stephen, who worked as a sailor. While employed as "housekeeper and waiting maid in Dr. Flint's family . . . the factotum of the household," as well as a night nurse for Mrs. Flint's children, Betty gave "premature birth to six children" and to "two feeble babes, one of whom died in a few days, and the other in four weeks."[46] We gain some insight into the impact of this history of thwarted Black maternity through Betty's unwavering support of Harriet's efforts to escape slavery.

Aunt Betty took tremendous risks and suffered serious personal losses in support of Harriet's freedom.[47] She served as the family's spy in Dr. Flint's household, reporting on his efforts to locate Harriet, and was briefly jailed after her escape to the attic.[48] Most devastatingly, she was deprived of her marriage. After Harriet's escape, as John Jacobs recounts in his slave narrative, Dr. Flint effectively dissolved her marriage:

> my uncle-in-law Stephen . . . had had several chances to make his escape from slavery, yet he had returned on every voyage. The doctor, who owned my aunt, forbad[e] his going to see her, although they had lived together for twenty years, and had never been known to quarrel. It was most cruel that they should be separated, not for their own, but for another's acts. The doctor was inexorable; they were strictly interdicted from seeing each other. The only tie that bound my uncle to slavery was his wife, to whom he was truly attached. When their sacred union—a union holy in the sight of God, however desecrated by wicked men—was broken, he would not longer submit to the yoke. He took advantage of his next voyage to release himself from it, and he returned no more. His wife was dead to him—nay, worse than dead.[49]

Despite what must have been the agonizing loss of her husband, on top of the prior deaths of their children, Aunt Betty was the one who fortified Harriet in her determination to escape.

> When my friends tried to discourage me from running away, she always encouraged me. When they thought I had better return to ask my master's pardon, because there was no

> possibility of escape, she sent me word never to yield. She said if I persevered I might, perhaps, gain the freedom of my children; and even if I perished in doing it, that was better than to leave them to groan under the same persecutions that had blighted my own life.[50]

In her advice to Harriet never to yield, Aunt Betty reiterates the claim of other enslaved mothers that death was preferable to the horrors of slavery. But she also encourages Harriet to pursue an enlarged vision of freedom that encompassed her children. Aunt Betty was prevented from raising her own children, but beyond the forced reproductive labor she was coerced into performing for the Flint household, she also chose to mother her niece and was a key member of the Jacobs/Horniblow family.[51] As Harriet recalled: "A word from her always strengthened me, and not me only. The whole family relied upon her judgment and were guided by her advice."[52] Indeed, in a family where her grandmother already looms large as a caring maternal presence, albeit one more wedded to respectability, Aunt Betty represents a more openly defiant model of insurrectionary Black maternity (while herself remaining enslaved).

The story of Aunt Betty's death and burial also reveals the denial of shared mourning as another form of loss chronicled in *Incidents*. Grief itself became a terrain of struggle for enslaved people. Not only did the Flints (a.k.a. Norcoms) seek to use the Jacobs family's sorrow at the death of Aunt Betty to force Harriet's return; the circumstances of her death and burial were suffused with repeated grievances amid grief. Dr. Flint's son, for example, dared to mention Aunt Betty's death in his reply to a letter from Harriet asking to be sold to her grandmother: "We cannot sell you to your grandmother; the community would object to your returning to live in a state of freedom. Harriet, doubtless before this you have heard of the death of your aunt Betty. In her life she taught us how to live, and in her death she taught us how to die."[53] Presumably Dr. Flint's son wanted to invoke the image of a faithful slave, but Aunt Betty, who as far as we know never tried to escape herself, was in fact anything but. Her death was another in a long line of losses inflicted by enslavers on the Jacobs/Horniblow family, as her grandmother observed in her reply to Dr. Flint's blatant attempt to manipulate her grief to secure Harriet's return. On Aunt Betty's deathbed, he told her: "'I wish . . . that Linda [Harriet] would come to supply her aunt's place. . . . I wish it for your sake also, Martha. Now that Nancy [Betty] is taken from you, she would be a great comfort in your old age.' . . . Almost choking with grief, my grandmother replied, 'It was not I that drove Linda away. My grandchildren are gone; and of my nine children only one is left. God help me!'" For enslaved mothers, loss was inescapable, either as foreclosed maternity (as in the case of Aunt Betty) or as maternal dispossession (as in the case of those whose children were sold away or who were prevented from caring for them). For her part, Harriet describes feeling both sorrow and rage at her aunt's passing: "To me the death of this kind relative was an inexpressible sorrow. *I knew that she had been slowly murdered*."[54] *Incidents* takes pains to name the kind of slow, quotidian violence that killed Aunt Betty.

Jacobs's narrative also shows practices of care and Black reproductive labor performed by various family members struggling to have their kinship rights acknowledged by enslavers who had inured themselves to Black suffering. Jacobs's family, for example, had to prevent Mrs. Flint, the cause of Aunt Betty's death, from burying her away from the rest of her Black relatives. "Mrs. Flint had rendered her poor foster-sister childless apparently without any compunction. . . . But now she became very sentimental. I suppose she thought it would be a beautiful illustration of the attachment existing between slaveholder and slave, if the body of the old worn-out servant was buried at her feet." Mrs. Flint's gesture, without any thought to the wishes of Aunt Betty's family, is a searing yet ordinary example of how white sentimentalism could be a form of cruelty rather than solidarity. "It had never occurred to Mrs. Flint that slaves could have any feelings," Jacobs writes. After the intercession of a white clergyman allowed her grandmother to express her desire that her daughter be buried next to her relatives in the Black cemetery, Mrs. Flint "graciously complied with her wish, though she said it was painful to her to have Nancy buried away from *her*. She might have added with touching pathos, 'I was so long used to sleep with her lying near me, on the entry floor.'"[55] In death, as in life, Aunt Betty was to be made adjunct to the whims of her white enslaver, who wanted only the appearance of benevolence. Instead, Jacobs's sarcasm ruthlessly exposed Mrs. Flint's actions as fueled purely by the narcissistic satisfactions of sympathy. By critiquing white women's wielding of sentiment to overshadow Black loss, Jacobs's text refuses white readers easy affective identifications.

Jacobs's description of Aunt Betty's funeral is a detailed accounting of the losses accrued in asserting the right itself to mourn. It shows her determination to make visible the hidden transcript of Black grief during slavery. "My uncle Phillip asked permission to bury his sister at his own expense, and slaveholders are always ready to grant *such* favors to slaves and their relatives. . . . It was talked of by the slaves as a mighty grand funeral." But Jacobs quickly moves to dispel any mistaken notions of sentimental attachment between enslavers and enslaved evoked by the "very plain, but perfectly respectable" funeral paid for by Aunt Betty's family, or of slave owners' care and benevolence conjured by the single tear shed by a supposedly "tender-hearted" Mrs. Flint at the graveside:

> *We* could have told them a different story. We could have given them a chapter of wrongs and sufferings, that would have touched their hearts, if they *had* any hearts to feel for the colored people. We could have told them how the poor old slave-mother had toiled, year after year, to earn eight hundred dollars to buy her son Phillip's right to his own earnings; and how that same Phillip paid the expenses of the funeral, which they regarded as doing so much credit to the master. We could also have told them of a poor, blighted young creature, shut up in a living grave for years, to avoid the tortures that would be inflicted on her, if she ventured to come out and look on the face of her departed friend.[56]

Here, Jacobs provides the facts that rend the comforting veils of enslavers' fictions. She details compounding Black material losses in the form of unpaid labor, the travesty of enslaved people being forced to buy their own freedom (i.e., manumission via self-purchase), and care for enslaved relatives as a means through which even free Black persons were indirectly dispossessed of their earnings. She also accounts for other types of loss: her physical loss of mobility (being confined to a "living grave" in her grandmother's attic in order to escape sexual violence), and the affective loss of the denial of the tactile consolations of shared mourning.[57] Jacobs mourns a variety of losses in *Incidents*, as Syedullah argues.[58] Her approach to Black loss makes space for grief even as it also centers Black life, not death.

If Jacobs is at pains to disclose the "chapter of wrongs" slavery imposed on Black families—and Black women in particular—there is also an important politics of concealment of the pained

Black body in Jacobs that is different from that in Wells. Wells's withholding of affect can be read as a refusal of exposure, of the sacrifice that comes with visibly talking about pain. But in other ways, as we will see, Wells did participate in the affective economy that required the exposure of the pained Black body to awaken white empathy and spur outrage at lynching. Wells gave detailed descriptions of white violence and mutilated Black bodies, even as she also archived Black lives prior to the violence and the violation. Jacobs sought white women's solidarity with enslaved women, but she did not offer up their violated Black bodies for abolitionist consumption. Jacobs's editor Lydia Maria Child (who helped get *Incidents* published) explicitly acknowledged the pleasure white abolitionist readers derived from consuming antislavery literature: "No incidents in history, or romance are more thrilling than the sufferings, perils, and hairbreadth escapes of American slaves."[59]

Beyond the pleasures of consuming action-packed tales of successful flights from slavery, abolitionists trafficked in an "iconography of abjection"—epitomized in the image of the kneeling slave pleading for freedom—that represented Black people as passive victims rather than active agents in their own liberation.[60] The scarred bodies of enslaved people were regularly featured in abolitionist literature to illustrate the brutality of slavery, and the rape of enslaved women was a central element of the moral condemnation of the peculiar institution. Black male authors of slave narratives participated in the representation of Black women's pained bodies as well, as Hazel Carby argues. Their descriptions of "mothers, sisters, and daughters as victims, of either brutal beatings or sexual abuse" were evidence not only of the brutality of slavery, but of the additional harm of "denial of, the manhood of the male slave" because of their inability to protect their female kin.[61] John Jacobs's slave narrative follows this pattern. The opening lines of his narrative introduce readers to slavery's harms in the following way:

> To be a man, and not to be a man—a father without authority—a husband and no protector—is the darkest of fates. Such . . . is the condition of every slave throughout the United States: he owns nothing, he can claim nothing. His wife is not his: his children are not his; they can be taken from him, and sold at any minute. . . . A slave's wife or daughter may be insulted before his eyes with impunity. He himself may be called on to torture them, and dare not refuse. . . . He must bear all things and resist nothing.[62]

Like other male slave narrative authors, John Jacobs depicts slavery's harms in terms of the impossibility of asserting patriarchal manhood, while Harriet Jacobs's *Incidents* centers enslaved women's struggles for self-emancipation and the collective freedom of the family unit.

In contrast to depictions of slavery in which the spectacle of the violated Black woman's body took center stage, Harriet Jacobs's *Incidents* focuses on quotidian rather than spectacular white violence and on Black women's agency, however constrained. As Syedullah observes, Jacobs tells

> a story of escape from slavery that did not center the spectacle of subjection [that] abolitionist literature had made familiar to antebellum audiences. . . . In *Incidents* . . . reference to such spectacular scenes are largely indirect . . . rather than circumscribe black suffering to the cause of abolition over and against the struggles for dignity and humanity [of] enslaved people. . . . *Incidents* insisted upon detailing the day-to-day implications of what it meant to live under constant threat of not only corporeal violence, but also sexual violation.[63]

For example, in the case of the unnamed slave girl whose deathbed scene is described in *Incidents*, the rape she suffered is only implied. Jacobs transgressed gender norms and racist convention by centering the question of Black women's sexual agency, just as Wells's antilynching texts were controversial because they disclosed consensual interracial relationships between Black men and white women. Of her relationship with Mr. Sands, Jacobs writes: "It seems less degrading to give one's self, than to submit to compulsion. There is something akin to freedom in having a lover who has no control over you."[64] This sentence is nestled within a chapter that tries to anticipate and preempt the condemnation of her readers by dwelling on her grandmother's (uncharacteristically) unsympathetic reaction to the disclosure of her relationship with Mr. Sands, even though she knew that Dr. Flint had prevented Harriet from marrying her preferred romantic partner, a free Black man. And yet, despite Jacobs's profuse apologies, this is as *un*sentimental an account of the limited sexual agency of enslaved women as one can imagine. *Incidents* highlights the fact that white men were rapists enabled by complicit white women focused solely on their own resentments. In this way, Jacobs shifts attention away from Black suffering as spectacle and onto white violence and complicity, particularly the collusion of white women, who for the most part did not use their greater agency to make common cause with enslaved women. The focus in *Incidents* is not on the violated Black female body; it is on Black survival. Jacobs was therefore strategic in both what she chose to reveal and what she chose to conceal about Black loss.

Incidents also does not contain a single pivotal moment where physical mastery is achieved over a slave owner. Instead, it centers moments of quiet resistance and psychological struggle. In her account of hidden, stolen moments of bodily pleasure as quotidian forms of resistance by enslaved people, historian Stephanie Camp suggests that viewing actions "other than organized rebellion or running away as only partial or even cooptative distracts us from interesting and important possibilities for understanding Black politics."[65] *Incidents* is attuned to precisely such possibilities. What, for example, is the counterpoint in Jacobs's narrative to Douglass's famous fight with Covey, which is widely viewed as the pivotal moment in his *Narrative*? Is it Jacobs's prolonged confinement in her grandmother's attic, which allows her to successfully elude Dr. Flint's attempts to rape her, but at the expense of being severely physically constrained? Or is it the moment when she asserts some degree of sexual autonomy by entering into a sexual relationship with a white man, Mr. Sands, who was not her legal owner? Neither of these pivotal events in Jacobs's narrative is a clear-cut victory. Nor are they singular occurrences, but rather ongoing processes. They are fraught, ambiguous steps in a text that refuses to offer a teleological account of the journey from slavery to freedom.

If Jacobs's struggle for self-emancipation in *Incidents* reveals something about the temporality of freedom, about its psychological and processual character, it also highlights it as a quotidian practice not necessarily restricted to singular heroic acts, in contrast to Douglass's initial account of his escape in his *Narrative*.[66] Syedullah, for example, reads Jacobs as a radical thinker in a Black feminist fugitive abolitionist intellectual tradition that refuses the seductions of "freedom's domestications." In her view, Jacobs is a theorist of freedom principally concerned with mourning "freedom's cost." Jacobs, she argues, "mourns the loss legitimized freedom costs fugitives. . . . Legal and legitimate freedom . . . came at a cost, both monetary and moral. There was no justice in this kind of freedom, particularly for a fugitive who would rather risk her life than remain enslaved. There was no glory, no redemption in this practice of liberation."[67] The losses associated with legal freedom revealed by Jacobs in *Incidents* have to do with refusing the seductions of national belonging and limited notions of liberal citizenship, as well as bourgeois fantasies of domesticity as modes of female place making. According to Syedullah, the fugitive abolitionist politics of Jacobs's text reveals "that political recognition and national incorporation are not always the primary or most advantageous aims for social acts of political resistance."[68] Like Douglass, then, Jacobs can also be read as pointing to alternative geographies of Black politics, beyond the domestic (read as both home and nation) out to the hemispheric.[69] In this vein, literary critic Maria Windell argues that prevailing understandings of Harriet Jacobs as wholly preoccupied with familial and national domesticity neglect her "efforts to conceptualize a black hemispheric imaginary." Jacobs "is as much engaged in envisioning African American elsewheres (writ large, beyond domesticity)" as her Black male contemporaries Douglass and Martin R. Delany were.[70] As exemplified by the seven years she spent immobilized in "the loophole of retreat," Jacobs's practices of flight disrupt easy demarcations between freedom and unfreedom and point to the fungible geographies of domination and resistance that attend to Black life "in the wake."

Jacobs's determination to account for "freedom's cost" is clear in the final chapter of *Incidents*, which—despite being exuberantly titled "Free at Last!"—maps the complicated ways in which her change in legal status (momentous as it was) did not equal escape from constraint, obligation, or subjection. Jacobs was dismayed, for example, that she gained her freedom by being purchased by her employer, Mrs. Willis, toward whom she thereafter felt bound by duty. This is how she described the moment in *Incidents*:

> Reader my story ends with freedom; not in in the usual way, with marriage. I and my children are now free! We are as free from the power of slaveholders as are the white people of the north; and though that, according to my ideas, is not saying a great deal, it is a vast improvement in *my* condition. The dream of my life is not yet realized. I do not sit with my children in a home of my own. . . . God so orders circumstance as to keep me with my friend Mrs. Bruce [Mrs. Willis]. Love, duty, gratitude, also bind me to her side.[71]

Jacobs is acutely aware of the various ways in which legal freedom is not enough; she continues to be bound by both labor and affective ties. As feminist readers of this passage have noted, the juxtaposition of freedom and marriage is an implied critique of marriage and its status as the telos of sentimental fiction. It also points to the ways unfreedom *exceeds* legal status, however. The claim that free Black persons and white citizens in the North continued to be subject to the power of slaveholders within the body politic was also a recognition of the limits of US democracy, of what John Jacobs ironically referred to as the "stars and *stripes* of America."[72]

Harriet Jacobs's critique of the distorting civic effects of white supremacy extended beyond the antebellum period. Presaging Wells's query more than fifty years later ("if this is democracy, what is bolshevism?"),[73] Jacobs also found herself wondering "Is this freedom?" while working to remedy the dire conditions faced by the suggestively named "contrabands" (the newly emancipated refugees on the frontlines of the Civil War).[74] Jacobs's work among the contrabands reflected the difficulties freedpeople faced in shaping their own lives even after emancipation. The debate over who would control the school founded by Jacobs and her daughter Louisa to educate the children at a camp for war refugees in Washington, DC, epitomizes this struggle for Black autonomy. As Jacobs explained:

> A question arose whether the white teachers or the colored teachers should be superintendents. The freedmen had built the school-house for their children, and were Trustees of the school. So, after some discussion, it was decided that it would be best for them to hold a meeting, and settle the question for themselves. I wish you could have been at that meeting. Most of the people were slaves, until quite recently, but they talked sensibly, and I assure you that they put the question to vote in quite parliamentary style. The result was a decision that the colored teachers should have charge of the school.[75]

In contrast to the paternalistic approach of white northerners at the time who sought to domesticate unruly freedpeople in various ways, Jacobs defended the capacities of slavery's fugitives and sought to help them enact their own practices of freedom and self-ownership. Her activism among the contrabands reflected lessons learned in her own life about the "burdened" freedom that followed legal emancipation.[76] Jacobs's careful accounting of freedom's lack points to a recognition that while certain losses cannot be repaired, they nevertheless need to be marked and grieved. She enacts a form of refusal. Turning from grief to grievance might imply that loss can be repaired, but Jacobs, in both *Incidents* and her later activism, suggests that some losses live on.

Ida B. Wells's Accounting of Black Life

Wells's relentless focus on lynching during the height of racial terror in the post-Reconstruction era was unmatched among her contemporaries. She is one of the African American thinkers to have most consistently grappled with anti-Black violence and Black death.[77] Most analyses of her writings on lynching and white racist violence rightly emphasize their social-scientific tenor and dispassionate presentation of facts supported by overwhelming statistical and qualitative evidence. But there are in fact different moments in which Black grief is more directly addressed, and others in which grievance takes center stage in Wells's work.

Wells wrestled with a conundrum shared by other Black intellectuals: whether to craft their rhetorical appeals in terms of fact or affect in hopes of transforming white public opinion. If one were to focus only on her most well-known antilynching texts, especially those where she is at her most "sociological" such as *A Red Record: Tabulated Statistics and Alleged Causes of Lynching in the United States, 1892-1893-1894* (1895), Wells could be read as emblematic of a strand in African American political thought that is relatively silent about grief and mourning for the sake of channeling loss into activism.[78] Throughout her writings, however—and indeed sometimes *within* a single text—we find a mix of sentimental and unsentimental elements in service of documenting myriad iterations of Black loss. While Wells's texts on lynching and white race riots undoubtedly foreground the Black dead, the violated and pained Black body, white violence, and white rage, she also repeatedly tells the stories of the lives of the Black victims and their families, such that her work itself becomes a site of grieving for Black loss. Wells narrativizes

Black suffering, even as she presents herself as an impartial purveyor of facts in order to navigate the skepticism of white readers primed to dismiss accounts of white violence and Black loss.

Wells, like Jacobs, navigated the epistemic inequalities Black women faced by aligning her work even more firmly with fact than affect, even as both were central elements of her lifelong commitment to telling the truth about Black loss. This was a deliberate rhetorical move on her part. She self-consciously fashioned herself as reliant on fact rather than affect, and her contemporaries described her rhetorical strategies in similar terms. Frederick Douglass's prefatory letter to *Southern Horrors: Lynch Law in All Its Phases* (1892), for example, lauds Wells's detached style and scientific rigor. "There has been no word equal to it in convincing power. . . . You have dealt with the facts with cool, painstaking fidelity, and left those naked and uncontradicted facts to speak for themselves."[79] While he initially ascribes her unmatched powers of persuasion to her firsthand knowledge of lynching, Douglass goes on to emphasize Wells's dispassionate style: her "cool, painstaking fidelity" to "naked" facts left to "speak for themselves." Wells echoes Douglass's description of her work. In the preface to *Southern Horrors*, she described the text as a compendium of facts. But immediately prior to that assertion, she makes an explosive comparison to a biblical story of love, lust, and deception evocative of sentimental fiction: "This statement is not . . . a defense for the poor blind Afro-American Sampsons who suffer themselves to be betrayed by white Delilahs. *It is a contribution to truth, an array of facts*."[80] Contrary to Wells's disclaimer, to cast stories of interracial intimacy into a well-known biblical narrative of female betrayal was to already make an affective appeal that condemned the role of white women in lynching. By the nineteenth century, the figure of Samson had become closely associated with

African Americans, and Wells's reference to "poor blind Afro-American Sampsons" echoed Henry Wadsworth Longfellow's sentimentalized portrait of Black Samson as a tragic figure in his antislavery poem "The Warning."[81] Wells builds on sentimental abolitionist depictions of Black Samson by adding the image of a white seductress to the biblical tableau of female betrayal. The reference to deceitful "white Delilahs" redirects the moral outrage spurred by fictive claims of rape by white women—for which the castration of Black male lynching victims was presented as proper punishment—onto innocent Black suffering instead.

Wells likewise portrays her work in terms of fact rather than affect in other texts. In *Mob Rule in New Orleans: Robert Charles and His Fight to the Death* (1900), she declared: "The publisher hereof does not attempt to moralize over the deplorable conditions of affairs shown in this publication, but simply presents the facts in a plain, unvarnished, connected way, so that he who runs may read."[82] Again, Wells subtly inserts a moral judgement while claiming not to do so by characterizing the conditions she is describing as "deplorable." More tellingly, she presents the text as an ethical test of readers by means of another biblical reference: "that he who runs may read."[83] Would her readers remain unmoved? Or would they act in response—not to a prophetic vision, but to a presentation of plain, unvarnished facts? Wells distances herself from any attempt to "moralize," but the aim of the text is clearly to condemn racist white violence. Rather than indicating a belief in the rhetorical power of fact over affect, this disclaimer reflects her concern that readers not succumb simply to "the satisfactions of sympathy," wallowing in feelings of empathy that made them feel good. Her self-presentation as a mere purveyor of fact was also strategic. While some white readers may have been open to being moved by accounts of Black loss, they did not necessarily want to be lectured to by a Black woman. Wells believed that the moral conscience of the nation would one day awaken to the atrocity of lynching, and when it did the full "red record" would be needed. "When this conscience wakes and speaks out in thunder tones, as it must, it will need facts to use as a weapon against injustice, barbarism and wrong. It is for this reason that I carefully compile, print and send forth these facts."[84] Wells's antisentimental method (or rather her depiction of it as such) was also a preemptive response to the specter of antidemocratic mourning, to the possibility that rather than condemn injustice, white readers would revel in anti-Black violence.

Given Wells's self-presentation as a mere expositor of unvarnished fact, it might be tempting to contrast her seemingly unwavering belief in the power of dispassionate accountings of Black loss to transform white moral understandings to Du Bois's shift from fact to affect, from scientific data to rhetorical appeals to emotion following the lynching of Sam Hose and the death of his son in 1899. Du Bois's elegy for his son, "Of the Passing of the First-Born" in *The Souls of Black Folk* (1903), is a text by a Black male thinker that centers grief and mourning. Annie Menzel has argued that "Of the Passing of the First-Born" is usually dismissed by commentators precisely because it "epitomizes this new [affective] idiom" in Du Bois's work.[85] Like Du Bois, Wells was horrified by Hose's lynching, which she described in gruesome detail in *Lynch Law in Georgia* (1899), calling it a "deed of unspeakable barbarism."[86] It would be a mistake to read Wells's consistent characterization of her work in terms of fact rather than affect as a failure to learn a lesson about the power of *pathos* over *logos* which Du Bois understood, however.[87] After all, racist violence had been Wells's central subject matter long before it became so for Du Bois, and she experienced it at close hand. Her commitment to unflinchingly confront and expose it was propelled by the lynching of a close family friend and the subsequent shutdown of her newspaper as a result of her activism on behalf of the victims. Both Wells and Du Bois were struggling with how to confront racist terror and white affective investments in making Black life disposable, but they faced different gendered constraints in doing so.[88]

Most importantly, Wells offers an important alternative to the framing, derived from Du Bois's account of his own rhetorical transformation, of a clear-cut distinction in the work of Black thinkers between dispassionate, scientific fact and more explicitly affective modes. When Wells claims to simply compile facts that speak for themselves, she is wrestling with the dilemma of how to expose pain and suffering that is political without falling purely into the ethical. Her overriding concern was to produce work that could serve as a "weapon against injustice." To do so, she skillfully combines *logos* and *pathos*. Her self-styled focus on cold, hard facts is also a way to reverse the dynamic whereby the Black body is seen as pure affect or emotion. If lynching (and notions of Black inferiority more broadly) were justified by painting Black people as animalistic and ruled by emotion rather than reason, Wells's relentless statistical catalog of Black death served to shift the focus onto the actions and affect of the white mob instead. In *A Red Record*, for example, Wells shifts attention onto the white perpetrators by arranging the *Chicago Tribune*'s lynching data in terms of the actions of the white mob rather than the Black victims, resulting in chapter headings such as "Lynching Imbeciles" (which contains subheadings such "An Arkansas Butchery" and "Tortured and Burned in Texas), "Lynching of Innocent Men," and "Lynched, or for Anything or Nothing." This inversion is part of her reframing of lynching as a problem of white violence rather than

Black death, but without losing sight of Black life. In other words, Wells sought to turn grief into grievance without eclipsing Black loss.

Even in Wells's emblematic texts on lynching and white race riots, there is an accounting of Black lives. In *A Red Record,* for example, where most of the text is devoted to presenting statistical data, she nevertheless reanimates the life before the lynching. The chapter "Lynching Imbeciles," which tells the stories of Hamp Biscoe in Arkansas and Henry Smith in Texas, does not include the names of the two male victims in the chapter subheadings. But in the text, Wells shares that Biscoe was a "hard working, thrifty farmer," that he had a thirteen-year-old son and a wife, that his wife was pregnant, that she "had a babe at the breast" when the family was killed, and that the white men who killed all but the breastfeeding baby took $220 dollars from Mrs. Biscoe's stockings after they killed her, among other details.[89] Similarly, Wells's pamphlet on an infamous early twentieth-century white race riot, *The East St. Louis Massacre: The Greatest Outrage of the Century* (1917), which prompted a Congressional investigation, is textually dominated by her compilation of the life stories of the Black victims. Unlike *A Red Record,* in which chapter titles and subheadings reference event types rather than individual victims—that is, "Lynching of Innocent Men (Lynched on Account of Relationship)," "Lynched Because the Jury Acquitted Him," and Lynched as a Scapegoat"—most of the chapters in *The East St. Louis Massacre* are named after the Black victims whose stories they tell. These chapters tell the individual life stories of the Black victims, and their titles reflect this: "Mrs. Ballard's Story," "Mrs. Lulu Thomas' Story," "Clarissa Lockett's Story," "Story of William Gould," "Story of James Taylor." Before the contemporary #sayhername campaign to name Black women killed by police officers and bring attention to the fact that they are also victims of state violence, Wells employed the same strategy to reanimate Black lives lost to white violence.[90] She told their stories and said their names.

Wells builds a litany of loss with each successive chapter on an individual victim in *The East St. Louis Massacre*. She provides an incredible amount of quotidian detail about the Black lives lived before the riot, thereby forcing her readers to grapple with the losses, both psychological and material, it produced. For example, in "Mrs. Willie Flake's Story," she writes:

> Mrs. Flake is a widow with three children, 11, 8 and 6 years old. She is a laundress who came to East St. Louis four year ago from Jackson, Tenn. She took care of her little family by taking in washing, and she worked from Monday morning until Saturday night at the ironing board. She too had three rooms full of nice furniture. Both of the two front rooms having nice rugs on the floor, a brass bedstead and other furniture to correspond. She had about a hundred dollars worth of furniture ruined, fifty dollars worth of clothing and about fifty dollars more of bedding, mattresses, etc. The mob had taken a phonograph for which she had paid $15.00 and twenty-five records for which she had paid 75 cents and $1.00 each.[91]

In this passage, Wells captures grief and loss without resorting to overtly emotional language. Noting the exact price of the musical equipment is a way to mark the riot's economic impact, but it also prompts the reader to imagine Mrs. Flake listening to music with her children, perhaps even taking a break from washing and ironing to dance or sing along to one of the twenty-five records she had purchased with her hard-earned wages. Mrs. Flake's losses and those of her children are also of safety and a home painstakingly built. Wells combines a laser-like focus on compiling a factual record of anti-Black violence with a detailed accounting of the Black lives upended or foreclosed by that violence. *The East St. Louis Massacre* is an example of what Dagmawi Woubshet calls the "poetics of compounding loss . . . narratives of mourning [that] do not recount, respond to, and reflect upon singular events of mourning, but instead explicitly underscore . . . the serial and repetitive nature of the losses they confront."[92] The accounting of Black loss that Wells undertakes is multivalent. For most of her white readers, who were unaccustomed to extending the same care and concern to Black people, the detailed lists of material goods lost could read as mere statements of fact, to be sure. But for those who had developed the civic capacity to care about the losses of racialized others, and for Black audiences, these inventories of dispossession were profoundly affective.

Narrating the facts of Black life in addition to white violence required both a Morrisonian ethical commitment to considering the terms of disclosure of Black suffering and distinct embodied journalistic/ethnographic practices on Wells's part. In her reporting on the East St. Louis massacre, for instance, she made a fateful decision that would shape whose voices dominated her account of the riot. When she arrived in town, she planned to interview the white officials in charge (the National Guard general and the mayor) but saw a group of Black women, "bareheaded and their clothing dirty," who had returned to try and recover what was left of their possessions. Wells immediately shifted strategy and spent all day compiling the women's stories as they traveled to the burned ruins of their homes. "I went with them and in this way went inside a dozen of their three and four room houses and saw the mob's work of destruction. . . . The women told me the following stories as we rode around the town."[93] Wells's ethical praxis of telling the stories of Black loss resulted in a strikingly different record from that of the official reports on the massacre and the coverage in white newspapers.[94]

In other texts, Wells navigated the epistemic challenges she faced as a Black woman writing about white violence by relying on white newspapers as her source materials. To blunt charges of exaggeration, for example, she explained that all the statistical data in *A Red Record* was taken from the *Chicago Tribune*. She noted that she had compiled "the facts of these lynchings, as they appeared from time to time in the white newspapers of America—the news gathered by white correspondents, compiled by white press bureaus and disseminated among white people."[95] But relying on white reporting as primary source material made it difficult to retrace the lives of Black victims; as a result Wells's most direct depictions of Black grief appear when she had firsthand access to Black victims. As we will see, her ability to interact directly with the victims and their families would also prove crucial to her ability to produce a capacious account of Black loss in the case of another white race riot, the riot in Elaine, Arkansas, in 1920. Wells's embodied presence in these spaces allowed her to marshal facts (enumerating Black loss) to produce affect.

Wells balanced grief and grievance and fact and affect across and within texts to tell the full story of Black loss. We see this clearly in two texts that bookend her career: "Lynch Law in All Its Phases," one of her early speeches against lynching in 1893 following her exile from Memphis, and *The Arkansas Race Riot* (1920). While there is significant overlap between "Lynch Law in All Its Phases" and *Southern Horrors*, the former is much more explicit in attending to Black grief. In "Lynch Law," she speaks directly about her own experiences with white violence. In this instance (as in the East St. Louis and Arkansas riots), she had direct access to the Black victims and their families.[96] In "Lynch

Law," Wells recalls the grief of her friend Betty Moss, who shed tears that fell "thick and fast" on their infant son as she contemplated the sad fate of her husband, Tom, who was lynched alongside his business partner by a white mob at the instigation of a rival white business owner. Wells also describes how Tom and Betty's baby daughter, Maurine, "toddles to the wardrobe, seizes the legs of the trousers of his letter carrier uniform, hugs and kisses them . . . and stretches up her little hands to be taken up into the arms which will nevermore clasp his daughter's form."[97] Her account of the Moss family's grief is so heartrending precisely because of the abundance of quotidian details of Black life: Tom's uniform, Betty holding her sleeping child, their toddler with outstretched arms. This poignant depiction of a Black family's grief stands in contrast to accounts of lynching in which the Black dead appear only as individuals surrounded by angry white mobs.

Wells's antilynching writings undoubtedly also shine a spotlight on white rage and brutality, however, and she does not shy away from sharing gruesome details about the tortured Black body. If her description of the Moss family's grief was a rare glimpse of the Black communities devastated by lynching, in other moments she directs the reader's eye to the gleeful white mob reveling in horrific anti-Black violence. Indeed, to reinforce the fact that it was a communal enterprise, Wells repeatedly points to white children's active participation in lynching. In her lectures abroad, she described gruesome scenes to a disbelieving European audience: "The British people took with incredulity my statements that colored men were roasted or lynched in broad daylight . . . and looked askance at statements that *half-grown boys* shot bullets into hanging bodies, and, after cutting off toes and fingers of the dead or dying, carried them about as trophies."[98] The white counterparts to little Maurine Moss are the young white boys who join in the torture and death of Black men, and the "little tot . . . [who] clapped her baby hands as her father held her on his shoulders above the heads of the people" to give her a better view of the mutilation, torture, and murder of Henry Smith. These white children, their "little faces distorted with passion," were initiated into white supremacy via active lynching spectatorship.[99] In contrast to Hannah Arendt's critique of Black parents who allowed their children to participate in desegregation battles, which she deemed a kind of political heroism more appropriate for adults, the white parents who brought their children to mass lynchings were not asking them to be heroes. They were teaching them to be monsters.[100] They did so by imparting important lessons about racial subordination, the disregard for Black life required to maintain it, and white impunity.[101] If Wells thus "gave powerful voice to . . . [the Moss] family's bereavement,"[102] she also showed how lynching distorted the moral and civic capacities of even the most innocent white persons.

There is a similar attention to both grief and grievance in one of Wells's last published works, *The Arkansas Race Riot*, a pamphlet chronicling a 1919 massacre in which white mobs killed hundreds of Black sharecroppers and their families as well as innocent bystanders.[103] The Black farmers were attempting to unionize to be able to sell their crops at a fair market price. The white landowners, farmers, and cotton brokers who derived their wealth from cheating Black sharecroppers of their profits fiercely opposed this organizing effort. Yet no whites were punished for the killings. Instead, over a hundred Black survivors were accused of plotting a Black uprising and arrested, with more than seventy charged with murder. Of these, the dozen or so initially convicted by all-white juries spent years on death row until they were eventually freed by the courts after a series of successful appeals. Wells traveled to Arkansas and systematically documented Black losses. Her pamphlet moves between grief and grievance, as the reader is bombarded with facts that disprove the official narrative justifying white violence, but is also presented with a moving portrait of Black suffering. Wells combines profuse statistical data (fact) with quotidian details (affect) in *The Arkansas Race Riot* to tell the story of Black loss.

Similarly to how she redirects the reader's gaze to white violence in her antilynching texts, Wells drew attention to how white wealth was directly built on Black dispossession in her pamphlets on white race riots. As with the lynching statistics she carefully compiled, in *The Arkansas Race Riot* Wells calculated the monetary losses suffered by the Black farmers in painstaking detail.[104] The statements of each of the Black sharecroppers she interviewed recounted the initial white mob attack on their union organizing meeting, the subsequent manhunt, how those who escaped were lured into returning under false pretenses, their mistreatment and torture in prison, and a precise accounting of the material losses they suffered. In his statement, for example, Ed Ware said: "I lost all of my household goods and 121 acres of cotton and corn, two mules, one horse, one Jersey cow and one farm wagon and all farming tools and harness and eight head of hogs, 135 chickens and one Ford car."[105] Wells calculated that "the white lynchers of Phillips County made a cool million dollars last year off the cotton crop of the twelve men who are sentenced to death, the seventy-five who are in the Arkansas penitentiary and the one hundred whom they lynched outright on that awful October 1, 1919!"[106] Wells also draws attention to the fact that white families as a whole, including wives and children, benefitted from violently stolen wealth. In the chapter, "What White Folks Got from Riot," she juxtaposes the condition of the Black farmers' families to the white consumption enabled by such acts of dispossession.

"The wives and children of the white men who committed this crime and robbed these Negroes are riding in automobiles, living in comfortable homes, enjoying good food and fine clothes. The wives and children of these Negroes are wandering from place to place, homeless, penniless, ragged and starving, depending on public charity."[107] White women were not just complicit, but active participants, in Black expropriation. Wells tells the story of Frank Moore's wife, who returned to try to retrieve their property. When she confronted their landlord's wife, "Mrs. Archdale told her she would get nothing even though Mrs. Moore saw some of her furniture and clothes in Mrs. Archdale's house."[108]

Wells attends to seemingly superfluous details, to "small, needful facts" that point to deeper truths—in this case, that white looting during massacres and race riots was not aberrant, but part of a larger pattern of racial dispossession. Mrs. Ware, for example, returned to reclaim her possessions after the riot only to find "her safe in a Mrs. Forsyth's house" and that "a Mr. George had her chairs."[109] Similarly, during the Palestinian Nakba, individual acts of plunder and settler colonial expropriation and expulsion went hand in hand. Historians have shown that looting of personal possessions such as musical instruments, livestock, agricultural produce, agricultural machinery, and antiquities by erstwhile Israeli neighbors and soldiers was rampant.[110] The inventories of loss Wells compiled likewise show that racial dispossession is central to US democracy. In the penultimate chapter of *The Arkansas Race Riot*, for instance, she contrasts the very different treatment meted out to striking white coal miners and that inflicted on the Black sharecroppers massacred for merely *trying* to unionize. Both groups were "working men" seeking "economic justice," but the Black farmers were "sentenced to death because they dared, in this democracy of ours, to ask relief from economic slavery." The disparity in the treatment of the white and Black workers laid bare white democracy's dependence on racial exploitation. This led Wells to conclude the pamphlet by asking: "If this is democracy, what is bolshevism?"[111]

As in *The East St. Louis Massacre,* Wells's embodied presence enabled her to collect contemporaneous oral histories of white violence and Black life that were missing from mainstream news accounts and official government documents. She was able to gather firsthand information about the massacre and the lives of the Black farmers and their families by passing as a relative and joining the wives and mothers of the incarcerated men during visiting hours at the state prison. In the opening pages of *The Arkansas Race Riot,* Wells writes directly about Black grief. She recounts the torture and isolation of the prisoners, who "during this time of terror" composed a song entitled "I Stand and Wring my Hands and Cry," which they sang "in heart-breaking tones":

> I used to have some loving friends
> to walk and talk with me,
> But now I am in trouble,
> they have turned their backs on me;
> They just laugh me to scorn and will not come nigh,
> And I just stand and wring my hands and cry. . . .
>
> And I just stand and wring my hands and cry,
> And I just stand and wring my hands and cry, Oh Lord!
> Sometimes I feel like I ain't got no friends at all.
> And I just stand and wring my hands and cry. . . .
>
> My heart is overwhelmed with sorrow,
> My eyes are melted down in tears;
> But I have called to the God of Heaven,
> And I know He always hears.

According to Wells, the Black farmers sang this modern sorrow song "in the most mournful tones ever heard."[112] Here, as in other texts, Wells moves between grief and grievance, between fact and affect.

While the lyrics of the imprisoned Black sharecroppers' lament share thematic similarities with other prison blues—grief, loneliness, abandonment by erstwhile friends—it differs from the "sonic radical blues tradition" that challenged norms of respectability and offered a "critique of legal moralism, incarceration, and physical and psychic violence in the legal sphere."[113] The song's emphasis on religious faith in its final stanza, as well as Wells's advice to the Black farmers to "pray to live and have faith" and her professed belief that such prayers would "strengthen the hands of the white people of the state who want to do the right thing,"[114] point to the influence of a philosophical anthropology derived from Christianity that posits that when confronted with undeserved suffering people with Christian commitments will seek to repair the wrongs that caused it.[115] Wells acknowledges that "the American thinking public cannot bring back the dead." But she calls on "the white people of Arkansas—the honest, law-abiding Christian men and women of that state" to help "open the prison doors" for the remaining unjustly incarcerated Black sharecroppers. Wells was not naive about the white public, but she nevertheless tries to call a democratic public into being that can face the truth of white violence. At the same time, hers is not simply a red record intended to shame the white public; it is an enumeration of loss that archives the facts of Black life.

Throughout her writings Wells presented the facts of Black loss unflinchingly but also reanimated the lives before the violence. This is evident not only in her depiction of the lives of the Black slain, but also in her pioneering use of lynching photography against itself. The use of such photographs became a key element of the NAACP's subsequent national antilynching campaign. But absent Wells's attention to the details of Black life, the fraught ethical calculus of using Black pain to elicit white solidarity shifted radically.

Wells began using lynching photographs to overcome the skepticism of white audiences. During her speaking tour to the UK, for example, the British public doubted the facts of lynching until "I showed them photographs of such scenes, the newspaper reports, and the reports of searching investigations on the subject. . . . They [then] accepted the evidence of their own senses against their wills."[116] Yet, despite Wells's assertion that certain kinds of evidence forced white audiences to accept the facts against their will, lynching photographs were semiotically unruly texts. According to Jacqueline Goldsby, for example, even when used oppositionally, "African-Americans' responses to lynching photographs, even to the prospect of viewing them, were varied and unpredictable."[117] For this reason, the Black press tended to use hand-drawn political cartoons to illustrate its diligent coverage of lynching rather than camera-made images, because the former afforded more control over the meaning of the images.[118]

The problem with the oppositional use of lynching photography was not simply the uncertainty over how the images would be read, but also the fact that they could not meet the challenge of showing the full personhood of lynching victims nor lynching's impact on Black families and Black communities.[119] According to historian Amy Wood, the antilynching narrative that solidified in the wake of World War I steadily displaced both the suffering of Black victims and white racism as the cause of lynching. The focus of antilynching activism shifted instead to the broader civic effects of lynching and "the savagery of white mobs, mobs that stood as abominations to American democratic ideals."[120] What became important was their violent behavior, not their racist motivations. Melvin Rogers argues that Wells (and other African American intellectuals) deployed horror to induce moral disgust in white audiences. The focus on bloodthirsty and ferocious white mobs aimed to horrify readers and make them recoil in revulsion at white barbarity and the culture of racial disregard.[121] Nevertheless, the emphasis on how white moral capacities were disfigured by racism shifted the *locus* of loss away from Black grief to the harms to US democracy, as figure 3.1 illustrates.

In this striking example, a 1935 NAACP antilynching pamphlet is visually dominated by a photograph of the lynching of Rubin Stacy. Rather than focus on the Black victim, however, who is only briefly named, the text highlights the white assailants and spectators and the effect of the lynching on *them*. The pamphlet instructs the reader: "Do not look at the Negro. . . . Instead look at the seven WHITE children who gaze at this gruesome spectacle. . . . Rubin Stacy, the negro who was lynched . . . suffered PHYSICAL torture for a few short hours, but what psychological havoc is being wrought in the minds of the white children? Into what kinds of white citizens will they grow up?"[122] While Stacy's dead body dominates the frame of the photograph, the NAACP's text draws the viewer's eye to the white adults and children who surround him. It briefly references the violence not captured in the image but does not dwell on it or its effect on Stacy's family and community. Instead, the pamphlet highlights the distorting effects of lynching on the civic capacities of the young white children who are stand-ins for a US democracy disfigured by lynching.

Do not look at the Negro.

His earthly problems are ended.

Instead, look at the seven WHITE children who gaze at this gruesome spectacle.

Is it horror or gloating on the face of the neatly dressed seven-year-old girl on the right?

Is the tiny four-year-old on the left old enough, one wonders, to comprehend the barbarism her elders have perpetrated?

Rubin Stacy, the Negro, who was lynched at Fort Lauderdale, Florida, on July 19, 1935, for "threatening and frightening a white woman," suffered PHYSICAL torture for a few short hours. But what psychological havoc is being wrought in the minds of the white children? Into what kinds of citizens

FIGURE 3.1. "N.A.A.C.P. Rubin Stacy Anti-lynching Flyer," 1935. Clippings file of the James Weldon Johnson Memorial Collection, James Weldon Johnson Memorial Collection in the Yale Collection of American Literature, Beinecke Rare Book and Manuscript Library.

Wells also highlighted white children's lynching spectatorship, but she simultaneously forced her audience to "look at the Negro" by reanimating the lives of the Black victims before they were foreclosed by violence. African American newspapers in the South adopted a similar stance. By the 1930s, lynching photographs were often used interchangeably, often with no accompanying details about the victims or the localities where the lynching occurred. In contrast, instead of reprinting photographs of lynched bodies, the Black press chose to publish photographs that humanized Black victims by showing their lives before they became interchangeable symbols of Black grief/white violence.[123] Female African American playwrights likewise authored lynching dramas that Koritha Mitchell argues constitute a counterarchive to white lynching photographs. In contrast to this "archive left by the perpetrators,"[124] African American lynching dramas written for Black audiences dramatized the impact of white violence on Black households and centered Black families and communities. "While the [white] mob's efforts centered on black death, African American dramatists helped their communities to live, even while lynching remained a reality."[125] Lynching plays were set in Black homes and were seldom formally staged. Instead, the community and domestic spaces in which they were performed echoed the subject matter, which was the impact of lynching on the survivors of the violence, the pain and grief of those left behind. "In contrast to mainstream photographers," Mitchell notes, "dramatists who lived and wrote in the midst of lynching often refused to feature physical violence; their scripts spotlight instead the black home and the impact that the mob's outdoor activities have on the family. Indeed, the dramas most commonly depict exactly what mainstream discourse denied existed: loving black homes."[126] The NAACP's oppositional use of lynching photographs is an example of the perils of turning grief into grievance. It shows how direct emotional appeals focused on white audiences could nevertheless still eclipse Black loss. In contrast, Wells used both *pathos* and *logos* to force her readers to reckon with Black grief, even as she also sought to impel them to grievance.

At a moment when Black Lives Matter protests have powerfully directed national attention to contemporary forms of lethal racist violence via militarized policing, Wells is viewed as a "a foundational thinker on racial criminalization" and a "pioneering necropolitical activist" whose strategies (such as challenging the meaning assigned to the bodies of the Black dead, calling out the complicity of the mainstream press, and compiling statistical data on anti-Black violence) have been successfully updated by contemporary activists.[127] Today's viral lists of "things you can't do while Black"—for example, the quotidian activities for which the police are called to discipline Black people or for which the police kill unarmed Blacks—echo the lists compiled by Wells of real and imaginary offenses for which Blacks were lynched a century ago.[128] These ranged from crimes such as suspected arson and theft, to "because they were saucy," "for a quarrel," for "enticing servant away," for "writing letters to a white woman," for "giving information," for "conjuring," and so on.[129] Wells had an expansive critique of racial disparities in the criminal justice system, and there are striking similarities between her hundred-year-old account of police impunity in *Mob Rule in New Orleans* and contemporary prison and police abolitionists' rejection of punitive carceral logics and Black criminalization.[130]

In *Mob Rule in New Orleans,* Wells tells the story of Robert Charles, whose refusal to submit to arbitrary arrest by the police triggered a white riot:

> Fortified by the assurance born of long experience in the New Orleans service, three policemen . . . observing two colored men sitting on doorsteps . . . determined, without a shadow of authority, to arrest them. . . . The colored men . . . had not broken the peace in any way whatever, no warrant was in the policemen's hands justifying their arrest, and no crime had been committed of which they were the suspects. *The policemen, however, secure in the firm belief that they could do anything to a Negro that they wished,* approached the two men, and in less than three minutes from the time they accosted them attempted to put both colored men under arrest.[131]

Charles refused to be arrested and was attacked by a police officer, whom he subsequently shot, triggering a manhunt in which he killed five additional policemen and injured a dozen more. This in turn inspired a white mob of thousands to join the search for Charles, resulting in random attacks on other Black residents of the city. Ultimately, the riot left twenty-eight people dead, most of them Black. As in her other texts, Wells humanizes Charles, challenging his depiction by white newspapers as a "desperado" suffused with racial hatred because he served as an agent for a Black emigrationist society to Liberia.[132] She reproduces his last known letter in full, observing that it "sounds like a voice from the Tomb," and describes him as a "hero" to Black people for defending himself against arbitrary white power.[133] Yet, as the redemptive Christian (rather than prison blues) sonic of the imprisoned Arkansas Black sharecroppers she transcribed illustrates, Wells's challenge to depictions of Black criminality did not go as far as more radical approaches to grieving deviance in the blues tradition. Nonetheless, it is precisely Wells's painstaking accounting of Black loss that compels us to see *all* Black lives as grievable.

How to "Look at the Negro"

It would be tempting to think that we have moved past the dilemma of how to make Black loss visible. But it continues to surface in mediums as varied as viral videos of police killings of unarmed Black persons—which are as semiotically unruly as lynching photographs—and the current revival of neo-slavery cinema. Two recent feature films, the critically acclaimed *12 Years a Slave* (2013) and the more formulaic *Harriet* (2019), illustrate the continued stakes of staging spectacles of Black suffering, particularly the pain and violation of Black women.[134]

Contemporary cinematic depictions of the horrors of slavery face the same ethical dilemmas Wells and Jacobs navigated: How and why should audiences "look at the negro?" And who is trying to speak via these depictions of Black pain and trauma and to what ends? *12 Years a Slave* and *Harriet* offer two distinct approaches to depicting Black grief and Black survival. Like the scenes of Black women's torture and violation in male slave narratives and white abolitionist texts, *12 Years a Slave* highlights visually brutal scenes of Patsey's rape and whipping.[135] The fundamental site of slavery's violence in *12 Years a Slave* is the violated Black female body, even as its fundamental harm is the denial of Black male freedom, which Solomon ultimately regains. In contrast, *Harriet* does not contain any pivotal scenes of sexual violence or physical torture. Instead, white cruelty is expressed by the threat of family separation (a danger most visibly faced today by undocumented immigrants in US detention). While it is a biopic of Tubman, *Harriet* centers Black women's struggles to preserve community and the collective freedom of the family unit. Even in the scenes depicting the daring, heroic rescues Tubman engineered on southern slave plantations, escape is presented as a collective endeavor that required the collusion of even seemingly "faithful slaves" who chose to remain behind, such as her sister Rachel. *Harriet* thus offers a depiction of Black agency—both spectacular and quotidian—and community survival.

The different approaches between the two films may have something to do with the different historical moments in which they were released. It is no coincidence that *12 Years a Slave* was released before Ferguson police left Michael Brown's dead body lying in the street, unattended, for hours in 2014, or before Breonna Taylor was killed by police in the middle of the night in her own apartment in Louisville, Kentucky, in 2020. As Mark Reinhardt has argued, telling stories of slavery ethically requires renouncing ventriloquism—speaking for enslaved people, presuming to know the details of their inner lives—but the question is not just: "What constitutes a responsible telling?"[136] It is also: Why tell these stories now? Who needs to see Black pain, and why? There is certainly no shortage of images of Black pain and suffering in contemporary US life, of grief that must be turned into grievance, of protests seeking racial justice. Like Jacobs and Wells, however, we are still struggling to find a way to tell the story of the Black lives before (and after) the violence and the violation.

Jacobs and Wells help us address these questions because they exemplify a strand of African American political thought on loss that does not forgo grievance, but makes space for a more capacious approach to Black grief. Their writings force us to consider how the spectacular and the quotidian operate in Black life and white supremacy. In analyzing Jacobs and Wells, this chapter breaks down several (presumed) oppositions: fact versus affect, grief versus grievance, and public versus private. Public, spectacular anti-Black violence has had an important mobilizing role in Black politics, but there is a tradeoff between eliciting white solidarity and attending to Black grief. While Jacobs and Wells are associated with chronicling spectacular violence (i.e., slavery and lynching), they also attend to ordinary white supremacy and quotidian Black life—highlighting, in the process, the domestic as an intensely political site of struggle.

Wells and Jacobs provide accounts of loss that are ultimately committed to accounting for Black life beyond grief and grievance, and they both utilize a combination of fact and affect in their rhetorical appeals to make Black loss visible. They each devise different strategies to refuse the seductive exchange of Black suffering for white sympathy: in Wells's case the withholding of Black feeling is a refusal of emotional exposure, while Jacobs refuses to offer violated Black women's bodies as spectacle. One of the central concerns of their approach to loss is grappling with how *not* to stage Black pain for white consumption (grief turned grievance) in exchange for solidarity (redress). Their politics of disclosure and concealment, their refusal of certain kinds of exposure, points to the importance of paying attention, not only to white audiences, but also to Black witnesses. Jacobs and Wells exemplify an ethics of truth telling about Black suffering, as well as a politics of withholding interiority from the white fellow citizens to whom, in a multiracial democracy, Black people must appeal for racial justice. Part of Black epistemic loss is having to navigate between fact and affect, grief and grievance. One of the lessons imparted by Jacobs's and Wells's accounts of Black loss is that Black people must grieve the very turn to grievance and not lose sight of Black life amid Black death. This is what it means to live on, while grieving, "in the wake."

INTERLUDE 4

(after the murder,
after the burial)
Emmett's mother is a pretty-faced thing;
the tint of pulled taffy.
She sits in a red room,
drinking black coffee.
She kisses her killed boy.
And she is sorry.
Chaos in windy grays through a red prairie.

—GWENDOLYN BROOKS, *THE LAST QUATRAIN OF THE BALLAD OF EMMETT TILL* (REPRINTED BY CONSENT OF BROOKS PERMISSIONS)

Everybody always asks: what's the next steps?
  What are y'all gonna do next?
What you gonna do next?
What you gonna do next?
You know what we're gonna do?
  We're gonna grieve.
Umhuh.
We're gonna *grieve.*

—FROM "HAPPY BIRTHDAY PHILANDO CASTILE" (HTTPS://VIMEO.COM/179535585)

4

Maternal Grief and Black Politics

THE DEATH OF activist Erica Garner in 2017 at twenty-seven from a heart attack provoked "profound sadness," "deep despair," and "rage" among Black women.[1] Garner was propelled into activism following the death of her father, Eric, after he was placed in a fatal chokehold by a New York City police officer. The viral video of Eric Garner's fatal interaction with agents of the state—which was prompted, as so many other police killings of unarmed Black persons have been, by a seemingly innocuous act, in his case selling unlicensed cigarettes—made "I can't breathe" one of the defining catchphrases of the Black Lives Matter (BLM) protests against police violence. Eric Garner's death scene, and Michael Brown's unattended Black body lying in the street for hours, became emblematic images of racial violence and racial terror in the United States in the twenty-first century. In turn, Erica Garner's death, less than four years after her father was killed, raised stark questions about the intergenerational costs of state violence, the burdens of activism, and the enhanced and unrecognized vulnerabilities faced by Black women. As Melissa Harris-Perry observed about Garner's death, "The abrupt loss of Erica Garner is more than an individual tragedy; her death, like her father's, is a public lesson in

American inequality wrought on a fragile human body for all of us to see."[2] If Eric Garner's death was emblematic of the kind of spectacular violence Black men are likely to suffer, Erica Garner's death was also emblematic of the more quotidian forms of slow death that also blight Black communities. As the child of a father who was repeatedly caught up in the punitive carceral state (prior to his death Eric Garner had been arrested more than thirty times by the NYPD), she, like the family members of other Black and brown people disproportionately targeted for criminalization and violent policing, endured the economic, psychological, and social costs of mass incarceration. Erica Garner also died six months after giving birth to her second child, which led to a postpartum heart attack after the pregnancy put too much stress on her already-enlarged heart.[3] Her death reflects the daunting rates of maternal and infant mortality Black women face as a result of both substandard medical care and the physical stress of racism. As Ruha Benjamin observes, "Erica Garner-Snipes, no doubt, was weathered. Not only by the senseless loss of her father, but by a lifetime of economic precarity and everyday racism."[4] Erica's body succumbed from the stress of carrying so many burdens, both medical and civic. Like other grieving Black women who became activists after losing loved ones to the carceral state, such as Venida Browder, mother of Kalief, her heart literally stopped beating.[5] Private grief turned public mourning has been a central feature of Black politics, but Erica Garner's tragic premature death points to the urgent need to consider the costs of "grieving activism," to consider that making Black loss visible often comes at the expense of surviving loss.[6]

Erica Garner's death at such a young age raises questions about the personal and physical toll of the kind of Black activism against racial injustice that is lauded as an exemplary democratic act. As a *New York Times* article about the untimely deaths of young Black activists noted, many social justice activists galvanized by the Movement for Black Lives (M4BL) are now being forced to ponder

> the most dire consequence of an activist life—untimely death. . . . With each fallen comrade, activists are left to ponder their own mortality and whether the many pressures of the movement contributed to the shortened lives of their colleagues. Along with the long hours, constant confrontation and frequent heartbreak they experience, activists work for little or no pay and sometimes struggle for basic needs like food and shelter even as they push for societal change.[7]

These young BLM activists died of a variety of causes ranging from homicide and suicide to "natural" causes, that, as in Erica Garner's case, obscure the toll of grief and accumulated racist disparities on their lives.[8] Yet, despite these pressures, Black activists are supposed to be passionate but not angry, decorous rather than messy in their grief. Black protesters who depart from this script are often harshly disciplined.

The outsize expectations of heroism and civility under which Black activists labor are reflected in how Erica Garner was perceived. Because of her "unapologetic style," she did not receive the same level of recognition or admiration as other activists of her generation, for example. For Joy James, however, it was precisely Garner's refusal to accede to demands for civility in her activism, her "challenges [to] decorum and convention with political rebellion," that mark Garner as one of those "ancestors [who] are so spirited that their fierce, radical critiques disrupt liberal and progressive politics and diverge from popularized forms of protest."[9] But viewing Erica Garner as "a warrior," as her mother described her, who "put her entire life into this fight" in the words of a fellow activist and friend, also minimizes her grief and pain.[10] She may now be a radical ancestor in the heroic frame we expect Black women to embody, but she was also a daughter who lost her father, and a mother who left orphaned children. Focusing on Erica Garner's justified anger at injustice keeps us from seeing her as simultaneously "hurting . . . and vulnerable."[11] The masculinist, martial, stoic, steely connotations of the term "warrior" and mottos such as "give me liberty or give me death" condition us to see death in service of a just cause as laudably heroic.[12] Such expectations of sacrifice illustrate how our templates for activism blind us to its costs and impede acknowledgment of activists' full humanity. Erica Garner's life was certainly grievable, but because of the political community's need to embrace her as a heroic warrior for social justice who was able to use her personal pain to further collective political aims, we tend to forget that she was also, above all, *grieving*.

What do we owe the grieving? If white supremacy materialized as police violence and state neglect literally makes it impossible for Black citizens to breathe, the deaths of Erica Garner and Venida Browder raise the uncomfortable possibility that attempts to transform white supremacy also exact an unacceptable toll on Black activists, especially Black women. For Black politics writ large, this raises several questions: What are the costs of grounding projects of racial justice in the public mourning of Black death oriented to democratic repair? How long will Black politics and movements for racial justice continue to rely on the venerable strategy of trying to catalyze white empathy by mobilizing Black grief? And, most centrally, what role should grief and grievance play in a politics of Black life? The complexity and high stakes of these questions are illustrated by the call from some grieving Black families of contemporary victims of police violence to "put an end to the political-economy's parasitism on Black death and poverty."[13] Turning Black loss into grievance is both a collective political desire of the political community and a strategy by Black people to endow their losses with meaning. But it is also one that grieving Black families do not uniformly accept: some push back against the instrumentalization of Black grief and refuse the expectation that their suffering will become a form of martyrdom.

The political mourning that has galvanized the contemporary M4BL is the latest iteration of a long tradition in Black politics, in which Black death has long played a central role because of the unremitting nature of Black loss.[14] For example, in her study of African American funerary practices, Karla Holloway argues that

> the anticipation of death and dying figured into the experiences of black folk so persistently, given how much more omnipresent death was for them than for other Americans, that lamentation and mortification both found their way into their public and private representations of African America to an astonishing degree. . . . Death was an untimely accompaniment to the life of black folk—a sensibility that was, unfortunately, based on hard facts.[15]

Holloway is not alone in claiming that Black people have become very adept at mourning owing to the tragic ubiquity of death in Black communities.[16] As historian Vincent Brown argues about "mortuary politics" in colonial-era Jamaica, "Relations with the dead, by virtue of their powerful symbolism and association with things sacred, have the ability to connect the private and public. . . . This linkage makes the dead central to both social organization and political mobilization."[17] Brown's analysis emphasizes the social world created despite, and in part by, the ubiquity of death during the era of transatlantic slavery. "In Jamaican slave society . . . death tended and nurtured the activities of the living. . . . Death helped to constitute life, and the dead were an undeniable presence."[18] Specific African beliefs about spiritual repatriation fed understandings of death as freeing in the context of slavery, but enslaved people also framed it as a release from racial subjection, and mourning became one of many sites of struggle for enslaved people. Since the era of slavery, Black people have had to reckon with the fact that "death is ever present, that death is somehow always impending, and that survivors can confront all this death in the face of shame and stigma in eloquent ways that also often imply a fierce political sensibility and a longing for justice."[19]

Given the central role grief has historically played in Black politics, it is important to pay attention to who is allowed to grieve and who is seen as grievable. Grief has been central to representations of Black womanhood.[20] As Jennifer Nash observes, there is "a pervasive racialized iconography where black women are represented as witnesses of violence and black men are represented as victims of violence, where black women raise the dead and black men are the dead."[21] This distribution of death and care labor is not coincidental. Feminist theorists have noted that the gendering of mourning is a recurring feature of the politics of lamentation. For Bonnie Honig, for example, "the historic alliance of mothering with mourning does not just maternalize lamentation, it also naturalizes motherhood and invests it with ideological power."[22] In the case of Black communities, widows and mothers have been the iconic symbols of Black grief. In her analysis of civil rights movement widows, Brenda Tindal argues that figures such as Myrlie Evers-Williams, Betty Shabazz, and Coretta Scott King "have lived most significantly in the national conscience as paragons of grief, exemplars of respectability and motherhood, and as custodians of their husbands' social memories." Their displays of dignity, grace, resilience, rectitude, and emotional control following the loss of their husbands, made "legible both the cost and legitimate aims of the black freedom struggle."[23] In addition to widows, mothers too have been emblematic Black mourners. In his slave narrative, for example, Solomon Northrup, a free Black man who was kidnapped, enslaved, and separated from his wife and children, observed about Eliza, who was also captured alongside him and whose children were subsequently sold away: "never have I seen such an exhibition of intense, unmeasured, and unbounded grief, as when Eliza was parted from her child."[24] From Mamie Till-Mobley to Lucy McBath and Venida Browder, the mothers of slain sons have become iconic lamenters of Black loss.[25] While it makes sense that parents would be the principal mourners of a child's death, the connection between maternalism and lamentation positions mothers as the principal bearers of loss, even in the case of adult victims. For Black communities, maternalism mobilized via mourning raises important questions about which losses can be grieved, and about who is recognized as a grieving subject. In other words, how are Black grief and grievance gendered and sexualized?

Mothers and widows are not the only ones who undertake grieving activism on behalf of dead loved ones. Black women, even when they are not the biological mothers of the dead, seem to predominantly fill the role of mourner in chief turned activist.[26] Erica Garner, for example, can be read as a daughter who symbolically mothers her father via grieving activism. A similar dynamic is present in the case of Tyrone West (a forty-four-year-old Black man killed while in police custody after a traffic stop led to an arrest for cocaine possession) in Baltimore, whose sister Tawanda Jones continues to lead family members and supporters in weekly protests to keep the spotlight on her brother's death. Those called on to perform the care work of mourning are not only cisgender women, however; they are all those positioned as what Joy James calls "Captive Maternals." These individuals can be "Black female, male, trans, or ungendered persons, feminized and socialized into caretaking within the legacy of racism and US democracy. . . . As caretakers who minister to the needs of their communities and families, Captive Maternals expend emotional and physical labor in stabilizing the social and state structures that prey upon them."[27] Children, for example, can be placed in the caretaking position of captive maternals. "Erica Garner noted that her five-year-old daughter would try to protect her mother (and herself) by turning her back to the television when the footage of her grandfather's death appeared; in brief moments of solidarity and care, the child became the Captive Maternal for the parent as she engaged her mother in conversation to check in on her feelings."[28] The "Happy Birthday Project" videos in memory of Oscar Grant, Philando Castile, and Mario Woods also feature a variety of mourners. While the Grant and Woods videos highlight their mothers' ongoing grieving, as a whole the videos show a community of mourners that includes not just relatives, but also friends and neighbors. It is not just mothers, but an entire community that mourns in these digital memorials.[29]

But while Black women have generally been positioned as the principal lamenters of the Black male dead, not all Black women have been recognized as grieving subjects. Middle-aged, "respectable" Black mothers are (sometimes) able to avoid pervasive archetypes of Black women as greedy, uncaring, and self-involved, images that pervade virtually all popular entertainment genres, from music to film. Stereotypes of Black women, and especially young Black women, as hypersexual make it difficult for them to be perceived as grieving subjects. They do not fit the mold of respectability through which mothers and widows make Black grief legible. Rachel Jeantel and Diamond Reynolds, for example, are two young women who are central to contemporary stories of Black death but who have not received the same visibility as "the mothers of the movement." Jeantel in particular, Trayvon Martin's friend who was on the phone with him while he was being followed by his killer, George Zimmerman, was subjected to state cruelty as she braved a courtroom in order to speak for Martin and to let him speak through her. Rather than being honored for her courage, however, or being shown empathy for the trauma and sorrow she was forced to relive, Jeantel was treated as an inauthentic, unintelligible witness who displayed improper affect and whose unconventional intimacy with Martin could not be recognized.[30] Reynolds was Philando Castile's girlfriend who broadcast the video that subsequently went viral and brought attention to his killing. Like Jeantel, she has not emerged as a visible icon of Black grief in the same way as the mothers of other victims of police violence. This is despite the fact that in addition to being a grieving family member, Reynolds was herself directly a victim of trauma, as she was literally forced to witness Castile's death.[31] In her reading of a visual artwork composed of portraits of Reynolds, Tina Campt argues that critics who condemn the piece for silencing her miss the fact that it captures her practices of adjacency and refusal, and in its quiet forces us, the audience, to interrogate our demand that Reynolds continually retell the story of disposable Black life.[32] In different ways, Jeantel and Reynolds challenge the dominant modes of Black female witnessing that have made Black grief legible.

Dominant conceptions of gender and sexuality shape not only who is legible as a grieving subject, but also who is grievable. Heteronormative prescriptions about Black life add additional layers of grief for queer Black subjects, who are also often seen as less grievable. Reflecting on the life and passing (in both senses of the word) of musician Little Richard, for example, Ashon Crawley described feeling "blackqueer grief," which we can understand as a distinct form of Black grief, "for an unresolved and restless life."[33] As the "#SayHerName" campaign to raise awareness about Black female victims of police violence also illustrates, some Black losses receive greater visibility and concern than others.[34] The deaths of Black trans persons, for example, do not garner the same level of visibility or care and concern as those of cis Black male victims of police violence, even though Black trans women are disproportionately the majority of trans women killed, and Black trans people face much higher rates of discrimination than other transgender individuals.[35] As Shatema Threadcraft has argued, "There are benefits and burdens, inclusions and exclusions, in centering the politics of death within black politics, in giving dead bodies pride of place in black politics, and even within that necropolitics to centering the slain body. A focus on the slain body privileges how cis men die, how young men die, how able-bodied blacks die, over all other black dead." She argues that part of the problem is that the kinds of violence and life-threatening discrimination Black women and LGBTQ+ Black folk face do not map easily onto a narrative of the state as "the death-distributing mechanism."[36] Not only that, but for queer and trans persons, how they are grieved, how their (Black) lives are made to "matter," often erases the truth of the lives they lived. For example, as C. Riley Snorton and Jin Haritaworn's analysis of the afterlife of Tyra Hunter illustrates, Black trans women are mourned and become the basis for broader grieving activism only when they are reappropriated into more intelligible frames.[37] Hunter was consistently misidentified as male in the media coverage and activism that followed her death. Snorton argues that this "translation" of transgender bodies to make them more legible has "payoffs," such as the successful negligence and malpractice lawsuit brought by Tyra's mother. "The sanitizing of Tyra's transgender body undoubtedly allowed her to be understood more sympathetically as a son." This simultaneous erasure and visibility of trans women of color is emblematic "of larger projects of reincorporating transgender bodies of color under a more legible sign; in this case, the representation of Tyra as a spectacularized gay male body."[38] If grief turned into grievance has been central to Black politics, it has also shaped the forms of mourning and terms of grievability in Black publics.

Historically, Black politics has been galvanized by private grief transformed into catalytic public mourning. Public grief can be simultaneously educative, strategic, and deeply felt; and African American thinkers and activists have approached it in diverse ways. Yet the imperative to channel grief into activism that has been the dominant approach to loss in African American political thought has paradoxically functioned to circumscribe Black grief in certain ways. There are two separate (albeit related) issues at stake here: one is the need to make Black grief legible to the broader public, and the other is the politics and ethics of mobilizing Black mourning in the service of democratic repair. Accounts of Black loss by Black studies scholars such as Saidiya Hartman and Christina Sharpe provide radically different answers to these questions from conceptions of mourning as a democratic resource put forward by contemporary political theorists. My analysis of the role of grief and grievance in Black politics argues that we can and should avoid activism that instrumentalizes Black grief in the service of democratic repair, and that this need not mean an inward turn to self-care that avoids formal politics.

Black Grief and Democratic Mourning

At a moment when Black thinkers have been grappling with the philosophical and political implications of recognizing the intractability of white supremacy, political theorists have been paying increasing attention to the politics of lamentation, with many arguing that we should view mourning as generative for democratic politics.[39] Alexander Keller Hirsch and David McIvor, for example, observe that "not all losses are made visible, let alone honored. As such, loss, grief, and mourning—and the exposure to vulnerability to which they attest—are distinctively political phenomena."[40] With the notable exception of Honig's worries about the politics of lamentation turning into a lamentation of politics, however, much of the recent literature on mourning in political theory has tended to focus on its productive potential in different ways. McIvor and Simon Stow, for example, focus on the civic effects of different forms of public mourning, while Judith Butler theorizes loss as shared ground for solidarity. Butler suggests that "loss has made a tenuous 'we' of us all. . . . This means that each of us is constituted politically in part by virtue of the social vulnerability of our bodies." In her view, rather than being privatizing and depoliticizing, grief "furnishes a sense of political community of a complex order, and it does this first of all by bringing to the fore the relational ties that have implications for theorizing fundamental dependency and ethical responsibility."[41] Yet, as others have noted, Butler does not pay sufficient attention to the differential effects of structural violence; that is, the kind of ethical recognition she hopes the awareness of shared vulnerability will generate appears to depend on spectacles of racial (and other forms of) suffering that are not guaranteed an ethical response by the dominant.[42] To the contrary, turning loss into the grounds for solidarity can impose additional forms of democratic sacrifice on those whose lives are already defined by racialized precarity.

The primary way in which Black grief appears in recent scholarship on mourning in political theory is overwhelmingly as a resource, as an alternative model of collective remembrance and public memorialization that can fruitfully alter the larger national political community's response to loss. Many of the contemporary meditations on the civic effects of mourning by political theorists emerged in response to 9/11, because they regard it as a defining shared catastrophe or instance of loss in the United States, one that is assumed to have been experienced equally by all citizens. Given the still disputed status of slavery (and other forms of white supremacy) as a defining national catastrophe, it is ironic that many of these accounts turn to Black grief as a corrective to the problematic forms of national mourning that emerged in the wake of 9/11. Stow, for example, identifies an "indigenous" tragic African American mode of mourning that he argues can serve as a corrective to the nationalistic, romantic, nostalgic mode of public mourning that has dominated US politics, with damaging effects for democracy, in "the postplanes era."[43] McIvor, meanwhile, drawing on a Kleinian psychoanalytic approach, contrasts the foreclosures of both consensualist (Periclean) and agonistic (Antigonean) forms of mourning to a third, in-between position that eschews certainty in favor of ambivalence, which he argues is more appropriate for complex, pluralistic democratic political communities. He points to the local truth and reconciliation commission created twenty-five years after a Ku Klux Klan massacre in Greensboro, North Carolina, as exemplary of a more democratically generative form of civic mourning that creates spaces for contact and dialogue, and encourages "an appreciation for ambivalence, or for the awareness of multiple powers, presences, and possibilities."[44] Ultimately, McIvor and Stow draw on Black grief to identify alternative forms of national mourning that might enhance the democratic capacities of the political community as a whole.

While African American mourning traditions might indeed provide a useful corrective to models of national public mourning that insist on unity and eschew complexity, this is a separate question from what an adequate response to Black grief is. For example, the United States' national understanding of the afterlife of slavery and ongoing white supremacy is marked precisely by ambivalence, entanglement, and lack of moral and political clarity, as current struggles over teaching critical race theory in public schools and the removal of Confederate monuments illustrate. What may be needed in the wake of racial disaster is not complexity or ambivalence. Put another way, the same mechanisms that might provide needed correctives to the foreclosures and erasures of nostalgic forms of civic mourning that insist on national innocence—that is, ambivalence, recognition of complexity, and so on—are precisely what *also* serve to obfuscate racial wrongs and limit the ability to right them. Those who turn to Black grief as democratically reparative thus risk reinscribing the harms it mourns if they do not also attend to the structural inequalities that shape grievability, that is, to how racial power determines who is forced to turn grief into grievance. National mourning and Black grief face different challenges and limitations and require different models. This is precisely what the work of scholars in Black studies seeking to grapple fully with Black loss suggests.

Writing about mourning during the height of the AIDS crisis before effective antiretroviral therapy, when LGBTQ+ politics was galvanized by grief (as has been true of Black politics historically), Dagmawi Woubshet highlights the different temporalities of Black and queer mourning, for example. He argues that "Black mourning evinces a particular temporal conception of loss that is very instructive in understanding both the aesthetics and the politics of early AIDS mourning, providing alternatives to the psychoanalytic model dominant in queer studies."[45] Black grief exceeds Freudian categories of mourning and melancholia because Black loss is unremitting. There is no fixed "calendar of loss." This was also true for AIDS mourners during the height of that pandemic, who confronted "not singular events of mourning" but instead had to respond to repetitive, "relentless serial losses [whose impact was experienced] not as cumulative, but as compounding."[46] Like the Black dead, queer AIDS victims were not initially deemed grievable by their co-nationals. Like Emmett Till's, many early AIDS funerals therefore became political funerals. The grief of AIDS mourners, like that of Black mourners, was neither respected nor empathized with. They are both examples of what Woubshet calls "disprized mourners—the bereaved who are denied the rites, honor, and dignity of public mourning, and whose losses are instead shrouded in silence, shame, and disgrace."[47] For Black people, when ongoing harm or violence makes it impossible to mourn, when it interrupts grieving, there is a similar pattern. Like Ida B. Wells, AIDS mourners responded by cataloguing their losses, by taking inventory and insisting on memorializing their dead. As Woubshet observes, they compiled "lists of the dead, series of names, estimates of body counts," which together constitute a "poetics of compounding loss."[48] Mourning thus emerges as profoundly political for Black and queer subjects, even as it is still important to question the costs and erasures that accompany the turn from grief to grievance.

This recognition of Black facility with mourning has been taken up in contemporary arguments about Black grief that emphasize resiliency and collective empowerment. For Stow, for example, the "tradition of black mourning in the United States . . . mourns the dead while also imagining and seeking to generate a better future for those left behind." African American vernacular mourning practices, he argues, exemplify a "constructive response to loss" in which the living embrace the memory of the dead in a "hopeful—but not optimistic—struggle against the conditions which produced it."[49] In contrast to accounts of Black mourning that focus on resilience, an important distinction that I want to make is that it can simultaneously be true that when Black people grieve for themselves they do it right, and that when their grief is made adjunct to democracy it is problematic.

Indeed, one of the striking differences between scholarship in political theory on democracy and mourning and the accounts of Black loss of scholars such as Saidiya Hartman and Christina Sharpe is the latter's different account of the work of Black grief. Hartman and Sharpe make two important moves that are at odds with the view of Black grief in the scholarship on democracy and mourning. They resist reparative approaches to Black loss that accord the state a central role and insist on the need to attend to how Black life persists even as Black death is an ongoing yet not fully acknowledged catastrophe. Sharpe is worth citing at length on this point:

> I want to distinguish what I am calling Black being in the wake from the work of melancholia and mourning. And though wake work is, at least in part, attentive to mourning . . . how does one mourn the interminable event? Just as wake work troubles mourning, so too do the wake and wake work trouble the ways museums and memorials take up trauma and memory. That is, if museums and memorials materialize a kind of reparation (repair) . . . how does one memorialize chattel slavery and its afterlives, which are unfolding still? . . . How does one, in the words so often used by such institutions, "come to terms with" (which usually means move past) ongoing and quotidian atrocity? Put another way, I'm interested in ways of seeing and imagining responses to terror in the varied and various ways that our Black lives are lived under occupation; ways that attest to the modalities of Black life lived in, as, under, and despite Black death. . . . I want, too, to distinguish what I am calling and calling for as care from state-imposed surveillance.[50]

As the distinction between what Sharpe calls "wake work" and the traditional Freudian categories of mourning and melancholia illustrates, Black grief is not easily assimilated into the categories of grief and mourning as they are usually understood in political theory because Black loss is both ongoing and unintelligible in certain ways. Not only does it trouble the presumed temporality of loss, as Woubshet argues early AIDS deaths also did; Black grief is ever present, even as "we strategize, organize, conjure, create and commune. And the world requires black folk simply continue."[51] Sharpe's resistance to thinking of care for Black life in the context of pervasive and ongoing anti-Black violence and Black death in terms of reparation or repair, especially by the state (which is in many cases the perpetrator of that violence), stands in contrast to the way political theorists writing about democracy and mourning tend to turn to Black mourning as *itself* reparative for national and democratic politics writ large.

Indeed, for Sharpe and Hartman, the point of grappling with Black loss is to nurture Black life and Black community, which they understand to be quite different from, for instance, national political projects or US democracy. As Sharpe observes, "if we [Black people, those living in the wake] are lucky, we live in the knowledge that the wake has positioned us as no-citizen."[52] For Sharpe, the statelessness imposed on Black people can be generative. Yet embracing this positionality entails the difficult task of dispensing with seeing the state—or fellow citizens finally moved by Black suffering—as the site through which the losses that are "the only sure inheritance" of slavery can be repaired. As Hartman writes about the experience of being African American:

> Nearly every day you are reminded of your losses. You keep waiting for it to get better, but then you see another picture of a dead boy in the newspaper or someone else has gone missing for fifteen to life and you get really tired. You're tired of being a problem, you're tired of loving a country that doesn't love you or hating the place you call home. . . . No one said what it has done to us or disclosed the terrible things we do to one another. . . . Nor did we share the best things . . . the miracle that we were still here.

Given this constitutive and unavoidable ambivalence regarding national belonging and the challenges to Black solidarity, Hartman concludes her futile search for traces of those lost to slavery in Africa by embracing "the fugitive's legacy. It didn't require me to wait on bended knee for a great emancipator. It wasn't a dream of a White House, even if it was in Harlem, but of a free territory. It was a dream of autonomy rather than nationhood. It was a dream of an elsewhere, with all its promises and dangers, where the stateless might at last thrive."[53] One of the ways in which Black grief, as articulated by Sharpe and by Hartman, exceeds dominant understandings of civic mourning in political theory is that it finds its political horizon beyond the state, the nation, and democracy, for that matter. Sharpe's claim that the aim of wake work is to excavate "the modalities of Black life lived in, as, under, and despite Black death" is a reminder that arguments that conscript Black grief into the democratic work of national mourning without accounting for differences in structural position among citizens become complicit in the original and ongoing harm.

Indeed, part of the paradox of Black grief is that pervasive anti-Black violence makes it impossible for Black folks to disentangle grief from grievance, to engage in public mourning that is not instrumentalized. Consider the following account of Black maternal grief and political activism by one of the Mães de Maio (Mothers of May) struggling against police violence that disproportionately impacts poor, Black, *favelado* youth in Brazil:

> Because the state will not protect us against the state . . . relying on the system is destined to fail. Our field of struggle is the streets. In this process, mothers are the main political actors to transform the Americas' zone of death into a demilitarized territory of peace. As in many parts of the continent, in Brazil mothers are the ones going after the disappeared, piecing together scattered bodies, collecting evidences to bring the killers to justice, and mobilizing terrorized communities to honor

> the dead. Black women's activist labor is what makes life possible in the Brazilian graveyard. To counteract the terrorist state, "fed with the blood of our children," mothering politics emerges . . . to organize the collective struggle to rescue black and brown lives from the shadows of death.[54]

The haunting observation that Black women's activist labor "makes life possible in the Brazilian graveyard" shows the significant civic burdens Black mourners shoulder. Some of these have to do with the legibility of Black grief, that is, whether their losses will be seen by their fellow citizens or if, as is often the case, they will be dismissed as the result of the victims' actions, or as the regrettable but necessary price of safeguarding public safety for the majority. In order to make their losses visible, Black mourners can display only limited affects: forgiveness rather than rage, civility rather than disruption. Most significantly, Black mourners cannot just grieve, since obtaining justice for their dead requires moving from grief to grievance. Christen Smith argues that accounts of anti-Black state violence should consider not only its impacts on the dead, but also "its devastating and lethal impact on the living." Black families contend with the loss of their loved ones and the fear and terror that permeate communities subject to enhanced state violence. When Black mothers become activists after the death of their children, they do so knowing that they too will likely become targets of state violence as a result of their activism on behalf of the dead and the living. In Smith's view, "the state hopes to prevent Black mothers from giving birth (politically, biologically, philosophically) to children (biological, communal, or revolutionary); if they do manage to reproduce, the necropolitical state will then have to kill [them] in order to perpetuate itself."[55] While they were not killed directly by agents of the state, activists like Erica Garner and Venida Browder still died from the strain of struggling for redress from the same state that killed their loved ones.

Black mothers might therefore become "willing" martyrs to try to preserve Black life, but that too is a loss. It is part of the ongoing, everyday violence of being "in the wake" that traditional accounts of mourning do not capture. In such a context, the notion of agency as traditionally understood is not useful or sufficient for trying to make sense of the losses (or gains) associated with becoming a subject of grief and grievance. As Anne Cheng has noted, "What is needed is a serious effort at rethinking the term 'agency' in relation to forms of racial grief, to broaden the term beyond the assumption of a pure sovereign subject to other manifestations, forms, tonalities, and gradations of governance."[56] The point is not that there is no such thing as agency, but rather, to interrogate what "agency" can mean in a context where equal grievability is not a given, and where the move from grief to grievance is itself a symptom of a democratic and ethical deficit. Black women's lived experiences complicate how we think about agency, as well as overly celebratory accounts of Black grief. Historian Sasha Turner, for example, challenges historical narratives of slavery that emphasize Black women's use of fertility control as "gynecological revolt" against sexual exploitation, and those that discuss their enduring maternal attachments as forms of resistance in a context in which reproduction was forced labor. She argues that such "romances of resistance" have the paradoxical effect of obscuring maternal grief. They focus on the heroic aspects of enslaved women's mothering,

> but with the result of obfuscating failure, rejection, grief, fear, and loss. . . . Did women need consoling after aborting their babies? Did women and community members celebrate

> infanticide as "heroic tragedies" where, despite loss, death secured a passage to freedom? All too often, narratives of motherhood among enslaved women are frozen in a "heroic pose," and the quest to capture the s/hero's "unbending defiance" sidelines the complexities and vulnerabilities of enslaved subjects.[57]

The focus on Black women's resilience comes at a cost. The figure of the strong Black mother in particular circumscribes what is viewed as a productive response to loss.

Because of the refusal to recognize enslaved women's maternal capacities in relation to their own offspring (as opposed to their ability to care for white children), Black mothers who were able to turn grief into grievance in subsequent historical eras were "speaking back" to the notion of the nonmaternal enslaved mother. Yet these new Black maternal archetypes carried their own limitations, as performance studies scholar Rhaisa Kameela Williams argues. She identifies two predominant representations of Black maternal grief: strong Black mothers and "icons of Black maternal mourning." The latter is epitomized by Mamie Till-Mobley, whose mobilization of her son's mutilated body "laid the foundational work in contouring our ideas of iconic Black maternal mourning where the mother articulates her anguish *through grievance*."[58] Turning Black maternal grief into grievance is powerful, she argues, because of "the significance of the nation recognizing a Black maternal affect capable of mourning." At the same time, however, "the privileging of redress forecloses the varied responses to trauma that Black mothers have taken up. In particular, we must account for grief without consigning the subject to notions of abandonment, weakness, or insanity."[59] In other words, Turner and Williams show how an emphasis on Black women's agency can occlude their pain and suffering. They ask us to consider how narratives of Black resilience (as important as they are) are also only partial accounts of Black humanity that may unintentionally downplay grief, loss, and desolation. They point to the need to probe how the emphasis on coping with loss by turning to political activism and prioritizing community and family cohesion represents a specifically gendered burden for Black women, one that devalues other responses to loss, such as turning inward and refusing to fulfill the role of pillar of strength of family and community.

Yet activism can also be a form of grieving. As Melynda Price's research on "black motherist politics"—the political work that Black mothers undertake after their children are killed or imprisoned—shows, grief and grievance are difficult to disentangle in the praxis of Black women who turn to activism in the wake of the killing of their children. Drawing on the example of SOSAD, Save Our Sons and Daughters, an organization that struggled against youth violence and the expansion of the carceral state in Detroit in the 1980s and 1990s, Price argues that in the post–civil rights era Black motherhood as a political identity emerged in contrast to the "welfare queen" and the "crack fiend," the dominant archetypes of Black womanhood at the time.[60] SOSAD was founded by Clementine Barfield, who was already a community organizer when one of her sons was killed and another severely injured. The community looked to Barfield for leadership: they expressed condolences for her loss but also asked her what she was going to do about it. Yet SOSAD is also an example of how activism created space to continue to grieve. Price points out that in addition to an emphasis on emotional health and programs that emphasized "life and growth" (in contrast to more traditional political strategies such as litigation or running for office), the mothers of SOSAD were willing to "publicly show pain, grief, and tears. The archives show that there is a lot of crying in SOSAD."[61] At the time, this emphasis on visibly continuing to grieve was not seen as productive. A local reporter, for example, criticized the weeping at SOSAD events, suggesting that they were emphasizing grief at the expense of activism: "What good does it do for us to cry a river of tears when a river of blood is flowing in our streets?" The praxis of SOSAD mothers disrupts easy dichotomies between grief and grievance.[62] But the frustration with their public displays of grief shows which response to loss has been viewed as more legitimate.

Examining the interplay between grief and grievance is not intended to be prescriptive, however. That is, my concern is not necessarily with prescribing an appropriate way for Black people to grieve, nor is this merely a claim that Black grief also matters, although of course it does. As Frederick Douglass sarcastically observed about establishing the humanity of enslaved persons in 1852: "Must I undertake to prove that the slave is a man? That point is conceded already. Nobody doubts it."[63] Black people's right to grief/grievability/grievance likewise requires perpetual reaffirmation despite being obvious. After the Tree of Life synagogue shooting in 2018, for example, a Black resident of Pittsburgh noted the striking asymmetry in public mourning compared to incidents when Black or brown residents of the city were killed:

> Do we see the same outpouring of support and unity when a victim or victims are Black? No. This is the city where the mayor goes out of his way to clarify that Antwon Rose II, a 17-year-old Black boy gunned down by a police officer, wasn't killed within city boundaries without offering condolences. . . . This is the city where its football team has decided to ignore

> players' right to protest police violence but readily emblazons "Stronger than Hate" on their cleats to honor the synagogue victims. Yes, the entire community should grieve over this tragedy [the Tree of Life shooting]. But why is there such a double standard? *If all lives matter, why aren't Black lives mourned this way?*[64]

Black lives are not equally mourned because racism continues to shape grievable life. The persistent disregard for Black life means that Black people are still "disprized mourners."[65]

What I am principally concerned with here, however, is a different question: What is the wrong kind of instrumentalization of Black grief? My claim is not that grief should play no role in Black politics, that is, that it should remain in the private sphere. Instead, what I am arguing is that there are costs and injustices when Black mourning is instrumentalized as a democratic resource, and this is an eminently political, not simply an ethical, question. As Ida B. Wells and Harriet Jacobs showed, as we saw in chapter 3, we need both noninstrumentalized accounts of Black grief as well as accounts of democratic mourning that attend to how race and structural inequality shape grievability and the imperative to move from grief to grievance. Put another way, in Arendtian terms, grieving can be a form of world making/world building, particularly grief that turns to activism. At the same time, the demand that grief be mobilized for the task of democratic repair exacts a cost that leads to parasitic world building; that is, insofar as this kind of democratic labor is unequally distributed it cannot be considered genuine action in concert.[66] As I argue in chapter 2, democratic theory must be critically attentive to when democratic repair becomes democratic sacrifice. The point is not to proscribe grieving activism, but rather to argue for an enlarged account of democratic mourning that takes Black losses seriously, and not simply as a democratic resource. This would entail making space for different accounts of Black grief that are not purely instrumental. It would also require a sincere accounting of Black politics' reliance on turning grief into grievance.

Distinguishing between grief and grievance is important for those seeking to open more space for responses to Black loss that do not overly privilege the turn to activism. Yet making space for grief that is not (only) grievance does not mean that we should understand grief and grievance as two poles in a dichotomous binary. As the centrality of the concept of "healing justice" to the praxis of the contemporary M4BL illustrates, grief and grievance are not an either/or choice; instead they should be conceived as a both/and construct.[67] This is part of the paradox of Black grief, even as Black politics has historically relied on public mourning (i.e., grievance) to catalyze struggles for racial justice. Erica Garner, SOSAD, and Mamie Till-Mobley are different iterations of Black politics activated by Black women's grief transformed into grievance. Like Elizabeth Alexander's claim that the toll of psychic and physical state-sanctioned violence has been and is the defining condition of Blackness, the poet Claudia Rankine suggests that "the condition of black life is one of mourning." This is because there is no way to convey "the daily strain of knowing that as a black person you can be killed for simply being black: no hands in your pockets, no playing music, no sudden movements, no driving your car, no walking at night, no walking in the day, no turning onto this street, no entering this building, no standing your ground, no standing here, no standing there, no talking back, no playing with toy guns, no living while black."[68] Mourning is central to Black life because the personal and collective cost of living with constant vulnerability makes loss a constant fear and inevitable experience. Just as Black life has been shaped by violence and mourning, Black politics has been bound up with grief. It is, however, a paradoxical, limited conception of Black grief transformed into grievance that has often been central to Black politics.

Black Mo'nin' and Black Politics

The iconic photograph (see figure 4.1) of Mamie Till-Mobley overcome with grief at the open casket holding her son Emmett's disfigured body is emblematic of the key role that private grief, transformed into catalytic public mourning, has historically played in Black politics.[69] Till-Mobley's decision to force the world to see the brutal violence visited on her child—to "let the people see what they have done to my boy!"[70]—has been credited with galvanizing the civil rights movement.[71] The affective power of the visual images of Till's funeral are widely seen as having played a central role in this successful mobilization of Black grief into grievance. According to Elizabeth Alexander, the reproduction of an image of Till's disfigured body cemented the story of his murder in the Black imagination. "A photograph of Till in the casket—his head mottled and swollen . . . —ran in *Jet*, and largely through that medium, both the picture and Till's story became legendary." The image had a lasting impact:

> For black writers of a certain age, and perhaps of a certain region, a certain proximity to Southern roots, Emmett Till's story is a touchstone. It was the basis for a rite of passage that indoctrinated these young people into understanding the vulnerability of their own black bodies, coming of age, and the way in which their fate was interchangeable with Till's. It

FIGURE 4.1. Mamie Till-Mobley at the funeral of her son, Emmett Till, September 6, 1955, Chicago. *Chicago Sun-Times* via AP Images.

> also was a step in the consolidation of their understanding of themselves as black in America.[72]

Till's mutilated body undoubtedly epitomized Black vulnerability and pervasive susceptibility to racist violence. Reflecting on the lasting impact of Till-Mobley's grief, however, Fred Moten focuses on the impact of the sonic rather than the visual. He argues that "the famous picturing and display, staging and performance, of his [Till's] death," had such powerful political effects because of the "phonic substance" of the photograph. The unspoken wail captured in the image of Till-Mobley epitomizes mourning, "wounded kinship," and Black life. As Moten eloquently summarizes: "*In the sound of the photograph: childless mother*."[73] The public performance of Till-Mobley's maternal grief was thus as central as the photographs of her son's dead body to the powerfully galvanizing effect of his death. As Ruth Feldstein observes, "constructions of gender were at the center of a case hailed solely as a landmark in the history of the civil rights movement. . . . Motherhood itself was a battleground on which the meaning of Till's death was fought."[74] The images of his mutilated body and the public performance of his mother's grief were both key to the impact of Till's political funeral, but it is the former that is usually recalled.

While they differ in important ways, lynching photographs and those of Till's funeral are both examples of using images of the Black dead to spur antiracist mobilization, a tactic pioneered by antilynching activists in the late nineteenth and early twentieth centuries.[75] But as Susan Sontag has observed, the reception of photographs of atrocity is complex, and the moral import of an image cannot be taken for granted. "No 'we' should be taken for granted when the subject is looking at other people's pain," she argues, in part because the meaning of the photograph "and the viewer's response—depends on how the picture is identified or misidentified; that is, on words. . . . The misreadings and the misrememberings, and new ideological uses for the pictures, will make their difference." She also points out that there is a limit to what images of the suffering of others can accomplish. "Such images cannot be more than an invitation to pay attention, to reflect, to learn, to examine the rationalizations for mass suffering offered by established powers."[76] Sontag's reflections on war photography remind us that we cannot know what effect images of Black suffering will have on Black or white spectators. Instead of spurring mobilization and repudiation, they could instead induce acquiescence and pleasure respectively. The use of images of Black death to spur antiracist mobilization thus raises important questions about the risks of representing the unrepresentable, and about whether there are forms of representation that allow us to see Black life rather than Black death, the quotidian rather than the spectacular.[77]

In contrast to Alexander's claim that it was the horrifying close-up of Till's disfigured face that rendered his death "legendary," for example, there are other images of Till's funeral, including some in which his mutilated body is not visible at all, that might also account for its galvanizing effect. On this reading, the images derive their affective power from the fact that they show "black pain, and thus black life" rather than Black death and anti-Black violence, as in the multiple photographs of Till in his Sunday best lining the casket and the indescribable pain etched in his mother's body language in figure 4.1. These images of Till's funeral register something lynching photographs could not, they "reveal something of the socio-political world of black people—in other words, black life. Lynching photography was intended to display black death for white enjoyment, and as such, their use by civil rights activists could only reveal black death."[78] One of the key differences between the images from Till's funeral and lynching photographs, in which the Black dead were emphatically *not* being mourned, is therefore the centering of Black community.

Likewise, by situating Till as part of a family that had suffered an irreparable loss, the images of his funeral registered Black grief. "The Last Quatrain of the Ballad of Emmett Till," the poem by Gwendolyn Brooks that serves as an interlude to this chapter, implies that what lives on after Till's death is his mother's grief. Brooks was a lifelong resident of Chicago, Till's hometown and the site of his funeral. She was thirty-eight when he was killed, and her poems about his death were published five years later. Her brief poetic depiction of Till-Mobley's maternal grief has been described as "unnerving."[79] Its companion poem, "A Bronzeville Mother Loiters in Mississippi. Meanwhile, a Mississippi Mother Burns Bacon," also does not focus on Till, but rather on the "steep undoing" of the life of the white woman who falsely accused him. Patricia Smith's poem "Black, Poured Directly into the Wound" takes up Brooks's call to pay attention to what comes "after the murder, after the burial" by focusing squarely on the impact on Till-Mobley:

> *Listen*. Once she was pretty.
> Windy hues goldened her skin. She was pert, brown-faced,
> in every wide way the opposite of the raw, screeching thing
> chaos has crafted. Now, threaded awkwardly, she tires of the
> *sorries*, the *Lawd have mercies*. Grief's damnable tint
> is everywhere, darkening days she is no longer aware of[80]

Smith's poem captures the way Till-Mobley's life was overtaken by becoming a grieving mother. She went from being "pretty," "pert, brown-faced" to a "raw, screeching thing chaos has crafted." Mamie was only thirty-three when "Bo" was killed. She felt a calling to become an activist in the aftermath of his lynching. After his death, wondering what to do with her life, she heard a voice saying: "Have courage and faith that in the end there will be redemption for the sufferings of your people and you are the instrument of this purpose. Work unceasingly to tell the story so that the truth will arouse men's consciences and right can at last prevail." She depicts her turn to activism in religious terms consistent with Black Christianity's notion of redemptive suffering. But like Wells and the mothers of SOSAD, she also reanimated the life of her son. She recalled small, quotidian moments of pleasure and joy such as "how funny he could be" when "imitating the commercial announcers on TV," their pretend fights at her jealousy over his future wife, and her joy at the prospect of his children, her grandchildren.[81]

In contrast to the view that his mother's grief was central to the impact of Till's murder, there are those who believe that there is a specific affective power in images of the mutilated dead body, of which Till's is the iconic example. For instance, in support of his call to show pictures of the bodies of the children massacred in the Uvalde, Texas, mass shooting to finally spur action on gun violence in 2022, Jeh Johnson (former homeland security secretary from 2013 to 2017), declared: "We need an Emmett Till moment."[82] For James Martel, unburied bodies—which appear to be absolute victims of state power—can serve as sources of resistance and defiance. In the case of Michael Brown, he suggests that politicized Black mourning allows "death to inform life, to make the dead something other than what the state tells them they are, thereby refusing one form of standing in order to (re)gain another."[83] Claudia Rankine also lauds the instructive power of the Black dead. Pointing to Till's funeral, she argues that

> Mobley's refusal to keep private grief private allowed a body that meant nothing to the criminal-justice system to stand as evidence. By placing both herself and her son's corpse in positions of refusal relative to the etiquette of grief, she "disidentified" with the tradition of the lynched figure left out in public view as a warning to the black community, thereby using the lynching tradition against itself. . . . By insisting we look with her upon the dead, she reframed mourning as a method of acknowledgment.

For Rankine, the refusal of the Ferguson police to move Brown's corpse out of the street, like Till-Mobley's decision to display her son's body, "made mourning his death part of what it meant to take in the details of his story."[84] She also suggests that the decision *not* to release images of the slain bodies of the Black victims of the Charleston church massacre perpetrated by a white supremacist in 2015 was a missed opportunity to provide visual proof of Black vulnerability that might counter the superhuman Black bodies in the white imagination that ostensibly cause police officers (and civilians) to kill unarmed Black people. In a similar vein, reflecting on the refusal of James Byrd's family to allow photographs of his mutilated corpse to be published, Ashraf Rushdy argues that "there are other considerations . . . that are at least as compelling as a family's grief," namely that "representations of it [racial hatred] are critical to the education of white Americans."[85] Why, however, must the development of an antiracist white moral imagination continue to rely on the instructive power of the Black corpse?

Additionally, what are the dangers and costs of the expectation that Black grief become a site of public mourning? Rankine acknowledges that mourning is not necessarily the response evoked by the Black dead, whose pained bodies can instead become "a spectacle for white pornography."[86] That is, they can satisfy desires for white dominance, which are very much alive in the Trump era. In addition to the danger that such images will incite racist mimicry or pleasure, there are costs exacted by the imperative to turn Black grief into occasions of public mourning. Till-Mobley's public mobilization of her grief made her son's loss legible to the world, but at considerable personal cost. Like Erica Garner and countless others, she chose to galvanize public mourning at a time when she might have found solace, however inadequate, in grieving anonymously amid the support of family and friends. The problem is not only the toll that turning private grief into public mourning exacts on the families of the dead, however; it is the very conception of Black politics that situates Black grief turned grievance as an antidote to the ills of the body politic. It is also not clear that national mourning can provide the kind of acknowledgment of Black grief that Rankine and others think is necessary. She argues that "a sustained state of national mourning for black lives is called for in order to point to the undeniability of their devaluation."[87] But can national mourning in fact provide this? Or are the ritual practices of national public mourning codified since Till's funeral aimed precisely at domesticating rather than catalyzing Black protest against racial violence, as well as other radical political formations?

National public mourning easily morphs into precisely the kinds of rituals of liberal inclusion and democratic standing that Martel argues unburied dead bodies subvert by revealing the limits of state power. One telling example of the genre is then-president Obama's nationally televised eulogy for the victims of the massacre at the Emanuel African Methodist Episcopal Church in Charleston, which has been hailed as a "counter-eulogy" that avoids the traditional pitfalls of the public funeral oration.[88] Yet it also precisely illustrates how national public mourning turns Black grief into an occasion to suture the wounds of the body politic instead. Obama's recurring theme of "grace" rather than "justice" wove one of the worst acts of white racist violence in the United States in the twenty-first century into a narrative of multiracial reconciliation and national resilience. In contrast, the spontaneous eruptions by Black citizens in Ferguson in 2014 and in Baltimore in 2015 following the killings of Michael Brown and Freddie Gray by the police sounded a very different note from Obama's off-key rendition of "Amazing Grace," a hymn penned by a slave trader turned curate whose principal themes are forgiveness and redemption. For Ferguson and Baltimore's Black protesters, who were also mourning their dead, grief at lives taken that could easily have been their own required public expressions of anger, not democratic grace. Yet accounts of the affective motors of Black insurrections past and present—such as the riots that followed MLK's assassination and the acquittal of the police officers who brutally assaulted Rodney King—focus on anger and overlook grief and loss. Debra Thompson is undoubtedly correct that US democracy is characterized by the dual "disavowal of black rage and the tacit acceptance of white anger."[89] But forms of Black grief that are not easily reconciled with the imperatives of national public mourning can be as illegible as Black rage. The hypervisibility of Black death and the imperative to channel grief into activism that has been the dominant approach to loss in African American political thought has paradoxically delegitimized Black grief that is not turned into grievance.

Seeking to transform Black losses into occasions of national public mourning has been an oft-utilized strategy in Black politics, but one of its unintended effects has been to circumscribe modes of grieving in Black public life. While anti-Black violence and Black death have been ubiquitous in Black life, noninstrumental accounts of Black grief—those that do not foreground the move to national public mourning to spur mobilization for racial redress—remain a minor key in Black politics, though examples of it can be found throughout African American political thought.

One of the paradoxes of Black grief is that Black people are forced to be both participant and witness to their losses. If to be Black is to be forced to look, as the title of Alexander's essay on

Rodney King (another iconic visual symbol of Black suffering) asserts, it also means that one cannot choose to look away. In a brief essay on her refusal to watch Diamond Reynolds's recording of Philando Castile's death, Alexandra Juhasz (a white media studies scholar) reflects on the ethical and political responsibilities that follow from witnessing viral images of Black death. Its title, "How Do I (Not) Look," references Alexander's and raises the question of what it means for white people to look away from Black death, and for that choice not to be available to Black people.[90] Reflecting on Black writers' memories of Till's murder, Alexander argues that "in order to survive, black people have paradoxically had to witness their own murder and defilement and then pass along the epic tale of violation."[91] What does it entail not only to suffer violence but also to have to be responsible for "passing along the epic tale of violation," as Till-Mobley did, in order to try to obtain elusive justice for one's dead? What is lost when the move to grievance leaves little room for grief? Alexander argues that endless iterations of lessons in Black vulnerability are both a requirement of survival in a white supremacist world, and instances of collective trauma that are (re)activated when witnessing each new spectacular or quotidian act of violence. "The conundrum of being unable to 'bear to think about' something which is 'always present to my mind' is precisely the legacy wrought by state-sanctioned violence against African Americans. . . . To see is unbearable, both unto itself as well as for what is means about one's own likely fate."[92] Black people are continually forced to witness the unbearable, to experience again and again their individual and collective vulnerability and death. "To see is unbearable" in part because Black grief must simultaneously become public mourning in search of justice, but also because it can be expressed only in severely limited ways.

Even as Black mourners are forced to turn grief into grievance, the parameters that regulate the public expression of Black grief are extremely constricted. This is true even of Till-Mobley, whose agency in politicizing grieving Black motherhood and turning the iconography of lynching against itself and inaugurating a new mourning tradition is now widely recognized. In the immediate aftermath of her son's death, however, she "could not control the terms of the debate or the ways in which she herself was a symbol." She had to be seen as "a respectable mother in order for her son to be cast as an 'innocent victim,' but she needed to do so along multiple valences: to emerge as protective to Emmett, yet not emasculating; fashionable and well-groomed, yet not ostentatious and luxury laden; hardworking, yet not ambitious; and 'universal' enough to attract the sympathy of whites without distancing herself from the black community."[93] Till-Mobley was hemmed in by the impossible expectations of both detractors and allies, as Ruth Feldstein has shown.[94] Like Margaret Garner, another iconic (if vexed) grieving Black maternal figure, many sought to speak through her.[95] Whites who saw her as a pawn of the NAACP portrayed her "as greedy and unmaternal, on the one hand, and hysterical and unrefined on the other," while the NAACP, which benefitted from her skills as a speaker and fund-raiser, would also "ultimately seek to contain . . . [her] and define the meaning of motherhood" in conventionally gendered terms that assigned Black women the role of emotional, domestic figures, not public actors in their own right.[96] Till-Mobley wanted to be more than a symbol or a silent testifier; she wanted to be an activist in her own right, which challenged patriarchal conceptions of Black politics.

In her time, Till-Mobley was viewed as displaying either insufficient or excessive maternal grief, and contemporary parents of slain Black teenagers continue to face similar racialized, gendered expectations. They walk a tightrope, where grief must be performed in public but only within certainly tightly defined parameters. For example, reflecting on the trajectory of Trayvon Martin's parents, Sybrina Fulton and Tracy Martin, who became activists following the murder of their son by George Zimmerman, Minkah Makalani observes that

> it is tempting to view them as acting heroically, though in doing so one risks losing sight of their humanity. . . . These were black parents whom the racial state would neither allow to grieve nor express the full range of their emotions. Fulton recalls the demands that she speak publically [*sic*] about Trayvon and remembers thinking, "I was still grieving and just wanted to withdraw from the world that killed my son, instead of confronting it."[97]

The costs Fulton, Martin, and other relatives of the Black slain have to bear consist not only in the impossibility of withdrawal from the world. To secure justice for their loved ones, they must become activists, often at the cost of their personal health and to the exclusion of all else, as with Erica Garner. They have to be stoic and tightly regulate their emotions, as showing anger or frustration lessens the sympathy of the general public for their loss. They must also endure the backlash spurred by their activism, including hate mail and threats of physical and sexual violence. Fulton could not retreat from the world, and both she and Martin could show sadness but not anger at the death of their child, or frustration at the elusiveness of justice. There is a personal cost to surviving family members of having the death of their loved ones become galvanizing events for a movement. Black grief catalyzed into public mourning has been a central template of Black activism, but it comes with a prescribed script and exacts a steep price.

If "to see is unbearable," as Alexander argues, and visual texts such as lynching photographs and other representations of the mutilated Black body risk becoming spectacles for white pornography as Rankine observes, and if the outsize ethical potential attributed to the act of witnessing them exemplifies the too-quick turn from grief to grievance, the sonic might allow for a more noninstrumental, contrapuntal approach to Black grief. Listening can be a way of registering and *feeling* the depth of loss. This is not to suggest that the sonic as an aesthetic form is not subject to some of the same constraints as the visual. No aesthetic form can guarantee a response, and the reception of the sonic too is complicated.[98] But as many Black thinkers have argued, the sonic allows for a certain kind of complexity. Tina Campt, for example, suggests that "listening to images" or attending to the sonic frequencies in identification photography (a medium created to enforce state regulation), reveals the ways in which Black people enact everyday forms of refusal and envision futurity. She argues for a different mode of engaging with images that challenges the equation of vision with knowledge.[99] Listening to images is "a practice of looking beyond what we see . . . [that] foregrounds the frequencies of images and how they move, touch, and connect us to the *event* of the photo."[100] Like Wells's and Jacobs's attention to "small needful facts," Campt's method of listening to rather than looking at images is a way to pay attention to Black interiority, to focus on the quotidian rather than the spectacular. The sonic allows us to sit with loss, to feel and acknowledge Black grief (and survival) without foregrounding the needs of the wider public. The sonic as a register for loss calls us to attend to Black grief without instrumentalizing it.

The sonic has been a central medium through which Black people have registered loss in noninstrumental ways. As Alexander observes, "Hearing, too, is central to witnessing. Sounds here haunt the mind as much as visual images."[101] Listening has been central to witnessing Black grief, and it was especially so during the era of enslavement, when Black grief had to be obscured or camouflaged. Audibly (and visibly) grieving meant (among other things) bearing witness to the ubiquitous racial violence that defenders of slavery sought to deny or erase. The sonic allowed a refusal of exposure that the visual did not, and a kind of concealment that was necessary to evade proscribed grief. Moten argues that Black grief—which he characterizes in sonic terms as "mo'nin'"—exceeds and disrupts standard categories of mourning:

> Black Art, which is to say Black Life, which is to say Black (Life Against) Death, which is to say Black Eros, is the ongoing production of a performance: rupture and collision, augmented toward singularity, motherless child, childless mother, heart-rending shriek, levee camp moan, grieving lean and head turn, fall, *Stabat mater*, turn a step, loose booty funk brush stroke down my cheek, yellow dog, blue trän, black drive. The ways black mo'nin' improvises through the opposition of mourning and melancholia disrupt the temporal framework that buttresses that opposition. . . . Is the display of the picture melancholic? No, but it's certainly no simple release or mourning either. Mo'nin' improvises through that difference.[102]

Black grief is complex not only because it has often been proscribed, but also because the ubiquity of Black loss required affirmations of Black life against death. James Baldwin made this point when he observed regarding Black people's "capacity for facing and surviving disaster" that (contrary to white perceptions) Black life is not defined solely by suffering even though loss is ubiquitous, and it is in Black music where this intermingling of joy and grief is clearest. "I remember . . . church suppers and . . . rent and waistline parties *where rage and sorrow sat in the darkness and did not stir, and we ate and drank and talked and laughed and danced*. . . . This is the freedom that one hears in some gospel songs, for example, and in jazz. In all jazz, and especially the blues, there is something tart and ironic, authoritative and double edged."[103] Black life is precarious and Black death is ever present, but Black community is also life affirming. It is simultaneously a space of rage and sorrow and laughter and dance, all of which are captured in Black sonics.

A sonic genre that exemplifies the proscription against Black grief and its illegibility to (some) listeners is the slave spirituals that W.E.B. Du Bois aptly termed "sorrow songs." As Frederick Douglass explained, the songs of enslaved people were deceptive. To the casual observer they appeared to reinforce the myth of the "happy slave" promoted by proslavery propagandists. But, in reality, they were evidence not of contentment, but of the pain and loss of slavery. Douglass confessed to being haunted by these sonic expressions of enslaved people's sorrow. He affirms the affective power of the slave sonic:

> I have sometimes thought that the mere hearing of those songs would do more to impress some minds with the horrible character of slavery, than the reading of whole volumes of philosophy on the subject would do. I did not, when a slave, understand the deep meaning of those rude and apparently incoherent songs. . . . They told a tale of woe which was then altogether beyond my feeble comprehension. . . . Every

> tone was a testimony against slavery, and a prayer to God for deliverance from chains. The hearing of those wild notes always depressed my spirit, and filled me with ineffable sadness. I have frequently found myself in tears while hearing them. The mere recurrence to those songs, even now, afflicts me. . . . To those songs I trace my first glimmering conception of the dehumanizing character of slavery. . . . Those songs still follow me.[104]

This is a striking admission from Douglass about the power of the slave sonic, given that his extensive literary output attests to his belief in the force of the written word and of political-philosophical argumentation. Moreover, the claim that he did not fully grasp the meaning of the sorrow songs while enslaved points to the complexity of the medium and its ability to convey something of the depth of Black loss that transcended immediate experience. Douglass was haunted by the sorrow songs—they "followed" him—because Black grief is ongoing.

The harrowing scene in the film *12 Years a Slave* (2013) when Eliza audibly mourns the loss of her children and Solomon cannot bear to listen to her wailing shows the power of sonic expressions of grief and shows which forms of Black grief are proscribed. Eliza's Black mo'nin' is unbearable to witness, for both Solomon and the film's audience. As originally written in the script, the scene reads:

> SOLOMON: Eliza. Eliza, stop!
> ELIZA: It's all I have to keeps my loss present.
> SOLOMON: You let yourself be overcome by sorrow. You will drown in it.
> ELIZA: Have you stopped crying for your children? You make no sounds, but will you ever let them go in your heart?

SOLOMON: They are as my flesh.
ELIZA: Then who is distressed? Do I upset the Mistress and the Master?
Do you care less for my loss than their well-being? . . .
Oh, Solomon, let me weep for my children.[105]

While Solomon has also lost his children, he hides his sorrow, hoping that by doing so he will not be undone by it. Eliza, in contrast, refuses to keep her grief hidden. Her retort to Solomon, "It's all I have to keeps my loss present," was edited out of the final version of the film. Yet Eliza's audible grief brings home the enormous losses of slavery as powerfully as the visually brutal scenes of Patsey's rape and whipping. Illustrating Alexander's observations about the difficulties of witnessing, most online comments about the scene on YouTube (of which there are hundreds), pan the performance of the actress playing Eliza while praising that of the male actor who portrays Solomon. In so doing, the commenters ascribe their discomfort with the scene to the respective acting abilities of the actors, rather than to the difficulty—embodied in Solomon's furious demand to Eliza to "stop your wailing!"—of being present with Eliza in her grief. This scene does not appear in Northup's autobiography, which is much more sympathetic to Eliza's sorrow. In it he attributes a kind of courage that he lacked to Eliza's open expressions of grief. About the moment when she was parted from her son, Northup writes: "It was a mournful scene indeed. I would have cried myself if I had dared."[106] In contrast, the scene between Eliza and Solomon in the film echoes gendered expectations of Black mourning that were also present in coverage of Till's funeral. The *Chicago Defender*, for example, described the crowds of thousands of African American mourners who viewed Till's casket as composed of "stern men [who] gritted their teeth and turned tear-filled faces away from the ghastly sight, while women screamed and fainted."[107] Traditional gender norms shape expectations about how Black grief is expressed and felt: Black women's pain is used to motivate and mobilize Black publics, while Black men are not allowed to visibly express grief.

Eliza's and Solomon's different approaches to grief could be read as reflecting the constraints of traditional gender norms that allow women to express their emotions while men are expected to suppress theirs. On this reading, Solomon's decision to deal with his grief by bottling up his emotions in order to survive is emblematic of male self-control even in the face of unendurable loss, while Eliza exemplifies the trope of the hysterical woman who succumbs to grief. Indeed, Eliza can be read as akin to another Black maternal archetype, the Black matriarch, whose excessive affect prevents the successful mobilization of grief into grievance. According to Rhaisa Kameela Williams, the Black matriarch's "excessive" grievance obscures her grief. "Overly emotional and always aggrieved, the mother-child bond is not denied to the matriarch; however, the need to react to her grievances is cast aside because her omnipresent anger and emotionality evacuates meaning from actions elicited by the loss of her child. Locked in a state of constant grievance, the perceptions of the Black woman as matriarch work to silence her demands for redress, particularly if her child is murdered by a state actor."[108] Eliza does not fit neatly into Williams's sketch of the Black matriarch because there is no possibility of successfully mobilizing grief into grievance under slavery, but she does display "excessive" emotion. Eliza's keening for her lost children reverberates in the dramatic and emotionally intense lamentation characteristic of the Black funeral practices that have developed in Black churches and southern Black communities in the United States, in which Black women's wailing plays a key role.[109] While the import of Black women's wailing can be read as emblematic of grief transformed into grievance, because it is a call to hold the powerful accountable for Black suffering, these inchoate sonic expressions of Black sorrow can also be read as less instrumental attempts to *feel* the depth of loss.

Eliza's wailing, like the poems by Brooks and Smith about Mamie Till-Mobley, all point to a different way of facing loss that resists the model of redemptive suffering epitomized by iconic depictions of Black maternal grief. Unlike Solomon's masculine reticence to dwell on loss, Eliza's insists, as she says, on keeping her losses present. In contrast to calls for Emmett Till moments that center the exposure of Black pain to generate white solidarity,[110] the poems by Brooks and Smith about his mother's grief, like Eliza's weeping, are about marking and remembering losses that cannot be repaired even if "justice" is achieved. Eliza's insistence on mourning her losses even when doing so could be viewed as unproductive because it would not result in the return of her children is emblematic of a different approach to grief in African American political thought. Grievance would not repair her loss, but mourning was nevertheless necessary.

Toward a Politics of Black Life

In the interlude that precedes this chapter taken from the "Happy Birthday Philando Castile" video, Castile's family and friends discuss the pressure to engage in activism. In response to questions about what they're going to do next, they emphatically declare: "You know what we're gonna do? We're gonna grieve." The repeated refrain, "We're gonna *grieve*," points to the tension between grief and grievance. Grieving activism can provide solace by keeping the memory of a loved one alive, but it also implicitly disallows simply feeling loss. As artifacts, the Happy Birthday videos themselves reflect the push and pull between loss and activism: they chronicle the grief of loved ones and the humanity of the dead, but they are also public digital memorials. There is no Happy Birthday video for Erica Garner, whose life and death embodied the tensions of grieving activism. Like her father, Erica also died not being able to breathe, as heart attacks lead to asphyxia. But in her case, the role of the state was indirect, and those of us who celebrate her activism must also reckon with its costs. As disability justice feminist Alison Kiefer points out, we often gloss over references to embodiment and disability, such as the moment in Black feminist Bernice Johnson Reagon's influential essay on coalition politics when she describes having difficulty breathing and feeling like she was about to "keel over any minute and die."[111] Erica, Eric, and Bernice all struggled to breathe, but we tend to focus on deaths that result from spectacular rather than quiet violence, and to not pay sufficient attention to the everyday embodied costs of heroic activism. We remember that Eric could not breathe, but we tend to forget that Erica, also, in the end could not.

This omission matters because the stories we tell about Black grief shape Black politics. As McIvor observes, the "stories that are told about the dead—the meaning that is ascribed to social traumas and struggles, and the practices that are commonly associated with those struggles—inevitably shape political identities, imagination, and outcomes in the present."[112] The predominant story we have told about the Black dead is that loss should be channeled into activism or instrumentalized in the service of projects of public, multiracial mourning that can perform the work of racial redress and democratic repair. The instrumental use of Black grief for democratic politics in national memorialization is not about grieving Black life for Black people and Black communities, but about healing the racial wounds of the body politic, a process that often seems to fall short of actually repairing the cause of the racist wrongs in the first place. As I have argued throughout this chapter, when grief and mourning are instrumentalized, that is dehumanizing in itself. Rather than asking what the broader polity can learn from Black mourning, a question we might ask instead is: What is democracy's responsibility to Black grief? At the most basic level, of course, one of these responsibilities is to redress racist wrongs without requiring displays of Black suffering. But most importantly, we will have allowed Black people to be fully human when Black grief must no longer be mobilized in service of repairing white democracy.

But the imperative to turn grief into grievance is not only externally imposed. The overarching argument of this book is that both Black and white people need to learn to sit with loss, for different reasons, and to different ends. For Black people, sitting with loss would mean setting aside expectations to immediately move from grief to grievance. At the same time, it is important to recognize that one of the potential pitfalls of not moving from grief to grievance is that it can have apolitical or antipolitical implications. I am certainly not arguing that Black people should respond to loss with resignation or apathy. But the dominant response to harm or injury in Black politics has not been a failure to engage in politics; it has been precisely the opposite. Making space for sitting with loss implies a different temporality. It forestalls the pivot to the future as the time when and the place where wrongs will be repaired. Instead, sitting with loss orients us to hold the unrepairable past in view and stay in the present. In the case of Black grief, this means that Black people need to mourn their losses without acceding to the demand—imposed by majority expectations as well as some strands in their own political tradition—to give them meaning by mobilizing them in service of projects of democratic repair that fix Black politics into a posture of appeal to the state. Jennifer Nash has argued that in a context in which Black maternity is represented as "a kind of metaphorical ground zero for black death, a kind of *ur*-text of black death," it is critical to mobilize other conceptions of Black maternal aesthetics that challenge accounts of "Left/anti-racist politics as necessarily tethered to grief, pain, and scarcity."[113] This call to rethink anti-racist politics encapsulates the dilemma of Black politics: on the one hand Black loss is ubiquitous but unacknowledged by the wider public, while at the same time Black life is about more than grief and suffering. The challenge is to craft a conception of Black politics that attends to both. Invoking Nash's plea that we disentangle prevailing conceptions of (maternal) Blackness from suffering might seem counterintuitive in an account of Black grief, but it can help us think more clearly about what the life of Black grief could be if it were not saving democracy or galvanizing Black politics. In other words, as important as it is to not become tethered to what Honig calls "the lamentation of politics," it is equally important to consider what role non-instrumental accounts of grief can play in Black life.[114]

This is not a call for an inward turn to self-care that avoids the realm of formal politics, nor is it a critique of grieving activism. As I argued in the previous chapter, thinkers such as Ida B. Wells and Harriet Jacobs have formulated capacious accounts of loss that reckon with democracy and freedom's costs, balancing grief and grievance in service of making space for Black life amid ongoing Black death. In a similar vein, contemporary scholars concerned with the way Black politics has been overdetermined by its association with suffering, and with the way Black culture is overwhelmingly defined in terms of resistance, point to how we might begin to conceive the life of Black grief beyond (only or mainly) grievance. Nash, for example, juxtaposes a "black maternal aesthetics" that emphasizes abundance and spirituality to "the attenuated notion of the political that the Left, including black feminist theory, has granted black mothers—insisting that black mothers perform their political work around death and dying, around grief and mourning."[115] Nash's concern with the way contemporary understandings of Black maternity have been limited to the necropolitical echoes my concern in this chapter with the way the scripts of democratic public mourning constrict the life of Black grief. Kevin Quashie has also interrogated the equation of Blackness with resistance, arguing that "black culture is celebrated . . . for its capacity to manipulate social opinion and challenge racism. This is the politics of representation, where black subjectivity exists for its social and political meaningfulness rather than as a marker of . . . human individuality."[116] Reformulating his question—"what else beyond resistance can we say about black culture and expressiveness?"[117]—for our purposes, we are compelled to ask, what role is there for Black grief beyond repairing white democracy or galvanizing Black protest?

Answering this question requires refusing certain versions of democratic mourning. It also entails paying attention to how Black grief can become an accounting of quotidian Black life beyond representations of heroic spectacle. The following poem about Emmett Till illustrates how his and other Black lives can be reanimated beyond the iconic images of his mutilated body and his mother's grief. Eve Ewing's poem "I Saw Emmett Till This Week at the Grocery Store" is set in Chicago, in a mundane location that echoes the site of the fateful encounter that led to his murder.[118] In her retelling, however, the space of the everyday does not become the site of trauma, as a park did for Tamir Rice, or a sidewalk did for Eric Garner. Instead, like Ross Gay's imagery of Eric Garner planting flowers, in the poem we see Till delicately inspecting and selecting fruit. Ewing, who "like[s] to use poems as what-if machines and as time-traveling devices,"[119] imagines what would be if Till had not been murdered. The poem depicts an alternate universe in which Emmett lives. It stages an encounter between the poet, a young Black woman, and Till, but it is focused on Till, who is going about the ordinary task of buying groceries. He is shown reveling in quotidian pleasures, such as carefully selecting fruit, and the poem lingers in great detail on these quiet moments of grace. "Bo" is not required to do anything. He is not a symbol or a rallying cry. He smiles, intact, unmutilated, and goes on. Living. It is an alternative imagining of Black life in a society that demands sacrifice and democratic labor, even of the Black dead.

looking over the plums, one by one
lifting each to his eyes and
turning it slowly, a little earth,
checking the smooth skin for pockmarks
and rot, or signs of unkind days or people,
then sliding them gently into the plastic.
whistling softly, reaching with a slim, woolen arm
into the cart, he first balanced them over the wire
before realizing the danger of bruising
and lifting them back out, cradling them
in the crook of his elbow until
something harder could take that bottom space.
I knew him from his hat, one of those

fine porkpie numbers they used to sell
on Roosevelt Road. it had lost its feather but
he had carefully folded a dollar bill
and slid it between the ribbon and the felt
and it stood at attention. he wore his money.
upright and strong, he was already to the checkout
by the time I caught up with him. I called out his name
and he spun like a dancer, candy bar in hand,
looked at me quizzically for a moment before
remembering my face. he smiled. *well*
hello young lady
    hello, so chilly today
    should have worn my warm coat like you
yes so cool for August in Chicago
    how are things going for you
oh he sighed and put the candy on the belt
it goes, it goes.[120]

INTERLUDE 5

how much is owed
to those who wore
the chains who tilled
the land who nursed
the babes who mixed
the grits who fried
the food who chopped
the wood who picked
the bolls who ran
the road who fought
the war who shared
the crop who made
the name who wore
the noose who Blacked
the codes who sparked
the schools who juked
the blues who showed
the soul who left
the south who stayed
the course who caught
the hell who marched
the march who broke
the strike who struck
the blow who took
the vote who held
the hood who housed

the club who queered
the notes who spun
the jams who funked
the flow who built
the thing who built
the thing who built
the thing? you know.

take the payment
you ain't give
for all that & press
it down, make it
overflow fiddy'leven
times & gimme that.
in my own numbers
of my own currency.

—"FIDDY'LEVEN" FROM *FINNA: POEMS* BY NATE MARSHALL ()

CONCLUSION

Reckoning with Democratic Debts

THERE IS NO RESPITE from mourning. Quotidian and spectacular loss are unremitting. In the midst of a deadly war in the Ukraine and the ever-mounting deaths from the Covid-19 pandemic, which large swaths of the United States seem to blithely forget in the rush to return to "normal," two mass shootings refocused attention on gun violence in May 2022. The news of the racist mass shooting of ten African Americans at a grocery store in Buffalo had barely begun to be absorbed when another horrific mass shooting, this time of nineteen elementary-age schoolchildren and their teachers in Uvalde, Texas, displaced it in the national news a mere ten days later. The death of nine-, ten-, and eleven-year-olds and the abysmal police response, following quickly as it did on the heels of the killing of mostly elderly Black people peacefully grocery shopping on a Sunday afternoon, prompted calls to redouble efforts to finally enact stricter gun control policies at state and national levels. Yet, if gun violence has reached epidemic proportions in the United States, so too has white supremacy, and yet there was not the same national urgency to address the racism that motivated the Buffalo shooter, in part because the white grievance that motivated him is shared by many. The Buffalo shooter was galvanized by fears of white replacement (the false conspiracy theory that whites are being demographically and culturally replaced by nonwhites via immigration, demographic growth, and a drop in the white birth rate) that air nightly on *Fox News*, the country's most watched news channel. As with the electoral "Big Lie" that the 2020 election was stolen, fears of white replacement fuel white rage. And, as is often the case, white grievance at imagined or anticipatory losses obscures and displaces compounding Black and nonwhite losses. The mass shooting at Tops grocery store was an instance of spectacular death superimposed on ongoing "slow deaths" in a predominantly Black neighborhood. Buffalo's East Side is similar to many other Black urban communities across the United States that have been blighted as a result of policy choices: redlining that enforced residential segregation by blocking minorities from homeownership; and urban renewal projects that destroyed thriving Black neighborhoods, depressed wages and property values, and created food deserts.[1] Black residents of Buffalo suffered from "food apartheid" long before a white gunman opened fire. As one local food activist observed, there is a saying: "'The fork will kill you faster than the bullet.' And here in Buffalo, we're experiencing both, both the fork and bullet."[2] On that fatal day in Buffalo, slow and spectacular death converged, and like the 911 operator who callously hung up on one of the terrified victims calling for help from inside the store, significant numbers of their fellow citizens refuse to see and value the lives of Roberta Drury, Margus Morrison, Andre Mackneil, Aaron Salter, Geraldine Talley, Celestine Chaney, Heyward Patterson, Katherine Massey, Pearl Young, and Ruth Whitfield.[3]

For Black politics, the hope has been that making Black grief visible will undermine white grievance, but instead the very visibility of Black loss can lead to escalating white resentment. Racial politics are not static, and during the past two years we have witnessed two very different white responses to loss. On the one hand, the mass losses of the coronavirus pandemic initially shifted the usual economies of suffering such that the murders of George Floyd and Breonna Taylor sparked unprecedently broad national and global protests against racism. But the very breadth of those protests, and the possibility that the United States might finally reckon with Black loss, spurred backlash among those determined to preserve white dominance. In 2021, the multiracial antiracist protests of the summer of 2020 gave way to majority-white, antimask, antivaccine protests that asserted a version of individual freedom that recognizes no obligations of care and concern for fellow citizens. At the same time, right-wing activists and GOP-controlled legislatures and school boards have whipped up a moral panic about the supposed teaching of critical race theory in schools whose ultimate goal is the whitewashing US history. They have also passed antitrans legislation that cruelly denies young people life-affirming medical care and the ability to freely express their gender identities. Fueling much of this aggrieved whiteness is the fact that, for some, 2020 has become an emblematic instance of white loss, which (as was the case with the Lost Cause after the Civil War) is fueling commitment to white minority rule and nonwhite subordination.

These aggrieved responses to the fleeting possibility of truly reckoning with the losses inflicted by white supremacy shows how the unequal distribution of loss within the racially dissected body politic has led to the development of different civic capacities: some citizens refuse to accept loss—however minor, necessary, or legitimate—while others have had to learn to be resilient in the face of loss, to find ways to balance grief and grievance. Black activists and intellectuals have moved between fact and affect to tell the stories of Black grief without losing sight of Black life. As Dagmawi Woubshet observes about the early years of the AIDS crisis, "the dishonored had to mount an insurgent mourning for survival."[4] Like Harriet Jacobs and Black mourners during the era of slavery, or Ida B. Wells during the era of lynching, or the present-day mothers of the movement who seek justice for their slain children, Black mourners have had to attend to the stories of Black life, not just Black pain, or Black death.

On the eve of passing from AIDS, the Black queer filmmaker, poet, and gay rights activist Marlon Riggs connected the mass losses of the AIDS pandemic to a previous catastrophe visited on Black people: slavery. In his "Letters to the Dead," one of which was addressed to Harriet Tubman, he asked her:

> Don't you now see—oh I know you do!—the chilling parallel between the means by which we were held captive in your time, and the methods of our enslavement today. Don't you see the chains, my Harriet, sweet Moses, the chains not so much of steel and the law, but more insidious: the invisible chains, linked over centuries, of silence and shame? In this latest crisis, our new master is the virus; his overseer—silence; and his whip—shame.[5]

The link Riggs establishes between slavery and the AIDS pandemic reflects the superimposition of loss, the fact that for those Woubshet calls "disprized mourners," loss is rarely singular but rather multiple and ongoing. Riggs articulated an intergenerational politics of care that honored Black and gay life in the midst of grief and death and called Black people to a praxis of active witnessing. He expressed his gratitude to Tubman as if to a close friend:

> To Harriet, my sweet Moses, especially, I thank you for having led me from the forest to the river and commanded me to wade. Repayment, my dear dead beloved . . . is impossible. But what I have learned from you I now pass on. As Harriet walked with me, I now walk with others. And as Harriet held my hand, we must hold each other's. . . . Each of us must be a witness. . . . Even now, as the virus continues its course through my veins, I know nonetheless I will reach the other side, one way or another.[6]

Riggs's connection to Tubman, his sense that she had guided him as he hoped his work and life would guide others after him, enacts an intergenerational community of Black witnessing to loss but also survival.

Riggs's concatenation of grief is emblematic of the approach to loss in African American political thought that this book has traced. The thinkers and activists highlighted in *Black Grief/White Grievance* sketch an alternative approach to Black grief that insists on feeling the depth of loss, and points to how we might conceive grief that is not only or mainly grievance. It refuses the turn to redemptive suffering to make sense of loss.

This attempt to balance grief and grievance could not be more different from the responses to loss of dominant groups. Many analyses of the contemporary resurgence of anti-immigrant and xenophobic sentiment in the United States today have argued that it is a response to the sense of loss of predominantly white male citizens attracted by visions of "sovereign freedom" rooted in "sovereign individualism." In this telling, the problem is that some citizens respond to loss by doubling down on a desire for mastery that encompasses both unbounded individual agency and the power to assert untrammeled dominance over others. According to Elisabeth Anker and William L. Youmans, Trump and Brexit supporters are attracted by the "promise that state power . . . can wipe away all individual experiences of vulnerability."[7] But if reveling in the assertion of state power over women, immigrants, Black and antifa protesters, and others assuages feelings of vulnerability, it is also the case that many of the same people decry state power as an infringement on individual freedom when it comes to mask mandates or gun control. In contrast to this doubling down on domination, the African American thinkers that are at the center of this book point to a different tradition of thinking about loss that accepts contingency and vulnerability. They point to what can come from loss beyond reinvestment in domination. They show us what it would mean to refuse the desire for mastery in favor of "freedom dreams" for all.[8]

Arguing that citizens need to learn to sit with loss, as this book does, contravenes the dominant genre expectations in democratic theory, which tend to emphasize democracy's potential to empower citizens.[9] But democracy is difficult precisely because it requires acceptance of loss. Democratic theory's tendency to downplay loss can lead to understating the anxieties and alienations of democratic life. More troublingly, it can also lead us to laud sacrifices for democracy, framing them in a reparative vein that has the paradoxical effect of minimizing ongoing and continuing loss. This leads us to view democratic sacrifice as a form of civic virtue, to diagnose the need for such acts as a symptom of civic health, rather than of democratic decay and domination. In contrast, one of the aims of *Black Grief/White Grievance* has been to show that democratic theory needs a more accurate account of loss. Loss is central to democratic politics, and learning to accept legitimate loss is a vital civic capacity. Democratic theory needs to be able to say what is democratic about loss, not just offer visions of democratic citizenship as the unimpeded exercise of freedom, agency, and sovereignty. Offering an account of how loss is central to democracy is crucial because it actually comports with how members of subordinated groups have experienced democratic life. If democratic theorists need to be clearer about why loss is central to democratic praxis, citizens also need to accept the democratization of loss (i.e., to renounce expectations that it will be unequally distributed).

Popular narratives and contemporary scholarship in political theory on mourning and democracy illustrate some of the deficits in our current democratic thinking. Mourning has become increasingly central to thinking about democracy by political theorists and the general public alike. Following 9/11, political theorists sought to identify forms of public mourning that were less prone to the dangers that beset dominant ancient models of public mourning and that could make shared grievability the ground for more democratic approaches to national memorialization and transnational solidarity.[10] But lauding the enhanced capacity to grieve in what are seen as civically productive ways that some groups have been forced to develop risks instrumentalizing grief and reducing it to grievance. Meanwhile, during the Trump presidency and following the January 6 insurrection and continued attempts by sectors of the Republican party to undermine key institutional elements of US democracy and the rule of law, many ordinary citizens have mourned the loss of their vision of the United States as a robust democracy insulated from the kinds of democratic deficits and breakdowns that befall other countries. The long-standing scholarship in comparative politics on de-democratization can no longer be assumed to apply only to countries in the Global

South; instead, the question of *How Democracies Die* is frighteningly relevant for the United States as well.[11] For many, this has meant being confronted—for the first time—with the reality that the United States is a democracy in need of repair.

Of course, for subordinated groups the United States has never been a full democracy in which they can expect to exercise equal citizenship or have their rights respected. For Black citizens and other subordinated racial groups suffering from a racist carceral apparatus that demonizes them and routinely subjects them to lethal police violence for the most imagined infractions, being treated as an internal enemy by a state whose role is ostensibly to protect its citizens is nothing new. Neither is the "psychic tax" of knowing that the country's political leadership is complicit in perpetuating these harms and that a significant number of their fellow citizens are intensely invested in denying that such injustices are even occurring. Moreover, Black people in the US body politic not only have not received the same level of care and concern from the state and their fellow citizens; they are continually asked to sacrifice for democracy. Voter suppression tactics, for instance, have long meant that minority voters must stand in line for hours to vote, while gerrymandering has diluted their political agency. Black citizens are sacrificing to participate in a political community that not only does not protect them, but is not committed to their thriving.[12] The continued, routine existence of such racist disparities in the most basic democratic activities must necessarily shape how we assess the health of US democracy. The flagrant violations of the rule of law during the Trump presidency, the Capitol insurrection, and the arbitrary rulings by conservative judges throughout all levels of the judiciary, as well as continued attempts to undermine the electoral apparatus at the state level, have led some to ask, for the first time, is US democracy broken? Yet US democracy has *always* been broken *for some*. What we are seeing today is that the racist democratic deficits that have been present since the country's founding are seeping in and eroding "white democracy" as well.

My critique of white democracy in this book will inevitably raise the question of whether US democracy is salvageable. Here, it is important to reflect on what "salvaging" might entail. The *Oxford English Dictionary* defines "salvage" as "to save from shipwreck, fire, etc.; to make use of (unattended property); to save and collect (waste material) for recycling." This is quite different from its definition of repair: "to restore (a damaged, worn, or faulty object or structure) to good or proper condition by replacing or fixing parts; to mend, fix."[13] Salvaging therefore seems more suited to the complex task of rethinking, remaking, or *building from scratch* a truly egalitarian democracy where one has not really existed. Repair assumes a baseline soundness of the thing being fixed, which requires only alterations to some of its parts. In contrast, salvaging has more unruly connotations: it involves making use of unattended property, recycling refuse. Salvaging on this reading is closer to refusal than repair, or at least gestures to what might come after refusal.

Many Black thinkers and activists have refused the script of democratic sacrifice and have worked on behalf of political projects that exceed what I am calling here white democracy. As much as it is key for Black politics to refuse the domestication of Black freedom to the project of saving white democracy, it is also important to acknowledge that Black intellectuals have articulated their own, more radical visions of democracy. W.E.B. Du Bois's notion of "abolition democracy," for example, emerged from his reinterpretation of Reconstruction (against the dominant narrative popularized by Lost Cause historians) as an attempt to truly establish meaningful democracy in the

United States that was violently discontinued.[14] More recently, Black feminist visions of the democratic labor of care for Black life and human thriving have provided other models for thinking about what democracy could mean. Shatema Threadcraft, for example, points to the democracy-expanding interventions made by "unruly women, single mothers, welfare mothers, lesbians, sex workers and the women who explicitly cast their lot with these women" in the twentieth century. Their efforts to extend care to marginalized and often criminalized Black people and to resist carceral logics concerning which lives are valuable have called forth different Black publics and paved the way for contemporary abolition feminism, Threadcraft argues. As such it is an important attempt to enact "an always fugitive (feminist) abolition democracy."[15] Similarly, Deva Woodly draws attention to the radical Black feminist pragmatic imagination of the Movement for Black Lives, which centers a politics of care "which holds that the activity of governance in a society that hopes to be just must be oriented toward the responsibility to exercise and provide care for those most impacted by oppression and domination." This alternative democratic vision, she argues, can help overcome the "politics of despair" that has taken hold in the United States today. In her view, social movements (such as the M4BL) are essential to revitalizing democracy, and overcoming its tendency toward stagnation and closure. The success of the M4BL, she argues, could portend "that the third decade of the twenty-first century might be a moment for reconstruction" despite the fact that the very success of the movement's vision is leading to fierce backlash.[16] These Black feminist visions show that there is more to democracy than white democracy, but achieving them requires dispensing with certain ingrained ways of thinking about what constitutes democratic health, success, and failure.

Indeed, the distinction between salvaging and repairing democracy is reminiscent of the distinction between frameworks of justice that envision reparations for the harms of slavery and Christina Sharpe's notion of "living in the wake," in which she uses the wake as a metaphor with multiple meanings applicable to Black life in the aftermath of slavery. It refers both to a mourning ritual and to the disturbances that follow movements of air and water, such as those caused by the travels of slave ships.[17] In contrast, political theorists who advocate reparations for slavery generally base their claims on the idea that a society, in order to be just, must seek to repair the wrongs it has committed. Thomas McCarthy, for example, has argued that "redressing past wrongs is essential to establishing conditions of justice in a society scarred by the enduring and pervasive effects of those wrongs."[18] Advocates of reparations nevertheless acknowledge that these measures cannot repair the immeasurable systemic and long-lasting effects of slavery. This caveat is the starting point for Sharpe's reflections on "living in the wake." She argues that the answer does not lie in seeking redress from the state, because you cannot repair an ongoing harm, and moreover how would we even begin to repair the kinds of losses that are the result of anti-Blackness, that continue to render Black life disposable? Instead, she argues for what she calls "wake work": attending to the dead, tending to the living, performing the work of care in Black communities that is central to Black survival. If we live in the wake of the slave ship, in a state of ongoing mourning, Black people have become adept at making something out of that which was discarded or not properly valued. This book argues for holding both these perspectives simultaneously: refusing the reconstitution of something assumed to be essentially healthy implied in the language of repair, while also attending to the quotidian practices of living and survival without abandoning claims of justice. The aim of salvaging is not to repair the ship, but to dismantle white democracy, to strive for a future in which the communities built from the wreckage can thrive.

As the poem by Nate Marshall that serves as an interlude to these concluding reflections suggests, the United States owes profound democratic debts to Black citizens. Marshall's poem is a litany, whose power builds through repetition, of what Du Bois called "the gift of black folk."[19] Marshall does not stop at enumeration, however; he goes on to ask, "How much is owed" to "those who built the thing"? If the thing is US democracy, this book is partly about the crucial role Black activism has historically played in catalyzing moments of genuine democratic renewal. But there are costs to transforming ongoing loss into civic excellence, to performing the *work* of democratic care. According to Lawrie Balfour, in Martin Luther King Jr.'s view, "U.S. democracy has been marked by illegitimate demands for payment. . . . King draws on the language of . . . debt to make vivid a history of the United States' unmet obligations."[20] Indeed, the United States has succeeded in inverting the creditor/debtor relationship that has marked its history by continually invisibilizing Black sacrifice and spinning fantastic accounts of Black civic deficit. The fact that racist depictions of Black citizens and nonwhite immigrants as lazy, greedy dependents on the teat of a US democracy financed by hardworking white citizens are such a recurrent dog whistle in electoral politics points to the continued power of this phantasmagoric inversion. As Eula Biss argues in her attempt to grapple with "white debt," the condition of white life (to paraphrase Claudia Rankine) is to be "moral debtors who act as material creditors."[21] But whiteness is not destiny, it can be refused, and "debt can be repaid incrementally, resulting eventually in ownership." Doing so, however, requires not living perpetually in default. We need to reckon, as Du Bois, King, and Marshall suggest, with these deep democratic debts. Importantly, that debt is not only or primarily about enlisting Black grief to repair US democracy. Instead, the payment that has not been given must be made, as Marshall affirms in the interlude that precedes this chapter, "*in my own numbers of my own currency*." Grappling with racialized political loss makes it clear that Black freedom dreams should not be constrained by the limits of democratic repair. United States democracy has always been entangled with Black grief and white grievance, and as Black thinkers have repeatedly observed, racial justice is always untimely. We should therefore not be afraid to dream and imagine differently. As the prison and police abolition activist Mariame Kaba suggests, the journey begins "not with the question 'What do we have now, and how can we make it better?' Instead, let's ask, 'What can we imagine for ourselves and the world?' If we do that, then boundless possibilities of a more just world await us."[22]

NOTES

Introduction

1. The Covid-19 pandemic seems to have spurred or at least enabled participation in the widespread racial justice protests of the summer of 2020, which were Black led but multiracial. This suggests that the losses of the pandemic heightened solidarity with preexisting racial losses. See Arora, "How the Coronavirus Pandemic Helped the Floyd Protests." Letetra Wideman, who is quoted in the first epigraph to this chapter, is a sibling of twenty-nine-year-old Jacob Blake, who was shot and seriously injured by police officers in Kenosha, Wisconsin. A white police officer shot Blake, who is Black, seven times in the back while three of Blake's sons were in the backseat of the car. Wideman's statement is transcribed in full in Feller, "Jacob Blake's Sister." The second epigraph is a statement of an unidentified participant in the January 6, 2021, insurrection/white riot at the US Capitol. Cited in Tavernise et al., "'Our President Wants Us Here.'"

2. A note on terminology: I have followed the recommendations of *The Chicago Manual of Style* regarding the capitalization of "Black," "Latinx," and "Indigenous" for all references to race/ethnicity (with the exception of direct quotations). In the case of Latinx, the official census category is "Hispanic or Latino," so I have retained that usage when the sources cited are referencing census categories. I am very sympathetic to La Mar Jurelle Bruce's qualms about capitalization, however. He explains: "Grammatically, the proper noun corresponds to a formal name or title assigned to an individual, closed, fixed entity. I use a lowercase *b* because I want to emphasize an *improper* blackness: a blackness that is a 'critique of the proper'; a blackness that is collectivist rather than individualistic; a blackness that is 'never closed and always under contestation'; a blackness that is ever-unfurling rather than rigidly fixed; a blackness that is neither capitalized nor propertized via the protocols of Western grammar; a blackness that centers those who are typically regarded as lesser and *lower cases*, as it were; a blackness that amplifies those who are treated as 'minor figures,' in Western modernity." Bruce, *How to Go Mad*, 6.

3. Then New York governor Andrew Cuomo repeatedly uttered this phrase during his popular pandemic briefings, even as it was later revealed that his administration underreported nursing home deaths. Weeklong absences from work due to Covid-19 were 3.5 times higher among those with 2019 household incomes under $25,000 than among those with household incomes of $100,000 or more. On the class disparities in vaccination rates and absences from work due to Covid-19 symptoms of workers or their loved ones, see Raifman, Skinner, and Sojourner, *Economic Policy Institute Working Economics Blog*. On the racial disparities in Covid-19 infection, hospitalization, and fatality rates across the United States, see the official data compiled by the Centers for Disease Control at https://www.cdc.gov/coronavirus/2019-ncov/community/health-equity/racial-ethnic-disparities/index.html. On racial disparities in vaccine access, see the analysis by the *New York Times*: https://www.nytimes.com/interactive/2021/03/05/us/vaccine-racial-disparities.html#methodology. On the gender composition of essential workers, see Robertson and Gebeloff, "How Millions of Women Became the Most Essential Workers in America."

4. A. Johnson, "In Alaska Native Villages."

5. For a compilation of Trump's racist statements over the decades, see Lopez, "Donald Trump's Long History of Racism."

6. Hajnal, *Dangerously Divided*, 6.

7. Allen, *Talking to Strangers*. While I disagree with some elements of Allen's account of democratic sacrifice, her analysis of loss as central to democratic politics has been extremely useful and influential on my own thinking.

8. Francis, "Can Black Lives Matter inside United States Democracy," 186, 188–89.

9. I leave it to others to consider how the dilemmas I identify here might apply to other varieties of racial grief. White loss, for example, is rarely unintelligible, as the different responses to the crack epidemic and the opioid crisis illustrate. One seeming exception to this pattern is the issue of gun violence, where there has been marked indifference to continuous white deaths, even of children. Historically, however, policies on gun ownership and gun control have been shaped by efforts to preserve white supremacy, which might explain why this is an acceptable instance of white loss.

10. Shilliam, *Race and the Undeserving Poor*.

11. Grieving activism by the parents of dead or disappeared children has been a prominent feature of politics in Latin America. The Mothers of the Plaza de Mayo in Argentina in the 1970s, for example, are an iconic example of motherist politics. On Black women's grieving activism in the region, see C. Smith, "Facing the Dragon." On current racist backlash across Latin America and its impact on racial justice mobilization, see Hooker, *Black and Indigenous Resistance*.

12. Butler, *Precarious Life*, 20. I share Bonnie Honig's concerns with Butler's "mortalist humanism" and the move to ground the possibility of political solidarity in shared corporeal and affective vulnerability. See Honig, *Antigone, Interrupted*.

13. Shklar, *Faces of Injustice*, 81–82. Thanks to Bonnie Honig for pointing me to Shklar's account of injustice and helping me think through how loss differs from harm.

14. The concept of affect is notoriously difficult to pin down, but it has been defined as "the name we give to those forces—visceral forces beneath, alongside, or generally *other than* conscious knowing, vital forces insisting beyond emotion—that can serve to drive us toward movement, toward thought and extension . . . that can even leave us overwhelmed by the world's apparent intractability." Gregg and Seigworth, *Affect Theory Reader*, 1. For Deborah Gould the term *affect* "indicate[s] unconscious and unnamed, but nevertheless registered, experiences of bodily energy and intensity that arise in response to stimuli impinging on the body." Emotion, meanwhile, "describe[s] what of affect—what of the potential of bodily intensities—gets actualized or concretized in the flow of living." Gould, *Moving Politics*, 19–20.

15. Douglass, *Narrative*, 24.

16. Campt, "Black Visuality and the Practice of Refusal," 80.

17. Wolfe, "Settler Colonialism and the Elimination of the Native."

18. The film is *The Neutral Ground* (2021), https://www.neutralgroundfilm.com/.

19. Allen, *Talking to Strangers*, 22, 28–29. Adorno likewise argues that the autonomy democracy promises cannot be achieved under capitalism and that this leads to susceptibility to fascism. Adorno, "Meaning of Working through the Past."

20. The United States is not unique in this regard. As Michael Hanchard argues, inequality has been central to the praxis of all existing democracies, from the Greek city-states to those considered the most advanced liberal democracies today, which have been simultaneously shaped by white supremacy and colonialism. Hanchard, *Spectre of Race*.

21. Allen, *Talking to Strangers*, 41.

22. National Partnership for Women and Families, *Black Women's Maternal Health*. Contemporary racial disparities in Black maternal and infant mortality reflect a history of medical racism in the United States that dates back to slavery. From medical experimentation on enslaved women to forced sterilization campaigns in poor communities, the vestiges of abuse continue to haunt the medical system and give rise to current racial disparities. Experimentation on enslaved women (as well as Irish immigrants) was central to the development of modern US gynecology during the nineteenth century. Physicians held Black and Irish women in disregard. They racialized them as "medical superbodies" that could be overused as experimental sexual surgery patients. Enslaved women, in particular, were seen as unable to feel pain, a common (and persistent) misconception about Black patients. See Cooper Owens, *Medical Bondage*.

23. Dumm, "Political Theory for Losers." He argues that both Emerson and Du Bois offer instructive lessons for democratic citizens about how to confront loss and develop a "political theory for losers" that does not necessarily "strive to turn losers

into winners," but rather is able to invoke loss, accept our inability to control action, and move forward. Dumm, "Political Theory for Losers," 155. For another account of the insights Emerson and Du Bois acquired in their moments of loss, see Mariotti, "On the Passing of the First-Born Son."

24. Dumm, "Political Theory for Losers," 156–57.

25. Menzel, "'Awful Gladness,'" 35.

26. Wolin, "Fugitive Democracy," 11. He distinguishes between politics and the political. In contrast to the episodic nature of the political, politics is continuous and involves contestation over resources.

27. Dumm, "Political Theory for Losers," 157, 159, emphasis added.

28. Peter Euben, "The Politics of Nostalgia and Theories of Loss," in Frank and Tambornino, *Vocations of Political Theory*, 61.

29. Sheldon Wolin, "Political Theory: From Vocation to Invocation," in Frank and Tambornino, *Vocations of Political Theory*, 3, 4.

30. Cane, *Sheldon Wolin and Democracy*, 4, 12. Notably, Wolin is at times critical of "identity politics" and argues that difference should be bracketed for the sake of broader democratic politics.

31. "Democracy grief" was used to describe the "civic sadness" of white liberals during the Trump era confronted with the fragility of what they believed was a robust US democracy. Goldberg, "Democracy Grief Is Real."

32. Wendy Brown, "Resisting Left Melancholia," in Frank and Tambornino, *Vocations of Political Theory*, 460, 463–64. The concept of "Left Melancholia" was originally formulated by Walter Benjamin. See Benjamin, "Left-Wing Melancholy."

33. Hirsch and McIvor, *Democratic Arts of Mourning*, xx.

34. McIvor, *Mourning in America*; Stow, *American Mourning*.

35. Locke, "Against Nostalgia," 55.

36. The moments when Douglass was most optimistic about the possibility of the United States becoming a true multiracial democracy, such as during Reconstruction, turned out to be opportunities missed rather than enabling celebrations of idealized radical pasts. On the different moments in his political thought, see Hooker, "'Black Sister to Massachusetts.'"

37. Moten, "Black Mo'nin'." For this reason, I do not find traditional psychoanalytic understandings of mourning and melancholia useful to conceive racialized loss. For an analysis of racial grief that centers these categories, see Cheng, *Melancholy of Race*.

38. Cornel West, "Hope and Despair: Past and Present," in Shelby and Terry, *To Shape a New World*, 325–37. Despair is generally viewed as a negative political emotion, but it can have multiple effects. It can be mobilizing or demobilizing. It can register a feeling of disappointment or disgust with the world, hopelessness because one's aims cannot be achieved, or disappointment at the limits of individual or group

action. As a reaction to loss, despair might be more appropriate than Panglossian hope or cruel optimism. If a situation seems hopeless, one reaction might be to do nothing, but another might be to try previously unimaginable tactics, be confrontational, etc. On the concept of cruel optimism, see Berlant, *Cruel Optimism*.

39. The *OED* defines grief as: "Mental pain, distress, or sorrow. In modern use in a more limited sense: deep or violent sorrow, caused by loss or trouble; a keen or bitter feeling of regret for something lost, remorse for something done, or sorrow for mishap to oneself or others." Its definition of grievance is: "A circumstance or state of things which is felt to be oppressive. In modern use, a wrong or hardship (real or supposed) which is considered a legitimate ground of complaint; something to complain of." *OED Online*, March 2021, Oxford University Press: https://www.oed.com/view/Entry/81389; https://www.oed.com/view/Entry/81399 (accessed May 13, 2021).

40. My understanding of Black witnessing is shaped by Elizabeth Alexander's work. Her account of how racial violence has fundamentally shaped collective Black identity relies centrally on the notion of witnessing. She argues that having to witness continual spectacles of anti-Black violence is both unbearable and necessary. Witnessing on her account is a practice that is traumatic for Black people, at the same time that this knowledge is also deeply necessary for individual and collective Black survival. E. Alexander, "'Can You Be BLACK and Look at This?'" I have also benefited from ongoing conversations with Damali Britton on the topic.

41. Dumm and Noëlle McAfee articulate two aspects of witnessing as a democratic activity. McAfee sees witnessing as something that those who have suffered political violence can do and offer up to other citizens via public talk (democratic deliberation that takes the form of narratives shared in the public sphere). In her view, telling stories of loss can enable transformation in listeners, but more centrally, it allows victims of political trauma to reinhabit the category of citizen. McAfee, *Democracy and the Political Unconscious*. Dumm focuses on witnessing as a form of listening that entails imperatives for action. He argues that those who seek to inherit Du Bois's insights must acknowledge the greater depth of his grief and take on "racism as our debt." Dumm, "Political Theory for Losers," 159. He frames witnessing as a responsibility of those who have not directly suffered racial loss, as something that white citizens can do for their Black fellow citizens. He never says this quite so clearly, however, since the identity of the "we" who must witness Du Bois's compounded grief is unspecified.

42. Consider the case of Darnella Frazier, the seventeen-year-old high school junior whose video of Floyd's murder in May 2020 has been called "one of the most important civil rights documents in a generation." Hernandez, "Darnella Frazier." She was awarded an honorary Pulitzer Prize for her undoubtedly heroic actions. Yet Frazier was a traumatized child whose loss is ongoing. During her testimony in the

Chauvin trial, which forced her to relive Floyd's murder, Frazier said that when she looked at Floyd, she saw her father, her brothers, her cousins, her uncles and thought about how it could have been one of them. A year later, in July 2021, Frazier's uncle Leneal, an innocent bystander, was in fact also killed by the Minneapolis Police Department during a high-speed chase. How much must one person witness?

43. Jenna Wortham and Wesley Morris of the *New York Times* suggest that the witnesses who tried to prevent Floyd's murder, and the collective work they did to record the event and later testify during the trial of his killer, could be read as creating a kind of community out of strangers that served a function akin to that of the Greek chorus in ancient theater. Jenna Wortham and Wesley Morris, "The People in the Neighborhood," *Still Processing*, podcast audio, May 13, 2021, https://www.nytimes.com/2021/05/13/podcasts/still-processing-derek-chauvin-trial-witnesses.html.

44. I use the term "white democracy" to draw attention to the fact that racism remains a central organizing feature of what are commonly viewed as the most advanced contemporary liberal democracies, including Britain, France, and the United States, such that none of them are full multiracial democracies in practice.

45. I take up the question of why this kind of solidarity of strangers is necessary for democracy at length in Hooker, *Race and the Politics of Solidarity*. My understanding of racial justice follows the accounts of Charles Mills and Shatema Threadcraft, to encompass both civic and intimate justice. See Mills, *Black Rights/White Wrongs*; Threadcraft, *Intimate Justice*.

46. Clinical understandings of anticipatory grief refer to grief that occurs prior to death or another great loss such as the loss of a partner, a change in familial roles, severe financial hardship, etc. Hirsch uses the notion of "anticipatory mourning" to describe the meeting between Priam and Achilles in Homer's *Iliad* to negotiate the release of Hector's body where Priam appeals not to Achilles's grief over the loss of Patroclus but to Achilles's father's potential grief had his body been desecrated, or his own grief had his son's body been defiled. Rather than a moment of shared mourning, "Priam [is] calling on Achilleus to envisage a potential mourning, an imaginable mourning, a mourning that could have been, or could still be, but is not yet." Hirsch, "Hope, without Guarantees." Anticipatory loss similarly scrambles the temporality of loss by making future (imagined) losses a problem of the present. White grievance orients white citizens to imagine and grieve now for something that is yet to be. It positions multiracial democracy as a loss from which they have nothing to gain.

47. My point here is not that the country remains unchanged, but rather that present conditions are not ones where whites as a group have been displaced from the apex of the US racial hierarchy. It is striking, however, that 40 percent of respondents in a recent Pew Research Center survey believe white people face some discrimination, and 14 percent that they face a lot of it. The results are driven by the

views of white respondents, who were far more likely to say that whites face discrimination, particularly white Republicans, who were 24 percent more likely than white Democrats to agree. Daniller, "Majorities of Americans."

48. Attitudes toward gun rights illustrate indifference to Black death, as exposure to Black gun deaths either fails to move white public opinion in support of gun control, or leads to greater support for gun rights. Because access to firearms is implicitly associated with white rights, it is only when presented with white gun deaths that white public opinion shifts in favor of gun control. H. Walker, Collingwood, and Bunyasi, "White Response to Black Death." This is consistent with public opinion research on other topics that shows that policies that disproportionately affect nonwhites received less support from white respondents.

49. Marjorie Taylor Greene et al., "No matter what @GOPLeader does it would never be enough for the hate America Democrats," *Twitter*, February 3, 2021, https://twitter.com/mtgreenee/status/1356949229483220992?s=21. Many white women subscribe to white grievance. On white women's political attitudes, see Junn, "Trump Majority."

50. Research on the Black Lives Matter uprisings has found that they were overwhelmingly peaceful, and when there was violence, it was most often directed *at* racial justice protesters by police or counterprotesters. Chenoweth and Pressman, "This Summer's Black Lives Matter Protesters."

51. The violent, militarized response to racial justice protests occurred in both Republican- and Democratic-controlled cities, from Ferguson (Missouri) in 2014 to Portland, New York City, and Washington, DC, in 2020.

52. Sophia Jordán Wallace and Chris Zepeda-Millán find that whites who feel culturally threatened by Latinxs, harbor racial resentment, and fear that the United States will become a majority-minority country are more likely to support harsh immigration policies such as family separation and child detention. Wallace and Zepeda-Millán, *Walls, Cages, and Family Separation*.

53. Empirical analyses by political scientists have clearly established that rather than being driven solely by the resentments of an economically precarious and forgotten white working class left behind by neoliberalism and globalization, it was Trump's hostile racist, sexist, anti-immigrant, and white nationalist rhetoric that resonated most with his supporters. See Hooghe and Dassonneville, "Explaining the Trump Vote"; Mutz, "Status Threat, Not Economic Hardship"; Schaffner, MacWilliams, and Nteta, "Understanding White Polarization in the 2016 Vote." For a critique of analyses of contemporary white grievance framed solely in terms of race or class, see Hooker, "How Can the Democratic Party Confront Racist Backlash?"

54. Pape and Ruby, "Capitol Rioters Aren't Like Other Extremists."

55. The term "Big Lie" was coined by Adolf Hitler to describe a propaganda technique for political purposes that was a colossal distortion of the facts (he argued that

it was used by Jews against Germany). Today, the term is used as a shorthand for the claim by Trump and sectors of the GOP that his loss in the 2020 election was the result of widespread fraud. Today's Big Lie could be used to turn a short-term loss into a long-term victory, as Jeffrey Tulis and Nicole Mellow argue that successful "losers" did in three previous "*anti*moments" (the antitheses of supposedly successful constitutional moments) in US political development. Tulis and Mellow, *Legacies of Losing in American Politics.*

56. Perhaps the most notable historical example of reparations for white loss is the fact that white slave owners received compensation after emancipation, while enslaved people were not compensated for their unpaid labor and the myriad other ways in which they suffered terror, exploitation, and dispossession. Compensated emancipation policies were enacted by the British Empire, France, Denmark, the Netherlands, most Latin American countries, and in the United States within the District of Columbia.

57. Anthony Pinn argues that the notion of redemptive suffering has been a major theme in Black Christian theology, with problematic political consequences because "they counteract efforts at liberation by finding something of value in Black suffering." Pinn, *Why, Lord?*, 17.

58. While she does not use it to discuss the workings of racism, I borrow the concept from Berlant, "Slow Death."

59. Honig, *Antigone, Interrupted.*

60. Refusal has become a central category in a variety of fields, including Black studies, Indigenous political thought, feminist theory, queer theory, anarchist political thought, etc. My understanding of refusal is derived from the work of Black feminists who theorize Black women's everyday practices of intimacy and sabotage as an archive of Black radicalism that can expand our understanding of Black politics. See, for example, Haley, *No Mercy*; Hartman, *Wayward Lives.*

61. Because of the reality of *Herrenvolk* democracy, Black thinkers have had a contested relationship to democracy. Affirmations of multiracial democracy have coexisted (and been in tension with) conceptions of Black freedom that focus on the creation of autonomous spaces, which I describe as traditions of fugitive democracy and Black fugitivity, respectively, in Hooker, *Theorizing Race in the Americas.* Black socialists in particular have advocated for more radical conceptions of democracy; see K.-Y. Taylor, *From #Blacklivesmatter to Black Liberation.*

Chapter One: White Grievance and Anticipatory Loss

1. Tracy, "Private Jet of Rich Trumpers."

2. According to statistics cited by *Vanity Fair* the poverty rate of Blacks (26.1 percent) and Hispanics/Latinxs (29.2 percent) in Memphis was more than

twice that of whites (9.3 percent). Similar racial disparities exist with regard to income, with the median non-Hispanic white Memphis household earning twice as much ($69,395) as the median Black ($35,668) and Hispanic/Latinx household ($38,864). Ibid.

3. Ibid.

4. Tracy, "New Photo Suggests Private-Jet Trumpers."

5. One could object that Republican party officials are simply trying to win elections, and the racist impact of these laws is simply a by-product of the different racial composition of the Democratic and Republican electorates. But this simply proves the point that the effect of a majority-white party seeking to suppress votes for a party whose voter coalition is multiracial will be to disproportionately suppress the votes of nonwhites. Moreover, many of these bills explicitly contain provisions making voting easier in white areas and more difficult in precincts with a large percentage of minority voters.

6. I use the terms "white refusal" and "white grievance" interchangeably throughout the chapter because I see white grievance as a form of white refusal.

7. See US Holocaust Memorial Museum, https://encyclopedia.ushmm.org/content/en/article/lebensraum.

8. Varela, "Trump's Anti-immigrant 'Invasion' Rhetoric."

9. For example, in 1969 the National Commission on the Causes and Prevention of Violence identified Black protest as threatening to US democracy: "With the ink still drying on the decade's landmark civil rights legislation, and the roar of the putatively illegal protests that catalyzed those laws still reverberating in their ears, the Commission reached the conclusion that disobedience 'is disastrous from the standpoint of the maintenance of a democratic society': *no matter how conscientious or nonviolent, the violation of law by protestors inevitably chips away at the foundations of a lawful democratic order* and encourages 'a climate of lawlessness' and violence." Pineda, *Seeing Like an Activist*, 25, emphasis added.

10. King, *Where Do We Go from Here*, 5–6, 8–9.

11. Ibid., 11–12.

12. There is evidence, for example, that younger white voters display lower levels of traditional measures of racism, such as racial resentment, but are more hostile to policies aimed at producing racial equity. "Younger whites, those who are part of the Millennial generation, may appear to have lower levels of racial prejudice, but these attitudes are more strongly linked to old-fashioned racial stereotypes than for older whites. In this sense, less is more; while the average level of racial resentment is lower among Millennials, racial resentment has a more virulent effect for this group in comparison to their predecessors. Racially resentful Millennials rely on old-fashioned stereotypes, adopt notions of 'reverse discrimination,' and are much less like likely to support policies that aim to produce greater racial equity than older,

prejudiced whites." DeSante and Smith, "Less Is More," 967. For similar reasons, the so-called browning of the United States also cannot be counted on as a panacea, because we should not assume that all nonwhites support racial egalitarianism (or share the same view of what this entails). Some may even participate in white grievance. Cristina Beltrán, for example, argues that we need to think in terms of a notion of "multiracial whiteness" that promises nonwhite voters the ability to also participate in a "politics of aggression, exclusion and domination." Whiteness, in her view, should be thought of not as a racial identity, but rather "a discriminatory worldview in which feelings of freedom and belonging are produced through the persecution and dehumanization of others." Beltrán, "To Understand Trump's Support."

13. For example, Deva Woodly argues that one of the ways that the Movement for Black Lives has "reshaped the political terrain" in the United States is by spurring changes in white political attitudes. For the first time in 2015 a majority of white Democrats agreed that racism was a major problem, while in 2020 a majority of white respondents agreed that Black people are treated unfairly by the police and judicial system. Woodly, *Reckoning*, 165, 167.

14. King, *Where Do We Go from Here*, 11.

15. The January 6 insurrectionists, for example, were galvanized by the antiracist protests of 2020: "In terms of what was motivating people on the ground, their willingness to be violent, their willingness to treat the moment as an existential threat—surely what happened in 2020 was an input. . . . The 2020 uprisings after George Floyd's murder have shaped their consciousness in a way that cannot be overstated. . . . For them those protests . . . felt like a real turning point, which contributes to this pervasive sense on the right that we're at the point of no return." Illing, "January 6 Should've Moderated the GOP."

16. On the history of ideas about whiteness, see Painter, *History of White People*.

17. Olson, *Abolition of White Democracy*, xix. In contrast to Olson's view that whiteness needs to be abolished, others argue that whiteness is a kind of social identity that can be transformed into a nonracist one. See Alcoff, *Future of Whiteness*. I do not take up this debate in this chapter.

18. The notion of citizens "giving things up for others" is from Danielle Allen's account of democratic sacrifice. Allen, *Talking to Strangers, 29*.

19. King, *Where Do We Go from Here*, 100–101.

20. See Hooker, "How Can the Democratic Party Confront Racist Backlash?"; Cohen, *Democracy Remixed*.

21. J. Harris and Appelbaum, "Blue States, You're the Problem."

22. The United States is not alone in experiencing resurgent racist backlash; similar trends are also shaping politics elsewhere in the Americas and Europe. On the racialized (re)construction of a forgotten "white working class" pervading contemporary anti-immigrant discourses in Britain, see Shilliam, *Race and the*

Undeserving Poor. On racist reaction to rights won by Black and Indigenous Latin Americans during an era of multicultural citizenship reforms, see Hooker, *Black and Indigenous Resistance*.

23. In the discipline of political science, for example, with the exception of scholars of race, ethnicity, and politics, the subfield of American politics has generally overlooked the fragility of US democracy, and approached ethnic and racial politics as peripheral to American politics, relevant only to work on ethnoracial minorities. Eckhouse, "White Riot." Notable exceptions include Abrajano and Hajnal, *White Backlash*; Hajnal, *Dangerously Divided*.

24. Anderson, *White Rage*, 3.

25. Papenfuss, "Ron Johnson Says He Would Have Been 'Concerned.'"

26. In the case of Indigenous peoples, disenfranchisement is infinitely more complex, as they are denied the ability to fully participate in a polity that was forced on them. For a historical overview of the challenges and barriers to Native American voting rights in the United States, see Wolfley, "Jim Crow, Indian Style."

27. My understanding of political imagination is similar to Woodly's: "imagination is the faculty or action of forming new ideas, or images or concepts of external objects not present to the senses. . . . Imagination is a normal political faculty, its opening is useful for political change and its closure is useful for the maintenance of status quo relations of power and privilege." Woodly, *Reckoning*, 52. See also Frank, *Publius and Political Imagination*.

28. Indeed, gains by nonwhites are experienced as losses because historically whites have been able to gain both materially and socially (in standing) from inflicting losses on other groups. In addition to the pleasures of domination, they obtained direct material gains from nonwhite expropriation and dispossession, as in the case of settlers on Indigenous lands or white race riots that also became occasions for looting. Ida B. Wells, for example, painstakingly documented the material losses of Black victims whose hard-earned possessions were appropriated by white rioters during early twentieth-century race riots/white massacres.

29. Rankine, *Citizen*, 135.

30. I refer to Black gains specifically here, but the argument applies to those of nonwhites in general. During the Trump presidency, for example, racial animus was also directed at Muslims and, in particular, Latinx immigrants, who were routinely depicted as poised to overrun the country and displace its white majority.

31. I follow Shannon Sullivan in using the term "white priority" rather than "white privilege" to acknowledge that white people can still accrue racial advantages from whiteness even if they are not spared financial hardship. She argues that white priority allows poorer white persons to "[feel] that s/he/they has more value than a black person even if some of black people have managed to work their way into the middle class (or the White House) and have more money or political power than the white

person does. White people come before them in terms of who matters in the great chain of being." Sullivan, "White Priority," 178. White persons who are not financially well-off and do not see themselves as privileged also enjoy other unjust advantages, such as not having to worry about being killed by the police when pulled over for a routine traffic violation or having their credentials and academic achievements questioned in professional settings. By white dominance I mean that despite demographic changes and the existence of poor and working-class white people, it remains the case that whites as a group are still economically, politically, and socially dominant in the United States.

32. Aristotle's classic formulation of political rule is rule among free equals. In book 3 of the *Politics,* he writes: "the good citizen must possess the knowledge and the capacity necessary for ruling as well as for being ruled, and the excellence of a citizen may be defined as consisting in 'a knowledge of rule over free men from both points of view' [i.e., that of the ruler as well as that of the ruled]." Aristotle, *Politics,* 105 (1277b15).

33. Allen, *Talking to Strangers,* 45.

34. Ibid., 41.

35. The term "*Herrenvolk* democracy" was originally coined by Pierre van den Berghe to refer to a political order that is "democratic for the master race but tyrannical for subordinate groups." In other words, these are political systems in which the equality enjoyed by members of the dominant racial group is dependent on the inequality between them and subordinate groups; it is not in contradiction with it. Van Den Berghe, *Race and Racism,* 18.

36. Allen, *Talking to Strangers,* 45.

37. Anne Norton has argued that Trumpism represents a desire for submission on the part of his followers: "What is most disturbing about Trump is . . . the avidity with which his followers seek to be ruled. They too have lived undemocratic lives. Perhaps they have come to value their slight ascendancies so much that they accept their larger subjection. Perhaps they have come to love their abjection." Norton, "King's New Body," 120.

38. Aristotle, *Politics,* 181 (1295b5–7). Thanks to Jill Frank for suggesting that I develop the discussion of social class and mastery in Aristotle.

39. Olson, *Abolition of White Democracy,* xx–xxi, emphasis added.

40. Ibid., 61–63.

41. Mills, "White Ignorance," 20.

42. Ibid., 21.

43. Manne, "Melancholy Whiteness," 238, emphasis in original.

44. As Manne observes, the investment in preserving a sense of moral innocence fuels "the desire, in part, of the historically privileged for barriers to mutual visibility—e.g., walls, screens, jail cells . . . —to interpose between themselves and

those with whom they have a shameful history. Such barriers both prevent the ethical impingement of the other, and also the loss of esteem in the eyes of moral authorities who side with the marginalized against the hitherto privileged." Ibid., 237. These barriers are not only physical; the current outcry against teaching critical race theory in schools, for example, is about preserving and passing on white innocence to future generations.

45. Ioanide, *Emotional Politics of Racism*, 1, 6. In a similar vein, Ashleigh Campi argues that conservative media has cultivated a desire for—and thereby manufactured consent for—punitive or authoritarian forms of rule in its viewers via gendered and racialized narratives of dominance and submission. Campi, "Cultivating Authoritarian Submission."

46. White vigilantes such as Kyle Rittenhouse in Kenosha, Wisconsin, who take it upon themselves to punish racial justice protesters in the name of protecting white property, or those who injure protesters with their vehicles, move from vicarious to direct participation in the pleasures of violent racial domination.

47. White nostalgia is also evident in the realm of cultural politics. According to Geoff Mann, for example, in the United States the genre of country music calls white people to whiteness through a process of "musical interpellation" in which nostalgic narratives that construct a historically innocent and besieged white subject play a key role. The genre's growing appeal to suburban and middle-class white listeners beyond its core western and southern working-class audience rests on a nostalgic construction of "naive victimhood" that is crucial to contemporary whiteness, he argues. Country music gives voice to "the perception of besieged-ness that organizes and shapes the performance of white conservatism in post–World War II American cultural politics." Mann, "Why Does Country Music Sound White?," 87, 89–90.

48. Maly, Dalmage, and Michaels, "End of an Idyllic World," 758, 764–65.

49. Du Bois, *Dusk of Dawn*, 671.

50. Du Bois, "The White World," in ibid., 673.

51. Du Bois, "White World," 679.

52. For an empirical analysis of contemporary white identity politics, see Jardina, *White Identity Politics*. As Du Bois's writing on the subject illustrates, however, recognition of and investment in white identity is not a new phenomenon.

53. Descriptive representation is not in and of itself a measure of political equality, but the lopsided composition of US elected officials as a group, especially at the highest levels, illustrates continued white preponderance. The representation of nonwhites and women in the US political establishment, for example, still lags far behind their proportions of the population, especially in the Republican Party. Moreover, given the minoritarian features of the US system that favor rural, mostly white geographic areas, greater numerical representation of racial minorities has not led to

meaningful power sharing, particularly at the national level. On the idea of representation, see Pitkin, *Concept of Representation*.

54. Hajnal, *Dangerously Divided*, 6.

55. Allen, *Talking to Strangers*, 22. She is clear about the complex role of imagination in democratic citizenship.

56. In 2008 there was "scant evidence of a decline in the racial divide. Blacks and Whites remain as far apart on racial policy matters in 2008 as in 1988. . . . Younger cohorts of Whites are no more racially liberal in 2008 than they were in 1988." See Hutchings, "Change or More of the Same?," 917. In fact, there was a resurgence in old-fashioned racist attitudes during Obama's presidency. Tesler, "Return of Old-Fashioned Racism."

57. Gilman, "Collapse of Racial Liberalism."

58. Browne and Carrington, "Obamas and the New Politics of Race," 117.

59. The notion of cancel culture panics refers to the grievances generated when public figures are critiqued for making racist, sexist, homophobic, transphobic comments and so forth. In most of these cases, so-called cancellation does not equal loss of employment or banishment from the public sphere. But the sense of being victimized is generated by the view that they should be able to make such claims without facing criticism or opprobrium.

60. Douglass, "Reminiscences of the Anti-slavery Conflict."

61. For example, the manifesto of the 2019 El Paso shooter described his killing of twenty-three mostly Latinx shoppers at a local Walmart as a last-ditch attempt to prevent white cultural and ethnic replacement due to an invasion of the United States by migrants. Varela, "Trump's Anti-immigrant 'Invasion' Rhetoric."

62. The rise of the modern carceral state is key to understanding the contemporary links between race, criminalization, and violent policing. See M. Alexander, *New Jim Crow*. As the US Department of Justice's 2015 report on Ferguson documented, there is also a clear link between neoliberal economic policies that lead to the use of police and court fees as sources of municipal revenue and the overpolicing of poor Black communities.

63. The Movement for Black Lives (M4BL) is a broad and diverse coalition of more than fifty organizations struggling for racial justice and Black freedom. It includes the chapter-based Black Lives Matter organization, but should not be equated with it. For the M4BL's policy platform and demands, see *"Vision for Black Lives,"* Movement for Black Lives, 2020, https://m4bl.org/policy-platforms/.

64. On the political philosophy, strategies, and impact of the M4BL, see Woodly, *Reckoning*; Mullings, "Neoliberal Racism and the Movement for Black Lives."

65. Long-standing socioeconomic gaps between white and Black/Latinx households in the United States persist. Black and Latinx households still have the lowest median income in the United States as well as higher unemployment rates,

and the gap between white and Black/Latinx income has increased since the 1960s. See Woodruff, "Income Gap between Blacks and Whites." Disparities in health and education also persist at all levels. To take but one example, Black children are more harshly and disproportionately punished in comparison to white children (via school suspensions, expulsions, etc.), creating a school-to-prison pipeline that disproportionately affects their life chances. According to the Department of Education, in 2011–12, across the United States, Black boys were suspended three times as often as white boys, and Black girls were suspended six times as often as white girls. Crenshaw, Ocen, and Nanda, *Black Girls Matter*.

66. According to data from the American National Election Study, 2016 Trump supporters were mostly affluent Republicans measured by household income, and even less educated Trump voters (those without college degrees) were relatively affluent, as nearly 60 percent of these voters were in the top half of the income distribution. Carnes and Lupu, "It's Time to Bust the Myth." Indeed, majorities of white voters at all income levels voted for Trump, while 53 percent of voters in households making less than $50,000 voted for Clinton. Clinton voters also tended to be much more economically distressed than Trump voters. Bump, "Clinton Voters Express More Economic Distress."

67. See Hooghe and Dassonneville, "Explaining the Trump Vote"; Mutz, "Status Threat, Not Economic Hardship"; Schaffner, MacWilliams, and Nteta, "Understanding White Polarization in the 2016 Vote."

68. Irwin and Katz, "Geography of Trumpism." Many of the indicted Capitol insurrectionists live in red areas within blue states, and the counties that were most likely to produce insurrectionists were those with the most significant declines in the non-Hispanic white population. Feuer, "Fears of White People."

69. This is true historically as well. An analysis of the exodus of southern whites from the Democratic Party following integration showed that racial attitudes played a much larger role and almost none for income growth or (non-race-related) policy preferences in explaining the partisan affiliation of white voters in the South from 1958 to 1980. The reaction of racially conservative white voters to the Democratic Party's belated support for civil rights explains virtually all the party's losses in the South. Kuziemko and Washington, "Why Did the Democrats Lose the South?"

70. Poor and working-class white communities are being affected by difficult social problems, such as unemployment and surges in drug and alcohol addiction, all of which have contributed to an increase in white mortality rates. Case and Deaton, "Rising Morbidity and Mortality." The impact of global economic trends, such as the loss of manufacturing jobs in the United States, has also been accompanied by social dislocations that have affected family structures. Economic changes that favored women's ability to gain jobs in the new economy have altered traditional gender roles and challenged traditional conceptions of masculinity. See Rosin, "End of

Men." The alarm produced by these trends has led to warnings about a crisis of white working-class values reminiscent of explanations of Black poverty rooted in Black pathology.

71. While all households suffered wealth losses during the 2008 recession, Black and Latinx households suffered larger losses and benefited less from the recovery, resulting in widening wealth inequality along racial and ethnic lines. See Kochhar and Fry, "Wealth Inequality Has Widened." The Covid-19 pandemic has had similarly disparate effects. According to the US Census Bureau non-Hispanic Black adults had higher rates of economic and mental health hardship than non-Hispanic white adults across several measures including housing, debt, food insufficiency, and mental health. Monte and Perez-Lopez, *Covid-19 Pandemic.*

72. Von Redecker, "Ownership's Shadow," 38–39. Thanks to Jan-Werner Mueller for bringing this article to my attention.

73. Ibid., 33, 35.

74. Ibid., 47, 49, 53. She identifies three strategies to defend phantom possession—institutionalization, self-defense, and restoration—that correspond to different strains of contemporary authoritarian mobilization.

75. For example, the "manosphere"—social media sites where individuals gather to mourn the loss of male power and enact aggrieved masculinity—has been central to the growth of contemporary white nationalism. "White nationalists use online venues to racialize homophobia and anti-feminism, affirming a normative white masculinity. They articulate a view of white racialization as both privileged and under attack; in this view, gender and sexuality are central to ideas about biological and cultural superiority. This provides a potent mix for both expanding the movement and inspiring outbursts of violence." Bjork-James, "Racializing Misogyny," 177.

76. These disaffected white voters believe that "minorities commit crimes with impunity, that illegal immigrants get benefits at higher rates than Americans, that gays and Muslims are afforded special status by the government," and they "lament that Confederate symbols, and the people whose heritage they represent, are sidelined while diversity is celebrated." Ball, "Resentment Powering Trump."

77. Freedom for All Americans, a bipartisan campaign to secure full nondiscrimination protections for LGBTQ+ people nationwide, created a tracker for all 2022 legislation related to LGBTQ+ discrimination; see "Legislative Tracker," Freedom for All Americans, last accessed October 6, 2022, https://freedomforallamericans.org/legislative-tracker/.

78. Manne, *Down Girl*, 282–83.

79. Honig, *Shell-Shocked*, 8, 12.

80. The centrality of participating in acts of domination to a politics of white grievance is illustrated by the spike in both hate speech and hate crimes during

Trump's presidency. See Feinberg, Branton, and Martinez-Ebers, "Counties That Hosted a 2016 Trump Rally."

81. Butler, "Endangered/Endangering," 16.

82. Cited in Marcus, "Pat Robertson."

83. For example, Tucker Carlson, the Fox network host who has been described as "the voice of white grievance," grew up in a very affluent household and credited his radicalization to an overly emotional first-grade teacher who was too concerned about social justice. Kranish, "How Tucker Carlson Became the Voice of White Grievance."

84. The addition of Tubman to the roster of those featured on US currency was part of a broader redesign meant to better reflect the country's gender and racial diversity. Besides Tubman, Sojourner Truth, Susan B. Anthony, Elizabeth Cady Stanton, Lucrecia Mott, Alice Paul, Marian Anderson, and Martin Luther King Jr. were also selected to join the existing lineup of white male founders and ex-presidents. Even after these additions, however, white males will still significantly outnumber women and racial minorities on US currency.

85. "For those who want to rescript the nation's past, American history is too male and too white. To correct that imbalance, heroes, symbols, and legends must conform to strict rubrics of race, class, and gender." In this apocalyptic vision, symbolic white loss is the Trojan horse for violent white subordination: "A regime whose creation stories and legends turn on 'enslavers' and 'invaders,' however, cannot long survive. Ritual shaming is not a nation builder. Sooner or later bold paladins will feel it's their duty to even the score with their oppressors, or failing that, their privileged descendants." Sewall, "Debasing of Our Civic Currency."

86. White backlash against symbolic loss can turn into material loss. For example, in a study of the impact of the politics of racial resentment on public health, Jonathan Metzl has shown that right-wing policies fueled by white backlash had negative effects on the health of the very white voters who supported them, making life sicker, harder, and shorter for them as well as others. White life expectancies fell, gun suicides soared, and school dropout rates rose after the implementation of the Affordable Care Act was blocked in Tennessee, the repeal of gun control laws in Missouri, and massive cuts to school and social service spending in Kansas. Metzl, *Dying of Whiteness*.

87. Garza, "Herstory of the #Blacklivesmatter Movement."

88. For an account of the important achievements to date of the broad Movement for Black Lives (as opposed to specific organizations such as the Black Lives Matter Global Network) and its role in transforming public opinion and policy, see Woodly, *Reckoning*.

89. Louisiana passed legislation in May 2016 making it a hate crime to target police officers or firefighters.

90. "US Protest Law Tracker," International Center for Not-for-Profit Law, last accessed October 6, 2022, https://www.icnl.org/usprotestlawtracker/. This site tracks legal initiatives since January 2017 that restrict the right to peaceful assembly. It defines such laws (or proposed bills) as those that include provisions that "constrain or narrow the means, methods, or venues used by individuals seeking to participate in or facilitate a peaceful protest." During this time period, 246 such bills have been considered in forty-five states, of which thirty-nine have been enacted and thirteen are pending. HB 1/SB 484, passed in Florida in 2021, "enlarges the legal definition of 'riot,' a 3rd degree felony, to include any group of three or more individuals whose shared intent to engage in disorderly and violent conduct results in 'imminent danger' of property damage or personal injury, or actual damage or injury. Notably, the new definition does not require that the individuals' conduct be disorderly or violent, or that they commit any actual damage or injury. Under the new law, a 'riot' consisting of 25 or more people, or one that 'endangers the safe movement of a vehicle,' is automatically an 'aggravated riot,' a new 2nd degree felony offense under the law." As a result, participants in large protests or protesters who block traffic (even temporarily), could face penalties of up to fifteen years in prison. "US Protest Tracker," International Center for Not-for-Profit Law, last accessed October 6, 2022, https://www.icnl.org/usprotestlawtracker/?location=12&status=&issue=&date=&type=.

91. For two recent normative defenses of rioting as a legitimate form of political activity in certain conditions, see Havercroft, "Why Is There No Just Riot Theory?"; Pasternak, "Political Rioting."

92. The two most sustained eras of confederate monument building were 1900 through the 1920s, when states were codifying Jim Crow laws reestablishing racial segregation and disenfranchising African Americans and the Ku Klux Klan was resurgent; and the 1950s and 1960s, as segregationists fought the civil rights movement. Confederate commemoration thus encompasses a set of rituals and objects that celebrated and cemented white rule in the South, where most confederate monuments were built. See Southern Poverty Law Center, *Whose Heritage?*

93. Tucker and Holley, "Dylann Roof's Eerie Tour of American Slavery."

94. Tuttle, "The 'Blood-Stained Banner' in Charleston," emphasis in original.

95. As of July 2021, a slim majority of all voters favor keeping confederate statues (51 percent), while a minority favor removal (30 percent). An overwhelming majority of Republican voters are against removal (83 percent), while a slim majority of Democrats are in favor (54 percent). Easley, "American Electorate Continues to Favor."

96. Moreover, the removal of the flag also fueled white grievance as "the strong backlash against the removal contributed to early support for Donald Trump's presidential campaign [in 2016]." Heather Pool, "Removing the Confederate Flag in South

Carolina in the Wake of Charleston," in Hirsch and McIvor, *Democratic Arts of Mourning*, 42.

97. The racist monuments removed in the United States also include some honoring individuals responsible for the genocide of Indigenous peoples in the Americas, such as Christopher Columbus. See "Removal of Confederate Monuments and Memorials," Wikipedia, last accessed October 6, 2022, https://en.wikipedia.org/wiki/Removal_of_Confederate_monuments_and_memorials. Racist monuments have also been removed globally. In the United Kingdom, for example, monuments were removed, and places renamed, that previously honored figures involved in the transatlantic slave trade, British colonialism, and eugenics. In Belgium, monuments to King Leopold II (who presided over massacres in the Congo) were defaced and toppled by protesters.

98. For antiprotest legislation proposed or enacted in Florida see the page on the state at "US Protest Tracker," International Center for Not-for-Profit Law, last accessed October 6, 2022, https://www.icnl.org/usprotestlawtracker/?location=12&status=&issue=&date=&type=.

99. Vozzella and Bethea, "'White Lives Matter' Painted on Arthur Ashe Monument."

100. J.T., "'I Lose Too,'" 2. I thank Jovonna Jones for alerting me to the existence of the letter and kindly sharing a copy.

101. Bell, "*Brown v. Board of Education* and the Interest Convergence Dilemma."

102. Indeed, we see this in legal rulings preventing the Biden administration from implementing racial equity provisions such as a loan forgiveness program for Black and minority farmers after decades of racial discrimination by the Department of Agriculture, and preferential access to business loans for minority-owned restaurants through the American Rescue Plan because the programs were supposedly discriminatory against whites. Shear, Cowley, and Rappeport, "Biden's Push for Equity in Government."

103. Douglass, "Why Is the Negro Lynched?," 492–93.

104. Ibid., 505.

105. Ibid., 506.

106. Ibid., 508.

107. I find psychoanalytic accounts that claim to grapple with the deeper affective motivations driving white grievance unhelpful because they tend to resort to therapeutic models that set aside racial power disparities. Kate Manne points to similar qualms at the end of her thoughtful analysis of how Sartre sought to reach white readers in his preface to Frantz Fanon's *Black Skins/White Masks*: "Sartre stages a performance which allows his ilk to reconceptualise themselves as somewhat heroic figures in a melodrama in which they star. They are not being stripped of something they're clutching; they're proudly choosing to relinquish their illicit sense of

unalloyed pride in their legacy. If I am right, then the effect (best case scenario) would be to transform their melancholic refusal to lose face—i.e., to grow shame-faced in the eyes of the historical other—into a subject whose very identity encompasses nobly facing such loss of innocence and reputation when a Fanon calls on them to do so. . . . This is a tale of facing one's shame . . . and being redeemed in the process. *But in the end, are we? By whose authority would we say so?*" Manne, "Melancholy Whiteness," 241, emphasis added.

108. Douglass, "Why Is the Negro Lynched?," 518.

109. Ibid., 520.

Chapter Two: Black Protest and Democratic Sacrifice

1. My analysis in this chapter draws primarily on Black activism in the United States. And while it certainly shouldn't be assumed that these patterns are replicated elsewhere, there has been a global wave of Black protest in recent years—from uprisings against police violence in the United States, the United Kingdom, Brazil, France, Canada, and Israel, to student protests in South Africa. Barnor Hesse and I have argued that these disparate Black protest movements originate from local concerns, but they "are responding in different ways to the inability of liberal democracy to deliver robust racial justice and inviolable equal rights, drawing attention to the unfinished project of decolonization and the unrelenting dehumanization of Black lives resulting from the precarity induced by global white supremacy (however much the latter may have morphed)." Hesse and Hooker, "Introduction: On Black Political Thought," 448.

2. The first version of the conference paper that became the article from which this chapter is drawn was written in early 2015, and the list of names of Black persons killed by police officers had to continually be updated throughout the publication process, as killings continued unabated. As I write this in 2022, there are so many names that would need to be added to the list, including those of Philando Castile, Breonna Taylor, George Floyd, Adam Toledo, and Ma'khia Bryant, to name only some of those whose cases have received the most national media attention. I chose to keep the list of names here as they first appeared in print in 2017 as a reminder that this is an ongoing disaster that is unceasing. Indeed, between January 1 and April 18, 2021—the day before closing arguments in the trial of Derek Chauvin for the killing of George Floyd—there were only three days when the police did *not* kill someone in the United States, according to data compiled by Mapping Police Violence, a nonprofit organization and independent research collaborative collecting data to quantify the impact of police violence. See "2021 Police Violence Report," Mapping Police Violence, last accessed October 16, 2021, https://mappingpoliceviolence.us/.

3. Many non-Black citizens have mobilized in support of the Black Lives Matter (BLM) protests, and the massive racial justice protests in 2020 in particular were Black led but multiracial. Yet BLM protests have also faced significant backlash, exemplified by the rejoinder that "all lives matter," and more dangerously, by the introduction of "Blue Lives Matter" bills that would make it a hate crime to target police officers, and the passage of legislation punishing protest participation and granting immunity to those who injure protesters. The backlash against racial justice protests has come mainly from those who reject both the aims of the protesters and their tactics, hence the fact that even the most peaceful protests (such as professional athletes kneeling while the national anthem is played) have also been condemned. More broadly, since reaching a high point in the summer of 2020, support for BLM has waned in the United States, in large part owing to a plunge in white and Republican support. Chudy and Jefferson, "Support for Black Lives Matter Surged Last Year."

4. By racialized solidarity, I mean "the diametrically opposed ethical-historical perspectives developed by [the members of] dominant (white) and subordinated (non-white) groups in a racialized polity." Hooker, *Race and the Politics of Solidarity*, 88.

5. Rogers, "Introduction: Disposable Lives." Disproportionate and consistent Black loss in US democracy is also the case in terms of political representation. According to Zoltan Hajnal, across a range of US elections, racial and ethnic minorities lose more regularly than other voters, and Black voters are the most likely to lose. Hajnal, "Who Loses in American Democracy?"

6. Working within a Rawlsian framework, for example, Tommie Shelby has argued that poor Black people who reside in "dark ghettos" do not have the same political obligations as other citizens as a result of the pervasive and systemic institutional injustice they face. See Shelby, *Dark Ghettos*.

7. The designation of a protest as a riot is itself racialized and serves to delegitimize the demands of Black protesters, not only in the United States, but globally. For example, Raven Rakia observes that citizen uprisings in Sudan were described as "riots" while those occurring at the same time in Egypt, Turkey, Brazil, Greece, and Spain were lauded as prodemocracy protests: "The decision to call one riots and the other protests has nothing to do with the amount of violence in the demonstrations. Violence is a realistic factor, and sometimes, a tactic, in all of these protests. Resisting is never peaceful. . . . But for the darker skinned (Africans and Blacks in the Diaspora), the violence of a few always represents the actions of the whole. In fact, it is our entire colonized history in a nutshell. For us, there is no nuance." Rakia, "Black Riot."

8. Lorde, "The Uses of Anger," in *Sister Outsider*. For a defense of Black anger, see Thompson, "Exoneration of Black Rage."

9. King, *Where Do We Go from Here*, 120, 27.

10. Baldwin et al., "Negro in American Culture," 205.

11. King, *Where Do We Go from Here*, 12.

12. For example, police officers rarely face charges when they kill someone in the line of duty, and the majority of those who do face charges are routinely acquitted despite evidence of use of excessive force or evidence of unnecessary escalation of encounters with civilians. Their defenses invariably invoke images of Black men as threats that are persuasive to predominantly white juries that share similar biases. When implicit bias prevents the humanity of Black victims from being recognized, it is impossible to gain redress via legal means, as the judicial system reproduces and magnifies bias at every stage, from arrest, to prosecution, to sentencing.

13. Baldwin, *Price of the Ticket*.

14. According to onetime Republican presidential candidate Mike Huckabee: "When I hear people scream, 'black lives matter,' I think, 'Of course they do.' But all lives matter. It's not that any life matters more than another. . . . That's the whole message that Dr. King tried to present, and I think he'd be appalled by the notion that we're elevating some lives above others." Bradner, "Huckabee."

15. Okeowo, "Can Stacey Abrams Save American Democracy?"

16. The image recalls the events of "Bloody Sunday," when Lewis was viciously beaten on the Pettus Bridge during the first march from Selma to Montgomery in 1965 to demand voting rights for African Americans in the South.

17. Moraga and Anzaldúa, *This Bridge Called My Back*.

18. Schouten, "'No One with Power Is Listening.'"

19. Jacob Frey (@MayorFrey), "George Floyd came to Minneapolis to better his life," *Twitter*, April 20, 2021, https://twitter.com/MayorFrey/status/1384619597576474625.

20. E. Brooks, "Nancy Pelosi Roasted for Bizarre Comments."

21. Kaba, *We Do This 'Til We Free Us*, 14.

22. On the idea of our indebtedness to the struggles of others in MLK's political thought, see Lawrie Balfour, "Living 'in the Red': Time, Debt, and Justice," in Shelby and Terry, *To Shape a New World*, 236–52.

23. Juliet Hooker, "Disobedience in Black: On Race and Dissent," in Schwartzberg, *Protest and Dissent*, 45–63. Contemporary theories of civil and uncivil disobedience in political theory and philosophy have relied on an often phenomenologically inaccurate understanding of the praxis of US civil rights activism, and also often reference MLK's views on protest. But the rich, complex, and sustained debates in Black political thought about the meaning and goals of dissent and the use of violence have not been as central to the framing of these accounts. Indeed, reductionist accounts of the debates in the 1960s between MLK and Black Power intellectuals about political violence as disputes between reformist and radical political visions, for example, ignore the richness and complexity of these intellectual exchanges. See

Brandon M. Terry, "Requiem for a Dream: The Problem-Space of Black Power," in Shelby and Terry, *To Shape a New World*, 290–324.

24. The concept of refusal has received wide uptake in a variety of fields in addition to Black studies, including Indigenous studies and various strands of political theory. Indigenous thinkers have written powerfully about refusal, including Simpson, *Mohawk Interruptus*; Coulthard, *Red Skin, White Masks*. On refusal in feminist theory, see Honig, *Feminist Theory of Refusal*.

25. Other thinkers have also argued that democratic politics can produce deep disappointments with dangerous potential consequences. Adorno, for example, argued that capitalism prevents the attainment of the autonomy promised by democracy and that this renders citizens vulnerable to fascism and totalitarianism. Adorno, "Meaning of Working through the Past," 98–99. In contrast, Ashley Atkins rejects the account of sovereignty underlying Allen's account of democracy and sacrifice; she argues that rather than being promised self-rule, democratic subjects are promised rule-with-others and are therefore inspired to collective, not possessive forms of love. Atkins, "Love and Death in Democracy," in McIvor et al., "Mourning Work," 176–82. It is telling, however, that Atkins's example of this kind of collective orientation is Mamie Till-Mobley's activism in the wake of the killing of her son Emmett, which I discuss in chapter 4.

26. Allen, *Talking to Strangers*, 22–23.

27. Allen is concerned with how democracies can manage the corrosive effect of congealed distrust among citizens. In the United States, she argues, interracial distrust is linked to a failure to develop civic habits that can contend with the fact that political decisions inevitably distribute burdens and benefits unequally among citizens. Her prescription is a form of political friendship that cultivates rhetoric, "understood as the art of talking to strangers as equals and of proving that one also has their good at heart." Ibid., 156.

28. On the concept of a racial polity, see Mills, *Racial Contract*.

29. See Steele, "Arendt versus Ellison on Little Rock," 186.

30. See Gines, *Hannah Arendt and the Negro Question*. In contrast to this dominant interpretation of Arendt's concerns in "Reflections," Ainsley LeSure argues that Arendt was in fact motivated by fear of "the rise of the white mob" in response to school desegregation, which presaged a destabilizing withdrawal of white commitment to equality and the rule of law whose consequence would be to further entrench racial domination for Black Americans. LeSure, "White Mob."

31. Arendt, "Reply to Critics," 179.

32. As Jill Locke has persuasively argued, even on her own terms, Arendt's misunderstanding of desegregation as Black "social climbing" depends on ignoring the fact that segregation served to ensure *white* social climbing, i.e., their dominant social status. See Locke, "Little Rock's Social Question."

33. Tessman argues that the kind of extraordinary courage required to resist oppression is a "burdened virtue" because it has steep costs. Additionally, the account of bravery lauded by resistance movements "tends to be based on a masculinist, military model (sometimes even within feminist organizing), which avoids rather than works through a question about what is really more noble: risking oneself in order to achieve victory in a battle against injustice or seeing to it that one returns home consistently, attentively, and safely enough to be able to love and care and be loved and cared for well." Tessman, *Burdened Virtues*, 126.

34. This account of Ellison's views is drawn primarily from an interview in which he directly addressed Arendt's "Reflections," and clearly articulated an "ideal of sacrifice" as a fundamental aspect of African American politics. In other texts such as *Invisible Man*, however, Ellison can be read as endorsing other responses to white supremacy in addition to political martyrdom, such as conspiracy and trickster strategies. See the chapter on Ellison in Lupino, "American Stasis." For an account of Ellison as a democratic theorist that draws primarily on his fiction, see Allen, "Ralph Ellison."

35. Interview with Ralph Ellison in Warren, *Who Speaks for the Negro?*, 342.

36. Ibid., 343.

37. Ibid., 341.

38. Ibid., 343.

39. Allen, *Talking to Strangers*, 28–29.

40. Ibid., 41.

41. Ibid., 110.

42. Johnston, "Two Cheers for Ferguson's Democratic Citizens." Another defense of confrontational modes of citizenship that can reinvigorate democratic participation and regime accountability is Sokoloff, *Confrontational Citizenship*.

43. King, *Where Do We Go from Here*, 72.

44. For example, the "nadir era" of US race relations following the dismantling of Reconstruction was characterized by open adherence to white supremacy, Black political disenfranchisement, heightened racial terror (including lynching and white race riots), the codification of racial segregation, and restrictive immigration policies.

45. Olson, *Abolition of White Democracy*, xxi.

46. Arendt, for instance, viewed school desegregation mandates as an illegitimate intrusion into a zone of private liberty that white parents should have been able to enjoy.

47. Arendt, "Reflections on Little Rock," 50.

48. This comparison implicitly assumes that the civil rights movement was popular in its time, but this was not the case. MLK, for example, was not viewed positively by a majority of the public in the 1960s. Only 28 percent of white polling respondents

expressed positive views of him in 1966 (when concerns about rioting were rising), compared to 76 percent in 1987. And in 1966, only 40 percent of the public expressed support for the civil rights movement. Setter, "Changes in Support for US Black Movements," 477, 481.

49. Many current members of the Black political establishment who participated in the civil rights movement in the 1960s have made this critique. It was also the subtext for the description of Baltimore protesters as "thugs" by President Obama and then mayor Stephanie Rawlings, for example.

50. Social scientific research on the impact of protests on public opinion and policy is extensive. Drawing on a global dataset, Chenoweth and Stephan find that nonviolent movements have been more successful than violent forms of resistance in the twentieth century. Chenoweth and Stephan, *Why Civil Resistance Works*. Research on the impact of Black protests in the United States specifically is divided between those who argue that white antipathy to Black uprisings fueled support for the GOP and "law and order" policies in the 1960s and 1970s (such as Wasow, "Agenda Seeding"), and those who find that minority protests have been successful in moving elite opinion and shaping policy (e.g., Gillion, *Political Power of Protest*). Conclusions about the efficacy of protest depend on how success and effectiveness are defined, however, and in particular on whether the success of dissenters should be judged solely on their ability to persuade their fellow citizens or bring about short-term policy change.

51. In her analysis of TV news coverage of BLM protests in 2014 and 2015, which coincided with commemoration of important civil rights movement anniversaries, Jackson documents the contrast between a homogenized collective memory of the civil rights movement and depictions of contemporary BLM activism almost wholly within the frame of "Black incivility." Jackson, "Making #Blacklivesmatter in the Shadow of Selma," 391.

52. "The white citizen is one who enjoys the status and privileges of a racial polity." It is a location in the racial order that is not defined solely by skin color or class position. Olson, *Abolition of White Democracy*, xix.

53. Terry, "Which Way to Memphis?"

54. Terry, "Requiem for a Dream."

55. The narratives that take hold about prior protest have a profound impact on the possibilities of subsequent mobilization. See Beckwith, "Narratives of Defeat."

56. Allen, *Talking to Strangers*, 115.

57. Ibid., 116.

58. Karuna Mantena, "Showdown for Nonviolence: The Theory and Practice of Nonviolent Politics," in Shelby and Terry, *To Shape a New World*, 99.

59. Ibid., 98–99.

60. Terry, "Requiem for a Dream," 306.

61. In the 1950s and 1960s, for example, segregationist politicians often condemned extremists on both sides, by which they meant the Ku Klux Klan *and* the NAACP.

62. Lynching publics, for example, are historical instances of active white spectatorship that had (to put it mildly) extremely uneven effects in terms of moral transformation, although of course these were not instances of willing Black sacrifice. In her study of lynching spectatorship, historian Amy Wood argues that "a spectator or a bystander becomes a witness when his or her spectatorship bears a legal, spiritual, or social consequence; when it can establish the true course or meaning of an event or action; or when it can confer significance or value on an event." For Wood, both white southerners whose sense of superiority and solidarity was buttressed by observing (which was a form of participation in) lynching, and antilynching activists who challenged the practice by focusing on loss and violence, were engaged in witnessing. Wood, *Lynching and Spectacle*, 4. I would instead reserve the term witnessing, and democratic witnessing in particular, for the latter political activity.

63. They presume a straightforward context of reception that ignores the fact that the act of reception is itself mediated by the very unjust conditions that dissent is supposed to make visible. As a result they do not sufficiently take into account the problem of epistemic injustice. See Dotson, "Accumulating Epistemic Power."

64. I use the term solidarity advisedly. There is a difference between empathy and solidarity. To have empathy is to be able to identify with the pain or suffering of others. Solidarity, meanwhile, implies willingness to take action to resolve the harm at issue, and even being willing to give up unearned privileges in order to do so. Where racial justice is concerned, the problem is not simply how to generate white empathy, but rather how to produce political solidarity. For a detailed discussion of the potential sources of such solidarity, see Hooker, *Race and the Politics of Solidarity*.

65. Butler, "Endangered/Endangering," 15–16.

66. For example: "In response to a September 1964 poll inquiring whether 'most of the actions' taken by 'Negroes . . . to get the things they want' had been violent or non-violent, 57% answered that 'most' had been violent." Pineda, *Seeing Like an Activist*, 28.

67. Gines, *Hannah Arendt and the Negro Question*, 16–17.

68. Arendt, "Reply to Critics," 181.

69. Arendt, "Reflections on Little Rock," 46.

70. Lebron, e.g., argues that shame can drive racial justice but does not explain how shame is induced. Lebron, *Color of Our Shame*. For a different strategy for inducing change in the moral orientations of white citizens, see Snyder, "'Marking Whiteness' for Cross-Racial Solidarity."

71. Poverty and mass incarceration already shape the lives of many Black citizens. For example, Blacks are overrepresented among the poor in the United States, and

Black and Latinx communities have the highest rate of mass incarceration. This is why scholars of the prison industrial complex see the expansion of the carceral state as a strategy for the reproduction of racial stratification. See M. Alexander, *New Jim Crow*.

72. Understandings of civil rights activism, both in public discourse and in academic philosophical defenses of civil disobedience, rely on a stylized, politically expedient narrative about the aims and tactics of the civil rights movement that is at odds with how civil rights activists understood their own actions, which complicate any facile understanding of nonviolence. See Pineda, *Seeing Like an Activist*.

73. Cited in Gines, *Hannah Arendt and the Negro Question*, 18, emphasis in original.

74. Apel, "'Hands Up, Don't Shoot.'"

75. I thank Anne Norton for pointing out this alternate reading of the gesture.

76. As Erin Pineda argues, one of the problems with liberal philosophical defenses of civil disobedience is the domestication of protest. For theorists like Rawls, "disobedience offers not a disruptive challenge to the prevailing order, but rather a necessary progression in its own core values—more a communicative act than direct action." Pineda, *Seeing Like an Activist*, 38. She calls this the problem of seeing disobedience "like a white state." The other problem with viewing protest as primarily communicative is that it becomes about what it does for observers, not what it does for protesters.

77. Angela Davis observes that in the United States: "There are multiple figurations of the enemy (including the immigrant and the terrorist), but the prisoner, imagined as murderer and rapist, looms large as a menace to security." Davis, *Abolition Democracy*, 42–43.

78. On the concept of the "epistemology of ignorance" that shapes the moral orientations of white citizens in a racial polity, see Mills, "White Ignorance."

79. For example, the urban uprisings of the 1960s are often blamed for the blighted neighborhoods home to communities of color in cities such as Chicago, but it was racist government and corporate responses to Black riots (namely, federal riot reinsurance policies) that fueled a wave of landlord arson in the 1970s. See Ansfield, "Crisis of Insurance and the Insuring of the Crisis."

80. The dependence of local municipalities on the fines and fees derived from racist policing was amply documented in the Department of Justice's scathing report on Ferguson, http://www.justice.gov/sites/default/files/opa/press-releases/attachments/2015/03/04/ferguson_police_department_report.pdf.

81. Black politicians have also been complicit in setting up predatory local governments that prey on poor Black citizens, and Black police officers have been involved in some of the deaths that galvanized Black Lives Matter protests. For example, three of the officers indicted in the death of Freddie Gray were Black, and one was a

woman, while one of the deputies who provided false testimony about how Walter Scott was killed in South Carolina was also Black.

82. In her analysis of low-income Black residents struggling against public school closures in Chicago and Philadelphia, Sally Nuamah finds that, despite repeated mobilization, many develop what she calls "'collective participatory debt,' a type of mobilization fatigue that transpires when citizens engaged in policy processes are met with a lack of democratic transparency and responsiveness despite high levels of repeated participation. . . . Each effort to participate in an unfair political process is remembered by those who had engaged and believed in it. With each negative experience that citizens have, it becomes more difficult to justify participating in the future, even if they have been successful at securing some policy 'wins.'" Nuamah, "Cost of Participating While Poor and Black," 1115–16.

83. On the role of anger in AIDS activism, see Gould, *Moving Politics*. She argues that the emotional habitus of queer communities, animated by concerns about how militant gay activism would be perceived, initially discouraged anger at the slow pace of scientific research and lack of government funding in response to the AIDS epidemic. This shifted with the emergence of ACT UP, which encouraged angry militancy. During its early years the organization's affective habits ruled out despair and encouraged anger instead, but this proved difficult to sustain when it was difficult to generate optimism amid accumulating death.

84. Nussbaum, *Anger and Forgiveness*.

85. Phoenix, *Anger Gap*, 25. He argues that African Americans tend to prioritize some forms of civic engagement more than others, such as activism rather than voting.

86. Gaonkar, "Demos Noir," 40, 51. Fear of the *demos*, which goes back to ancient political thought, blurs with fear of the mob after the French Revolution, but under more palatable garb, he argues.

87. Cave, "Defining Baltimore."

88. Havercroft, "Why Is There No Just Riot Theory?," 916.

89. Havercroft's proposed criteria for justified rioting include: that the action promote equality rather than hierarchy, that it is freedom preserving, that it gives voice to the grievances of marginalized communities, that the crowd is orderly, that the polity has systematically violated the basic rights of a liberal democratic regime, that it fails to guarantee genuine conditions of reciprocity to its most disadvantaged, that the rioters are targeting property or persons who either have caused the injustice or are threatening the protestors, that the actions of the rioters are proportionate to the injustice they are contesting, that they are contesting an unjust law, etc. Ibid., 12.

90. Pasternak, "Political Rioting."

91. Delmas, *Duty to Resist*.

92. José Medina, "No Justice, No Peace: Uncivil Protest and the Politics of Confrontation," in Schwartzberg, *Protest and Dissent*, 122–60.

93. The criteria set forth by the scholars cited here would generally disallow rioting by the powerful, but as the January 6 insurrection shows, political rioting is a weapon not only of the weak. For an account of the varied ideological and moral commitments of violent civil disobedients in US history, focusing on the historical examples of frontier vigilance committees, lynch mobs, and militant abolitionists, see Kirkpatrick, *Uncivil Disobedience*.

94. In contrast to these cultural prescriptions against Black anger, displays of ostensibly righteous anger, even when clearly deployed in bad faith, are a very effective strategy for privileged white men, as demonstrated by now Supreme Court justice Brett Kavanaugh's by-turns histrionically aggrieved, contemptuous, self-pitying—and above all, overabundant-in-affect—performance at his Senate confirmation hearing in 2018.

95. Cited in Traister, "Summer of Rage."

96. For a discussion of the difference between reparation and repair that likens repair to refusal, see Thomas, *Political Life in the Wake of the Plantation*.

97. M. U. Walker, "Moral Vulnerability and the Task of Reparations," 126.

98. As Terry observes, these defenses were made on both pragmatic and aesthetic grounds, as well as the more expansive claims that there was no duty to obey the law in a racist society or that violence (following Fanon) had a creative psychological effect on the oppressed. Terry, "Requiem for a Dream," 304–11.

99. For example, Saidiya Hartman's "intimate chronicle of black radicalism, an aesthetical and riotous history of colored girls and their experiments with freedom," brilliantly reimagines an archive of ordinary Black women's waywardness and refusal. Hartman, *Wayward Lives*, xv.

100. Haley, *No Mercy Here*, 200.

101. The play *Blueprints to Freedom*, which premiered in 2015, is about the gay civil rights movement leader Bayard Rustin. For a nuanced account of Rustin's political ideas, particularly his shift from being a key organizer, innovator, and promoter of nonviolent direct mass action to his searing critique of protest as merely performative—in contrast to "politics," which is concerned with wielding power and transforming political economy—in his 1965 polemic "From Protest to Politics," see George Shulman, "Bayard Rustin: Between Democratic Theory and Black Political Thought," in Rogers and Turner, *African American Political Thought*, 439–59.

102. For a critique of the limits of dominant LGBTQ+ politics focused on winning legal recognition and equal rights, and arguing instead for a "critical trans politics" that is attuned to the way the law functions to administer life and death instead, see Spade, *Normal Life*.

103. Davis, *Abolition Democracy*, 92.

104. The Supreme Court's decision to overturn *Roe v. Wade* in 2022 is a case in point. Before the ruling went into effect and news stories about the impact of state abortion bans began to appear, many commentators were more concerned about the damage that leaks of the draft opinion would cause to the court's legitimacy or about civil protests at the homes of the justices than about the effect of the ruling on citizens' lives.

105. The interview appears in the documentary *The Black Power Mixtape 1967–1975*, directed by Göran Hugo Olsson, which premiered in 2011, and aired on PBS in the United States.

106. King, *Where Do We Go from Here*, 2, 5.

107. Akbar, "Toward a Radical Imagination of Law," 409, 426.

108. As mentioned in chapter 1, the M4BL is a coalition of more than fifty organizations working for racial justice and Black freedom, including the chapter-based Black Lives Matter organization, which is credited with popularizing the hashtag, along with other previously existing racial justice organizations. For their policy platform and demands, see again Movement for Black Lives, "Vision for Black Lives." For scholarly analyses of the movement's praxis and its political impact, see Mullings, "Neoliberal Racism and the Movement for Black Lives"; Woodly, *Reckoning*.

109. Quashie, *Sovereignty of Quiet*.

110. Baldwin, "How to Cool It."

Chapter Three: Representing Loss between Fact and Affect

1. Morrison, "Unspeakable Things Unspoken," 149–50.

2. The Holocaust, for example, has often been deemed aesthetically "an unrepresentable—that is to say, inimitable and intransmissible—experience." Chow, "Sacrifice, Mimesis," 135.

3. In the case of AIDS, for instance, markers such as the first one hundred thousand deaths from the disease illustrate the quantification of loss, whereas a project like the AIDS quilt illustrates the turn to affect and the telling of individual victims' stories.

4. Du Bois attributed his shift from *logos* to *pathos* to the fact that "Sam Hose had been lynched, and they said that his knuckles were on exhibition at a grocery store farther down on Mitchell Street, along which I was walking. . . . I began to turn aside from my work . . . Two considerations thereafter broke in upon my work and eventually disrupted it: first, one could not be a calm, cool, and detached scientist while Negroes were lynched, murdered, and starved; and secondly, there was no such definite demand for scientific work of the sort that I was doing as I had confidently assumed." Du Bois, *Dusk of Dawn*, 602–3.

5. For divergent assessments of Du Bois's rhetorical appeals, see Menzel, "'Awful Gladness,'"; Rogers, "People, Rhetoric, and Affect." According to Menzel, Du Bois's shift from fact to affect was also motivated by grief over the death of his son, a month after Hose's lynching. Thereafter, he combined scientific inquiry with direct political activism and experimented with literary styles that allowed for more explicitly affective appeals. He famously argued that art could shape the political imagination of citizens in "Criteria of Negro Art" in 1926 (reprinted in Du Bois, *W.E.B. Du Bois: Writings*, 993–1002).

6. Literary critics have written extensively about Jacobs, but she has received comparatively less attention among political theorists, with the important exception of Black feminists. See Carby, *Reconstructing Womanhood*; Tate, *Domestic Allegories of Political Desire*; Threadcraft, *Intimate Justice*. Recent work by political theorists and philosophers on Wells has focused on the utility of her antilynching writings for a comprehensive account of reparations for slavery, antinostalgic politics, and use of publicity to induce shame. See Balfour, "Ida B. Wells and 'Color Line Justice'"; chapter 1, "American Shame and Real Freedom," in Lebron, *Making of Black Lives Matter*; and Locke, "Against Nostalgia."

7. Syedullah, "Kind of Loss Her Freedom Cost." I have benefitted immensely from Syedullah's brilliant reading of Jacobs and thank her for sharing this early version of this portion of her book manuscript with me.

8. Jacobs's narrative is one of the paradigmatic accounts of the female experience of enslavement and fugitivity. Jacobs escaped from slavery in 1842 and thereafter lived the tense and uncertain life of a fugitive slave in the North, especially after the passage of the Fugitive Slave Act of 1850. She became legally free in 1852, when her employer purchased her freedom. In the 1860s, Jacobs devoted herself to relief efforts on behalf of former slaves who had become refugees of the Civil War, and of freedpersons in the South until she was driven out by white supremacists. As was common with slave narratives, Jacobs initially published hers under a pseudonym with the endorsement of a prominent white abolitionist, Lydia Maria Child. This fueled doubts that it was a work of fiction or that it had been written by Child. *Incidents* remained in obscurity until the late twentieth century, when it was recovered by Black women scholars and its authenticity was finally indisputably verified by the literary historian Jean Fagan Yellin in the 1980s. See Yellin, "Introduction," in H. Jacobs, *Incidents*, xix–liii.

9. Wells became a journalist in an era when there was a thriving Black press. She founded her own newspaper in Memphis and later worked for or published mainly in African American publications.

10. Deborah Nelson identifies unsentimental writing as a literary mode that insists on confronting painful reality and suffering unflinchingly, without displays of feeling. The twentieth-century female intellectuals she analyzes—Diane Arbus,

Hannah Arendt, Joan Didion, Mary McCarthy, Susan Sontag, and Simone Weil—didn't so much subvert or challenge gendered expectations of sentimentality as refuse them outright. They felt they had a duty to face reality, but that emotions should be contained while doing so. Nelson does not directly address race, so it is left to us to consider how racism might shape the imperative to "face suffering with clarity" while resisting the seductions of excessive emotion. The female figures she writes about were all either ambivalent or hostile to feminism, and those with Jewish ancestry recognized it but did not embrace Jewish identity. Nelson, *Tough Enough*, 3–7, quote on 10. I thank Linda Zerilli for pointing me to Nelson's work.

11. Ibid., 6.

12. Sharpe, *In the Wake*, 10–11.

13. Wells, who abandoned early attempts at writing fiction in favor of journalism, was praised by one of her Black male contemporaries, the *New York Age*'s T. Thomas Fortune, for writing "more as a man, with firm, vigorous resolve in graphic, frank language about the pressing issues of the time." Cited in Goldsby, *Spectacular Secret*, 60. According to Jacqueline Goldsby, "Wells refused to adopt her female peers' impassioned but restrained styles of writing. . . . [She] preferred hard-hitting, blunt-sounding prose."

14. Despite the fact that men also participate in the genre, sentimental fiction has been associated with women to the point that the output of nineteenth-century women writers in the United States has been "arbitrarily and inaccurately and, until recently, always derogatorily" labeled as such, "regardless of its actual content, tone, style, or themes." Davidson, "Sentimental Novel."

15. Goldsby, *Spectacular Secret*, 46.

16. Sentimental literature has been framed as both a subversive vehicle for white women's claims to citizenship in the United States, and as a settler colonial form that sought to suture over hierarchies of race, class, nationality, and imperial power. I cannot do justice to the extensive scholarship by feminists and literary scholars on sentimentalism, but it is widely accepted that it was a deeply influential structuring idiom in literary, political, economic, and social spheres in the eighteenth- and nineteenth-century United States. For this reason, African American writers were forced to contend with it. In political thought, accounts of the political role of emotion and sympathy include Adam Smith's *The Theory of Moral Sentiments* (1759), and Jean-Jacques Rousseau's account of compassion in *A Discourse upon the Origin and Foundation of the Inequality among Mankind* (1755).

17. See, for example, Stern, *Plight of Feeling*. A similar overlap between the domestic and the political is present in nineteenth-century Latin American novels. According to Doris Sommer, these heterosexual (and at times interracial) national romances functioned as allegories of nonviolent consolidation in societies wracked by conflict. Sommer, *Foundational Fictions*. In her account of hemispheric sentimentalism, Maria

Windell argues that nineteenth-century Native American, African American, and Latin American writers—such as Martin Delany, Frederick Douglass, John S. Jacobs (brother of Harriet), John Rollin Ridge, and Cubans Cirilo Villaverde and José Martí—were able to informally represent and negotiate transnational encounters in texts written in a sentimental mode. Windell, *Transamerican Sentimentalism.*

18. On the focus on civic rather than intimate harms in dominant accounts of racial injustice, see Threadcraft, *Intimate Justice.* Tate argues that Jacobs and subsequent post-Reconstruction-era African American women writers—such as Francis E. W. Harper, Pauline Hopkins, and Amelia Johnson, who were Wells's contemporaries—were part of a genre of Black women's domestic fiction focused on courtship, marriage, and family formation that nevertheless reflected African American aspirations for political equality. Tate, *Domestic Allegories of Political Desire.*

19. See Dotson, "Conceptualizing Epistemic Oppression."

20. Carby, *Reconstructing Womanhood,* 32–35.

21. Franny Nudelman, for example, argues that Jacobs moves between sentimentality and realism within the text: "Throughout *Incidents in the Life of a Slave Girl,* Jacobs vacillates between the highly stylized and oblique language that characterizes the sentimental and domestic fiction of the antebellum period, and a direct, succinct and descriptive style." Nudelman, "Harriet Jacobs and the Sentimental Politics of Female Suffering," 939.

22. Black feminist readers of *Incidents* such as Carby, Tate, and Threadcraft have highlighted its transformation of the slave narrative genre by centering the specific harms faced by Black women and articulating what freedom and justice meant for enslaved and free Black women. Tate, for instance, argues that, in contrast to the "presumably nongendered humanistic petition for black civil liberty" in male slave narratives such as Douglass's, Jacobs "gave that petition black and female specificity by presenting it as a domestic discourse about black female sexuality." Tate, *Domestic Allegories of Political Desire,* 32.

23. This is so much the case that at the time of its publication an abolitionist periodical, the *National Anti-slavery Standard* (the official weekly newspaper of the American Anti-slavery Society), praised *Incidents* for its "lack of sensationalism." Yellin, "Introduction," in H. Jacobs, *Incidents,* xxxiv.

24. H. Jacobs, *Incidents,* 1, emphasis added.

25. Letter from Mrs. Willis to Stowe on Jacobs's behalf cited in Yellin, *Harriet Jacobs: A Life,* 121, emphasis added. Jacobs also wrote separate letters to Stowe about the matter.

26. This contrast between the facts of slavery and abolitionist fiction was echoed by William C. Nell in his endorsement of *Incidents* in the *Liberator,* the most influential abolitionist newspaper of the time. Nell, a prominent Black abolitionist, praised

Jacobs's text, "stressing its careful adherence to fact." In contrast to the "mingling of fiction with fact" in prior texts "purporting to be histories of slave life in America," he explained to the newspaper's readers, Jacobs's "record of complicated experience . . . surely need not the charms that any pen of fiction, however gifted and graceful, could lend." Yellin, "Introduction," in H. Jacobs, *Incidents*, xxxiv.

27. H. Jacobs, *Incidents*, 2.

28. As Gabrielle Foreman observes, "Jacobs writes absences and gaps into the events which she chooses to present. . . . She evades personal revelations and shields, indeed veils herself, in the move from private to public." Foreman, "Spoken and the Silenced," 317.

29. Nelson, *Tough Enough*, 10.

30. See, for example, Hartman, *Scenes of Subjection*.

31. See Franchot, "Punishment of Esther."

32. The added burdens that flight posed for enslaved mothers are evident when we compare Harriet's narrative to her brother John's. After being taken north by his enslaver, he had to choose whether to escape or remain in the South to try to assist his sister and other family members. He asked friends for advice about what to do: "'Now tell me my duty,' said I. The answer was a very natural one, 'Look out for yourself first.' I weighed the matter in my mind, and found the balance in favour of [escaping]. . . . If I returned along with my master, I could do my sister no good, and could see no further chance of my own escape." J. Jacobs, "True Tale of Slavery," 280.

33. Syedullah, "Kind of Loss Her Freedom Cost," 3, 7, 13. Elsewhere Syedullah argues that Jacobs practices a form of fugitive, abolitionist homemaking. "Finding escape within the constraints of the places she called home became a practice of survival." Syedullah, "No Place Like Home," 470.

34. Nash, "Political Life of Black Motherhood," 700.

35. Ibid., 701.

36. Ibid., 702.

37. Ibid., 703.

38. As Claudia Tate observes: "the text characterizes freedom not so much as a political condition as the domestic desire for the nurturance of free black children." Tate, *Domestic Allegories of Political Desire*, 27.

39. Jacobs describes both the everyday and also the most devastating (and ever-present) losses suffered by enslaved mothers. Among them was being prevented from caring for one's children: "my mother had been weaned at three months old, that the babe of the mistress might obtain sufficient food." The loss of children who were sold away is also a recurring theme in the book and the cause of widespread, collective maternal grief: "Notwithstanding my grandmother's long and faithful service to her owners, not one of her children escaped the auction block"; "to the slave mother New Year's day comes laden [with] peculiar sorrows. She sits on her cold

cabin floor, watching the children who may all be torn from her the next morning; and often does she wish that she and they might die before the day dawns." Jacobs repeatedly describes the agony of enslaved mothers and the idea that death would offer reprieve from slavery's horrors, as in the unnamed woman whose religious faith faltered after the loss of her children: "They've got all my children. Last week they took the last one. God only knows where they've sold her. They let me have her sixteen years, and then—O! O! Pray for her brothers and sisters! I've got nothing to live for now. God make my time short!" H. Jacobs, *Incidents*, 7, 9, 18, 91.

40. Ibid., 16.

41. Jacobs repeatedly describes her own maternal ambivalence because of the enslaved status of her children. After her son recovered from a childhood illness, she suffered a persistent "dark cloud over my enjoyment. I could never forget that he was a slave. Sometimes I wished that he might die in infancy." Later, after a fall, "when the brown eyes at last opened, I don't know whether I was very happy." She had similar thoughts about her daughter, with the added burden of knowing how much "more terrible for women" slavery was. "When I lay down beside my child, I felt how much easier it would be to see her die than to see the master beat her about." Ibid., 80, 100, 105, 112.

42. Ibid., 16.

43. Ibid.

44. Jacobs's departure in naming this chapter is later paralleled by Wells's use of the personal names of victims as chapter titles in *The East St. Louis Massacre: The Greatest Outrage of the Century* (1917), signaling a moment when she more fully depicts the Black lives and families affected by white violence. Wells, *The East St. Louis Massacre*, in Wells-Barnett, *Light of Truth*. All subsequent texts by Wells cited in this chapter are from this volume of her collected works. After her marriage in 1895, Wells changed her surname to Wells-Barnett, and subsequent publications appear under that name. But as she had already published extensively under her maiden name, for consistency I refer to her as Wells throughout.

45. For instance, Harriet was not allowed to mourn her father's death as a child: "I thought I should be allowed to go to my father's house the next morning; but I was ordered to go for flowers, that my mistress's house might be decorated for an evening party. I spent the day gathering flowers and weaving them into festoons, while the dead body of my father was lying within a mile of me. What cared my owners for that? he was merely a piece of property." H. Jacobs, *Incidents*, 11.

46. Ibid., 184.

47. She is not alone. Many people act selflessly on behalf of the freedom of others in *Incidents*, such as Harriet's friend Peter, who helps her escape to the North.

48. Yellin, *Harriet Jacobs: A Life*, 51, 57.

49. J. Jacobs, "True Tale of Slavery," 271–72.

50. H. Jacobs, *Incidents*, 184.

51. Horniblow was the surname of Harriet's grandmother, Molly, and her children.

52. H. Jacobs, *Incidents*, 185.

53. Cited in J. Jacobs, "True Tale of Slavery," 284.

54. H. Jacobs, *Incidents*, 186, emphasis added.

55. Ibid., 186–87. According to Yellin, the Black (enslaved and free) residents of Edenton had collectively purchased a tract of land called "Providence" that served as their meeting place and included a graveyard and church. Yellin, *Harriet Jacobs: A Life*, 19. Mrs. Flint proposed to have Aunt Betty buried in Dr. Flint's plot in the white cemetery.

56. H. Jacobs, *Incidents*, 187, emphasis in original.

57. *Incidents* archives the dispossession of wealth that has been a quotidian aspect of Black life since slavery. In addition to the unpaid labor and monetary gains slave owners accrued from holding other human beings as property, enslaved and free Black people suffered innumerable monetary losses, such as the hefty fees Harriet's grandmother paid to purchase her freedom and that of one of her sons, and the loan to her mistress for which she was never repaid and that was used to purchase items that were then passed on as family heirlooms. She also clothed and fed her enslaved children and grandchildren at her own expense so that they might be better protected in inclement weather, and Harriet's uncle was forced to pay jail fees to secure his release, even though Dr. Flint could not prove that he had conspired in her escape. Ibid., 7, 12–13, 23, 32; J. Jacobs, "True Tale of Slavery," 274.

58. Syedullah, "Kind of Loss Her Freedom Cost."

59. Cited in Reinhardt, "Who Speaks for Margaret Garner?," 91.

60. Savage, *Standing Soldiers, Kneeling Slaves*, 52.

61. Carby, *Reconstructing Womanhood*, 35.

62. J. Jacobs, "True Tale of Slavery," 266. John's narrative also gives a detailed account of the cruel whipping of a pregnant enslaved woman. Ibid., 288–89. He is silent both about the threat of sexual violence his sister faced, however, and about her relationship with Mr. Sands (who became his last enslaver). He implies that Harriet escaped because she feared being whipped: "I left my sister in the doctor's family. Some six or eight years have passed since I was sold, and she has become the mother of two children. After the birth of her second child, she was sent to live on his plantation, where she remained for two or three months, and then ran away." Ibid., 269.

63. Syedullah, "Kind of Loss Her Freedom Cost," 19–20.

64. H. Jacobs, *Incidents*, 70. Jacobs's argument that there was something akin to freedom in exercising even a constrained form of sexual autonomy departs from twentieth-century feminist accounts of the coercive character of women's sexuality in patriarchal societies. Catharine MacKinnon, for example, concludes her account

of sexuality as the site of male dominance and female subordination by citing Ti-Grace Atkinson: "I do not know any feminist worthy of that name who, if forced to choose between freedom and sex, would choose sex. She'd choose freedom every time." MacKinnon, "Sexuality, Pornography, and Method," 344. This radical feminist framing echoes the plot of sentimental novels, whose white heroines preferred death rather than to suffer sexual violation. By contrast, enslaved women's survival of institutionalized rape branded them as unfeeling or sexually promiscuous. See Carby, *Reconstructing Womanhood*, 34–35. As Emily Owens brilliantly argues, not only were enslaved women excluded from the legal category of consent, but more broadly the logic of rape law—with its emphasis on consent and therefore—transaction, makes it nearly impossible to prove rape cases. Owens, *Consent in the Presence of Force*, 157.

65. Camp, "Pleasures of Resistance," 535–36.

66. This is an insight that Neil Roberts has attributed to Douglass. See Roberts, *Freedom as Marronage*.

67. Syedullah, "Kind of Loss Her Freedom Cost," 1.

68. Ibid., 10.

69. On Douglass as a Black hemispheric thinker, see Hooker, *Theorizing Race in the Americas*.

70. Windell, *Transamerican Sentimentalism*, 136–37. She views the Jacobs siblings, Harriet and John, as exponents of a "transamerican sentimental mode" that allowed them "to process and thereby construct alternative visions for nineteenth-century hemispheric relations . . . [and] human connection." Ibid., 10.

71. H. Jacobs, *Incidents*, 259. Jacobs had long objected to the idea of purchasing her freedom. She had earlier refused her grandmother's offer to sell her house so she could purchase Harriet's freedom and that of her children: "I resolved that not another cent of her hard earnings should be spent to pay rapacious slaveholders for what they called their property." She was "unwilling to buy what I had already a right to possess." Ibid., 193.

72. J. Jacobs, "True Tale of Slavery," 269, emphasis in original. After her escape, Harriet received assistance but also encountered racism in the North. On the train ride from Philadelphia, for example, racial segregation was enforced, and Black people were not allowed to sit in first class. "This was the first chill to my enthusiasm about the Free States. Colored people were allowed to ride in a filthy box, behind white people, at the south, but they were not required to pay for the privilege. It made me sad to find how the north aped the customs of slavery." H. Jacobs, *Incidents*, 209.

73. Wells-Barnett, *The Arkansans Race Riot*, in Wells-Barnett, *Light of Truth*, 553.

74. Letter from Harriet Jacobs to William Lloyd Garrison, "Life among the Contrabands," August 1862, in H. Jacobs et al., *Harriet Jacobs Family Papers*, 401.

75. Letter from Harriet Jacobs and Louisa Matilda Jacobs to Lydia Maria Child, March 26, 1864, in H. Jacobs et al., *Harriet Jacobs Family Papers*, 559.

76. Hartman argues that the double bind of emancipation was the "burdened individuality" that conferred on ex-slaves obligations without entitlements. Hartman, *Scenes of Subjection*, 121.

77. According to Goldsby, Wells's antilynching pamphlets experimented with and parodied different journalistic forms, such as "the autobiographical 'stunt,' the sociological treatise, the wire report, and the serial investigative story," in order to show how newswriting's representational practices at the end of the nineteenth century abetted white violence and valorized the deaths of Black people. Goldsby, *Spectacular Secret*, 70–71.

78. Wells was a capacious thinker who wrote on numerous aspects of Black politics and racial justice in the United States. As her collected writings from 1885 to 1927 reveal, her interests encompassed women's roles, Black leadership, party politics, racial segregation, African American emigration, criminal justice reform, and more. See Wells-Barnett, *Light of Truth*. Amid this wide-ranging and extensive oeuvre, however, her texts on lynching are her most well known and commented on, especially *Southern Horrors: Lynch Law in All Its Phases* (1892) and *A Red Record: Tabulated Statistics and Alleged Causes of Lynching in the United States, 1892–1893–1894* (1895), both in Wells-Barnett, *Light of Truth* (57–82; 218–312).

79. "Hon. Fred. Douglass's Letter," in Wells-Barnett, *Southern Horrors*, in Wells-Barnett, *Light of Truth*, 59. In this letter, Douglass, whose own rhetorical prowess was widely recognized, described his own efforts as "feeble" in comparison to Wells's denunciation of lynching. Douglass's letter was also reproduced in *A Red Record*.

80. Wells-Barnett, *Southern Horrors*, in Wells-Barnett, *Light of Truth*, 58, emphasis added.

81. Junior and Schipper, *Black Samson*, 13–14, 21. The Bible contains minimal descriptions of Samson's physical appearance, none of which include the phenotypical characteristics commonly associated with race, yet by the eighteenth century he was regularly conceptualized as Black. According to Junior and Schipper, who trace the way Black Americans identified with and were identified by others with Samson, "generations of American interpreters understood Samson as an enslaved man forced into labor. His death became a final act of resistance against his oppressors. For some interpreters, it represents the ultimate sacrifice of a heroic martyr. For others, it is the foolish consequence of a selfish vendetta. In the end, however, there is no clear victor amid the rubble of the Philistine temple." Ibid., 10. A well-known Black spiritual about Samson, "If I Had My Way I'd Tear This Building Down," also seems to paint Delilah as white: "Samson's mother replied to him, 'Can't you find a woman of your kind and kin?" https://www.lyrics.com/lyric/4854356/Blind+Willie+Johnson

/If+I+Had+My+Way+I%27d+Tear+the+Building+Down. The song has generally been interpreted as a call to Black insurrection.

82. Wells-Barnett, *Mob Rule in New Orleans: Robert Charles and His Fight to the Death*, in Wells-Barnett, *Light of Truth*, 341.

83. Ibid. The phrase "he who runs may read" is from the Bible, Habakkuk 2:2, which is rendered in the American Standard edition as: "And Jehovah answered me, and said, Write the vision, and make it plain upon tablets, that he may run that readeth it." https://biblehub.com/asv/habakkuk/2.htm.

84. Wells-Barnett, *Mob Rule in New Orleans*, in Wells-Barnett, *Light of Truth*, 341.

85. Menzel, "'Awful Gladness,'" 33.

86. Wells-Barnett, *Lynch Law in Georgia*, in Wells-Barnett, *Light of Truth*, 322. Hose was savagely tortured and burned alive. His lynching culminated "in castration and incineration, with strips of Hose's liver cooked and sold for ten cents." Capeci and Knight, "Reckoning with Violence," 733.

87. Indeed, despite the praise Du Bois has received for his experimentation with genre in texts such as *Darkwater* (1920), his account of the East St. Louis massacre in it is actually much less affecting than Wells's pamphlet. In the chapter "Of Work and Wealth," Du Bois critiques the complicity of the white working class and clearly depicts white violence: "five thousand rioters arose. . . . They killed and beat and murdered; they dashed out the brains of children and stripped off the clothes of women; they drove victims into the flames and hanged the helpless to the lighting poles." Du Bois, *Darkwater*, 46. Yet his account does not have the same affective power of Wells's, because it lacks the attention to quotidian Black loss that Wells's profusion of seemingly unimportant details was able to capture.

88. Unlike Du Bois, Wells struggled with lack of recognition during her lifetime. Despite the fact that subsequent antilynching activists would model their activism on her pioneering strategies, Wells was viewed as difficult to work with by her contemporaries and was marginalized by both the NAACP and Black women's organizations owing to a combination of elitism, sexism, and her radical politics. She had a "vexed relationship with the NAACP," from which she was marginalized after having been a cofounder, even as its subsequent antilynching campaign "replicated her earlier strategies." Giddings, "Missing in Action," 2, 15. Her "radical politics and aggressive personality" also did not fit in well with the conservative ideology of the National Association of Colored Women (NACW) founded in 1896. Nevertheless, after the NACW became involved in the NAACP's campaign for federal antilynching legislation following World War I, "the tactics and arguments she [Wells] advocated were increasingly the ones adopted by black clubwomen." See Feimster, *Southern Horrors*, 118–19, 212–13, 28.

89. Wells-Barnett, *A Red Record*, in Wells-Barnett, *Light of Truth*, 236–39.

90. Wells-Barnett, *East St. Louis Massacre*, in Wells-Barnett, *Light of Truth*. See also Crenshaw and Ritchie, *Say Her Name*.

91. Wells-Barnett, *East St. Louis Massacre*, in Wells-Barnett, *Light of Truth*, 461.

92. Woubshet, *Calendar of Loss*, 3.

93. Wells-Barnett, *East St. Louis Massacre*, in Wells-Barnett, *Light of Truth*, 459.

94. Wells's pamphlets on white race riots recall the "shadow reports" civil society organizations submit to the Committee on the Elimination of Racial Discrimination (CERD)—which monitors implementation of the United Nations Convention on the Elimination of All Forms of Racial Discrimination—that supplement and often refute the official reports submitted by member states. See https://www.ohchr.org/en/treaty-bodies/cerd. For an example of a shadow report, see https://rfkhumanrights.org/reports/shadow-report-to-the-committee-on-the-elimination-of-racial-discrimination-cerd.

95. Wells-Barnett, *A Red Record*, in Wells-Barnett, *Light of Truth*, 281.

96. "Lynch Law" echoes Wells's first public lecture on lynching in New York City in 1892. While delivering this initial antilynching lecture Wells succumbed to tears recalling the grief of the Moss family, who were close personal friends. This overt display of feeling (and of appropriately feminine sentiment according to prevailing gender norms) made her a sympathetic figure to the audience of middle-class Black women at Lyric Hall and to the readers of subsequent accounts of the event in African American newspapers. Yet Wells, "who prided herself on her composure," was "mortified" and "chagrined" at this display of emotion, which she viewed as weakness. See Bay, *To Tell the Truth Freely*, 117–19. For an analysis of Wells's rhetorical strategies in the Lyric Hall speech, see August, "Shaping Presence."

97. Wells, "Lynch Law in All Its Phases," in Wells-Barnett, *Light of Truth*, 101–2.

98. "She Pleads for Her Race: Miss Ida B. Wells Talks about Her Anti-lynching Campaign," in Wells-Barnett, *Light of Truth*, 215, emphasis added. This 1894 newspaper article in the *New York Herald Tribune* transcribed Wells's first speech in New York City after her return from a UK lecture tour.

99. Wells-Barnett, *A Red Record*, in Wells-Barnett, *Light of Truth*, 246.

100. The term "monsters" is a reference to the genre of horror that Melvin Rogers argues Wells and other African American intellectuals utilized to try to incite the correct moral response to lynching in white citizens. Rogers, "Lynching and the Horrific." The current renaissance in Black horror cinema (*Get Out*, *Us*, *Lovecraft Country*)—in which racism is as menacing as creatures and threats conventional to the genre, if not more so—continues this tradition.

101. Mass public spectacle lynchings were "rituals of people-making" that helped affirm and constitute "the notion that the sovereign people were white, and that African Americans were their social subordinates." This is, in part, because there was

no clear demarcation between participants and spectators at most lynchings, and the crowd was an active participant in the act of collective violence. See Gorup, "Strange Fruit of the Tree of Liberty," 819, 825.

102. Bay, *To Tell the Truth Freely*, 117.

103. The pamphlet contains a description of the real causes of the riot, the facts of the massacre, the individual stories of some of the prisoners, a detailed recounting of the material losses sustained by the Black sharecroppers and their families, an enumeration of some of the material gains of the white rioters, an account of four prosperous Black citizens not involved in the proposed union killed by the rioters, the transcript of the initial trial, legal documents related to the case such as various motions and rulings, the constitution of the proposed sharecroppers' union, and a comparison to the very different treatment accorded unionized white labor.

104. She created two tables that list the total amount of acres of cotton and corn cultivated by thirty-four of the seventy-five Black farmers, as well as how much they should have been paid per bale of cotton. Wells-Barnett, *An Arkansas Race Riot*, in Wells-Barnett, *Light of Truth*, 516–18.

105. Ibid., 507.

106. Ibid., 519.

107. Ibid., 505–6.

108. Ibid., 513.

109. Ibid., 514.

110. Tzoreff, "Carpets, Books, and Jewelry."

111. Wells-Barnett, *An Arkansas Race Riot*, in Wells-Barnett, *Light of Truth*, 549–50, 53.

112. Ibid., 499–500. "Sorrow songs" is the term used by Du Bois to describe slave spirituals. See Du Bois, "Sorrow Songs," in *Souls of Black Folk*.

113. Haley, *No Mercy Here*, 212, 214, 219.

114. Wells-Barnett, *An Arkansas Race Riot*, in Wells-Barnett, *Light of Truth*, 500.

115. Scholars of African American religion have explored the key role of Christianity in US Black politics at length. They have pointed to the centrality of notions of redemptive suffering to Black Christianity in the United States, which shaped the tactics of thinkers and activists (such as MLK) who believed that suffering was purifying and would lead to white moral transformation. But critics of this strand of Black Christian theology have argued that the notion of redemptive suffering is an impediment to Black liberation because it relieves oppressors of accountability and prevents the oppressed from developing a proper understanding of suffering as unquestionably wrong. See Pinn, *Why, Lord?* While an in-depth analysis of the role of religion in Wells's political thought is beyond the scope of this chapter, Pinn sees Wells as someone who at times partakes of the notion of redemptive suffering but

does not fully embrace it. He notes that Emilie Townes draws on Audre Lorde's distinction between pain (a process that leads to change) and suffering (a cycle of reliving pain) to argue that Wells's activism is an example of the first, more productive approach. Unlike Townes, however, Pinn argues that "Ida Wells-Barnett does not, in actuality make a clean break with the redemptive suffering (read redemptive pain) idea. However, she does not make this argument as strongly as some." Ibid., 71.

116. Wells quoted in, "She Pleads for Her Race," in Wells-Barnett, *Light of Truth*, 215. Photographs of US lynchings also circulated outside the United States, including in Latin America. For example, "In 1934, the NAACP sent its report on Claude Neal's lynching, including the photographs of his nude, hanged body, to 144 international newspapers in forty countries, and at least one, *El Nacional*, Mexico City's leading newspaper, published the report and a scathing critique of U.S. racism on its front page." Wood, *Lynching and Spectacle*, 203. Leading Latin American intellectuals such as Cuban José Martí and Mexican José Vasconcelos wrote about lynching in the 1890s and 1930s, respectively. Vasconcelos mentions lynching briefly in a 1937 text, *Bolivarismo y Monroísmo*, in which he writes extensively about race relations in the United States, while Martí published an essay (in another Mexico City newspaper, *El Partido Liberal*) about the infamous lynching of Edward Coy in the Texarkana borderlands in 1892, which Wells also wrote about. See Martí, "A Town Sets a Black Man on Fire."

117. Goldsby, *Spectacular Secret*, 251.

118. Goldsby argues that political cartoons were "no less graphic than camera-made images . . . but . . . differ from photographs in a crucial way. In their insistence on hyperbole and caricature, hand-drawn illustrations allowed viewers to see lynching's violence in ways that documentary photographs did not. . . . The inexplicable smiles and unseemly calm that often charge lynching photographs turn into curdled sneers and frenzied excitement in anti-lynching political cartoons." Ibid., 252.

119. For a call to historians to be more innovative in their use of archival sources so that they can better tell the full stories of lynching victims, see K. Williams, "Writing Victims' Personhoods."

120. Wood, *Lynching and Spectacle*, 202. The displacement of Black victims and white racism allowed the white press to condemn lynching as lawlessness without addressing its racial dimension.

121. Rogers, "Lynching and the Horrific."

122. "N.A.A.C.P. Rubin Stacy Anti-lynching Flier." Available from the James Weldon Johnson Memorial Collection at the Beinecke Library, Yale University, https://brbl-dl.library.yale.edu/vufind/Record/3833735, emphasis in original. I have redacted the image so that Stacy's body is not visible. For more on the NAACP's lynching campaign and its impact on the organization's trajectory, see Francis, *Civil Rights*.

123. In an example that closely recalls Wells's detailed description of the Moss family, the *Atlanta Daily World*'s coverage of the lynching of Lint Shaw in 1936 included "an image of his home, a portrait of his wife and eleven children—their names and ages provided—and a close-up of their wife holding his youngest child." Wood, *Lynching and Spectacle*, 210.

124. Mitchell, *Living with Lynching*, 6.

125. Ibid., 1.

126. Ibid., 2.

127. See Naomi Murakawa, "Ida B. Wells on Racial Criminalization," in Rogers and Turner, *African American Political Thought*, 214; Threadcraft, "North American Necropolitics and Gender," 560.

128. Similarly, contemporary tabulation of the Black dead by M4BL activists and news organizations harkens back to the lynching statistics compiled by newspapers such as the *Chicago Tribune* that Wells repurposed. In the absence of comprehensive data collection by the federal government, media and nonprofit organizations have stepped in to create their own independent databases to track police killings, such as "Police Shootings Database," *Washington Post*, last accessed October 11, 2022, https://www.washingtonpost.com/graphics/investigations/police-shootings-database/.

129. Wells-Barnett, *A Red Record*, in *Light of Truth*, 256–58, 306.

130. Wells was not a prison or police abolitionist, but she is hailed as an important reference by contemporary activists. She advocated against the use of solitary confinement in prisons and also worked as one of Chicago's first adult parole officers. Bay, *To Tell the Truth Freely*, 289.

131. Wells, *Mob Rule in New Orleans*, in Wells-Barnett, *Light of Truth*, 341–42, emphasis added.

132. Ibid., 383–85.

133. Ibid., 386–87.

134. McQueen, *12 Years a Slave*; Lemmons, *Harriet*. This is a case where "bad" art in aesthetic terms is politically or ethically superior, despite the argument of many philosophers that aesthetic and political judgment are linked.

135. Rizvana Bradley argues that "McQueen's film actively relies upon tropes of mastery and domination, pain and trauma, in order to construct what Saidiya Hartman has referred to as a 'spectacle of sufferance,' while visually qualifying 'an embrace of pain' that engenders pleasure in the viewer. A certain line is blurred between what happens on-screen and our libidinal investment in an economy of pain that comes to stand in not only for a history of black subjection, but also of anti-black violence. *12 Years a Slave* exploits a sadomasochistic gaze." R. Bradley, "Close-Up: Fugitivity and the Filmic Imagination," 163.

136. Reinhardt, "Who Speaks for Margaret Garner?," 117.

Chapter Four: Maternal Grief and Black Politics

1. Harris-Perry, "Erica Garner Died of a Heart Attack."

2. Ibid.

3. Black women are disproportionately affected by heart disease and are more likely to die from heart attacks and strokes. They also have higher rates of breast cancer, cervical cancer, fibroids, diabetes, premature birth, etc. D. Williams, "Death of Erica Garner."

4. Benjamin, *Viral Justice*, 29.

5. Kalief Browder was arrested as a sixteen-year-old for allegedly stealing a backpack. He was jailed for three years, because his family could not afford bail, and spent two of those years in solitary confinement at Rikers Island. Shortly after finally being released, he committed suicide as a result of the trauma he suffered, and his death had a lasting impact on his mother. According to his surviving brother: "My mother, who had already grieved for her son when he was detained, then had to grieve for him for the rest of her life. To cope with her pain, she threw herself into the role of an activist—a role she never expected or wanted. Determined to make sure that her son was never forgotten and that the abuse he suffered wouldn't happen to other children, she partnered with Jay-Z and the Stop Solitary For Kids campaign, and she made numerous appearances discussing the injustice of Kalief's detention and the criminalization of children and poor families, especially those of color. The stress of fighting for justice and the pain over her son's death literally broke my mother's heart, resulting in her premature death at age 63 from complications of a heart attack." Browder, "My Mom Died Trying to Preserve the Legacy of Her Son."

6. By "grieving activism" I mean activism propelled by grief that in turn is also a way of mourning loss. In Black communities, grief and activism have not been seen as necessarily distinct, as the examples in this chapter illustrate. This is in contrast to the way mourning was contrasted to militancy in the early years of AIDS activism.

7. Eligon, "They Push."

8. Previous generations of Black activists also bore the costs of their "brutal sacrifices" on behalf of the struggle against white supremacy, from political assassinations and government persecution to contending with trauma. On the experiences of one young activist in the civil rights movement, and the ethical questions raised by trying to tell these stories, see Hamlin, "Historians and Ethics," 496.

9. James, "Abolitionist and Ancestor," e28.

10. Ibid., e29, e31.

11. Harris-Perry, "Erica Garner Died of a Heart Attack."

12. Others have argued that the way the term "social justice warrior," particularly in its abbreviated form—SJW—is deployed as a meme in online alt-right communities evokes "the monstrous feminine": an unwieldy, out-of-control, dehumanized

female figure. Massanari and Chess, "Attack of the 50-Foot Social Justice Warrior." On the pejorative use of the term in right-wing circles, see Ohlheiser, "Why 'Social Justice Warrior,' a Gamergate Insult, Is Now a Dictionary Entry."

13. "Official Statement from Samaria Rice." The statement specifically criticizes celebrity activism disconnected from local grassroots organizing and takes aim at BLM activists and donors who show no concern for the well-being of the families of the dead, while profiting from Black people's death. Such critiques have been aimed in particular at the Black Lives Matter Global Network, which has come under increased scrutiny for the personal enrichment of some of its leaders and for using some of the extensive funding it received to make questionable purchases. This, however, is not the reality of most activists, who do their work without adequate support in challenging circumstances, nor is it true of many of the Black Lives Matter chapters, which work independently at the local level. As mentioned elsewhere, the official chapter-based BLM organization is also distinct from the Movement for Black Lives (M4BL), which is a broad and diverse coalition of more than fifty organizations struggling for racial justice and Black freedom.

14. My focus here is on the United States, but grieving activism is present elsewhere as well. In France, for instance, female relatives of young Black men killed by the police have also led racial justice protests. A notable example is Assa Traoré, whose younger brother Adama died in police custody in 2016. Walt, "How Assa Traoré Became the Face of France's Movement for Racial Justice." In Latin America, feminist resistance to the combined crises of racism, femicide, ecocide, homophobia, etc., has been described as grieving activism. See Icaza Garza and Leyva Solano, *En tiempos de muerte*; Rodríguez Aguilera, "Grieving Geographies, Mourning Waters."

15. Holloway, *Passed On*, 6.

16. This dynamic is captured by historian Brittney Cooper's tweet on the passing of the novelist Toni Morrison: "What I love about Black people is that we know how to mourn. We know how to stop Western time and honor our ancestors. We know how. How and why we know how so well is the whole story. But I am grateful for our knowing. #ToniMorrison taught us. Hey Celestial." Brittney Cooper, "What I love about Black people is that we know how to mourn," *Twitter*, August 6, 2019, https://twitter.com/ProfessorCrunk/status/1158741949379219462.

17. V. Brown, *Reaper's Garden*, 6.

18. Ibid., 255.

19. Woubshet, *Calendar of Loss*, 5.

20. The prominence of Black women in grieving activism is notable given the masculinism that pervades Black political thought. See Carby, *Race Men*.

21. Nash, "Unwidowing," 752.

22. Honig, *Antigone, Interrupted*, 15–16. She suggests that "decentering maternalism and pluralizing kinship" might allow us to escape maternalism's allure.

23. Tindal, "'Its Own Special Attraction,' 264–65, 268.

24. Northup, *Twelve Years a Slave*, 85.

25. Lucy McBath is the mother of Jordan Davis, a seventeen-year-old who was shot and killed after an argument at a gas station in Florida about playing loud music; his killer cited Florida's stand-your-ground laws in his defense. She became a gun control advocate after her son's killing, and was elected to Congress in 2018.

26. Given the gendering of mourning, it is ironic that this phrase is used to describe one of the roles of the US president, an office to which no woman has yet been elected. Barack Obama, the only Black president, was seen as an exemplary mourner-in-chief despite his generally "cerebral" affect. See Ehrich, "President Obama, Mourner in Chief."

27. James, "Abolitionist and Ancestor," e29. See also James, "Womb of Western Theory." On invocations of the Black maternal that index the ungendering of Blackness as the ground for transness, see Snorton, *Black on Both Sides*.

28. James, "Abolitionist and Ancestor," e31.

29. The videos were created by filmmakers Mohammad Gorjestani and Malcolm Pullinger at Even/Odd Productions. They were filmed a year after Grant, Castile, and Woods were killed, as friends and family gathered to mourn them on their birthdates. The videos are available on the video hosting, sharing, and services platform Vimeo: "Happy Birthday Philando Castile," Even/Odd Productions, https://vimeo.com/179535585; "Happy Birthday Mario Woods," Even/Odd Productions, https://vimeo.com/184151687; and "Happy Birthday Oscar Grant," Even/Odd Productions, https://vimeo.com/127217499; last accessed October 12, 2022.

30. Nash, "Unwidowing." Jeantel could literally not be heard; she was mocked for her accent and repeatedly accused of speaking too softly.

31. Castile was killed when pulled over for a routine traffic stop with Reynolds and her four-year-old daughter in the car. The Latinx police officer who killed him was charged and tried (a rarity), but subsequently acquitted.

32. Campt, "Black Visuality and the Practice of Refusal."

33. Crawley argues that this is a specific form of Black grief because queer practices of joy and pleasure are interrupted by Christian theology and social norms. "Little Richard was not allowed to sustain the joy he found in Blackqueerness, because the doctrine of queerness as a condition to escape was an unresolved and restive journey he continually traversed." Crawley, "He Was an Architect."

34. As the African American Policy Forum report that launched the campaign explained: "None of these killings of Black women, nor the lack of accountability for them, have been widely elevated as exemplars of the systemic police brutality that is currently the focal point of mass protest and policy reform efforts. The failure to highlight and demand accountability for the countless Black women killed by police over the past two decades, including Eleanor Bumpurs, Tyisha Miller, LaTanya

Haggerty, Margaret Mitchell, Kayla Moore, and Tarika Wilson, to name just a few among scores, leaves Black women unnamed and thus underprotected in the face of their continued vulnerability to racialized police violence." Crenshaw and Ritchie, *Say Her Name*, 1.

35. National Black Justice Coalition et al., *Injustice at Every Turn*; Human Rights Campaign, *Violence against the Transgender Community in 2019*.

36. Threadcraft, "North American Necropolitics and Gender," 554, 569.

37. Hunter died because of the transphobia of first responders and medical personnel, who did not provide adequate treatment after a car accident.

38. Snorton and Haritaworn, "Trans Necropolitics," 69–70.

39. Some of the contemporary texts by political theorists on democracy and mourning include Butler, *Precarious Life*; Hirsch and McIvor, *Democratic Arts of Mourning*; Honig, *Antigone, Interrupted*; McIvor, *Mourning in America*; Stow, *American Mourning*.

40. Hirsch and McIvor, "Introduction," in Hirsch and McIvor, *Democratic Arts of Mourning*, x.

41. Butler, *Precarious Life*, 20, 22.

42. Butler attends more to these questions in "Between Grief and Grievance."

43. Stow, *American Mourning*.

44. He argues that by sublimating grief in the interest of social cohesion, the Periclean, consensualist mode of public mourning encourages civic passivity, while agonistic, Antigonean forms of mourning that fashion solidarity out of sorrow and channel private grief into public grievance encourage activist rage and "support the formation of rigid and moralistic political identities." McIvor, *Mourning in America*, 16–22, 28.

45. Woubshet, *Calendar of Loss*, 17. Douglas Crimp, for example, rejected the distinction between mourning and activism in queer politics, but he did so while drawing on Freud's categories. Crimp argued that insofar as healthy mourning, for Freud, was supposed to heal the loss suffered and offer a return to normalcy, this formula did not work for queer people since they were not allowed to grieve: "Seldom has a society so savaged people during their hour of loss. . . . The violence we encounter is relentless, the violence of silence and omission almost as impossible to endure as the violence of hatred and outright murder. Because this violence also desecrates the memories of our dead, we rise in anger to vindicate them. For many of us, mourning *becomes* militancy." Douglas Crimp, "Mourning and Militancy," in *Melancholia and Moralism*, 137.

46. Woubshet, *Calendar of Loss*, 3.

47. Ibid., 4.

48. Ibid., 3.

49. Stow, "From Upper Canal to Lower Manhattan," 693–94.

50. Sharpe, *In the Wake*, 19–20. For an argument that racial grief is ongoing and therefore disrupts the conventional Eurocentric categories of clinical psychology, and that as a result the occupation of grief and loss can be a powerful antiracist resource for a global intersectional Black feminist movement, see Nayak, "Occupation of Racial Grief."

51. Armah, "From I Can't Breathe to I Can't Grieve."

52. Sharpe, *In the Wake*, 22.

53. Hartman, *Lose Your Mother*, 103, 98, 234.

54. Alves and Silva, "Rebellion in the Brazilian Graveyard," 33. There is an extensive history of maternal activism in Latin America, of which the Mothers of the Plaza de Mayo in Argentina are the most iconic example. Black mothers are part of this tradition, but they are also positioned differently by virtue of their Blackness.

55. C. Smith, "Facing the Dragon," 32, 43.

56. Cheng, *Melancholy of Race*, 15. While I disagree with other elements of Cheng's analysis, we agree about the need to complicate the notion of agency.

57. Turner, "Nameless and the Forgotten," 233. Uncovering the interiority of Black women is made difficult by the silences of the archive, which enacts its own violence. See Hartman, "Venus in Two Acts."

58. R. Williams, "Toward a Theorization of Black Maternal Grief," 24, emphasis in the original.

59. Ibid., 22.

60. Price, "What Would Mama Do?," 22. Organizations like SOSAD illustrate the opposition within Black communities to law enforcement efforts that used the "War on Drugs" as a justification for the militarization of policing and the explosion of mass incarceration. Ibid., 21. Another organization created by parents in California that resisted the expansion of the carceral state is Mothers Reclaiming Our Children, discussed in Gilmore, *Golden Gulag*.

61. Price, "What Would Mama Do?," 22. Price argues that SOSAD's public mourning had both personal and strategic dimensions. "The mothers of SOSAD devote a lot of time to telling the stories of the children they have lost: who they were, what their likes and interests were, what events led to their deaths, how their deaths have affected their families. This constant relaying of their children's biography is part of the mourning process, but it is also an effort to make sure their children are visible to police, prosecutors, and the courts. They are working to make child victims of violence visible as persons whose lives are worthy of vindication and a zealous pursuit of justice. Even in Detroit, which was already by that time a majority Black city with key Black stakeholders, the efforts of SOSAD to focus attention on the value of the lives of their children was necessary, in part because some of the children who were killed in Detroit during the SOSAD years were participants in the drug trade." Ibid., 15–16. Like Ida B. Wells, SOSAD mothers insisted on focusing on not only the

deaths, but also the lives of their children. Like contemporary Black activists, who have insisted that we must "#SayHerName" and that "*all* Black Lives Matter," SOSAD also claimed the lives of their children were valuable regardless of their possible participation in illicit activities. Indeed, according to Price, the SOSAD chapter in Philadelphia was one of the first to take up the case of Trayvon Martin and bring attention to his killing in 2012.

62. A similar dynamic is evident in the case of Karen Hylton, who was on the front lines of antipolice protests in DC in 2020 simultaneously seeking justice for her son, grieving, and keeping his memory alive. He died in a scooter crash while being chased by police officers in a cruiser. C. Williams, "Pepper-Sprayed, Arrested, Grieving."

63. Douglass, "What to the Slave Is the Fourth of July," 117.

64. Idia, "Tree of Life Shooting," emphasis added.

65. Woubshet, *Calendar of Loss*, 4.

66. For an insightful elucidation of how my argument here potentially troubles agonistic accounts of democratic politics committed to permanent contestation that celebrate the democratic capacities of marginalized citizens, see Threadcraft's essay and Honig's response in Maxwell et al., "'Agonistic Turn.'"

67. M4BL activists adopted and enlarged the "healing justice" framework from the disability justice movement. It "is a collection of commitments and movement practices promoting the health, healing, and joy of Black people, by acknowledging the trauma that oppression and domination cause, and by trying to understand and address both the historical root and proximate causes of the structural violence that impacts Black lives." Woodly, *Reckoning*, 121–22.

68. Rankine, "Condition of Black Life Is One of Mourning."

69. Another instance of this kind of mobilization of private grief into public mourning as a catalyst for Black activism involving children is MLK's eulogy for the four little girls killed in the Sixteenth Street Baptist Church bombing in Birmingham, Alabama, which risked reducing them solely to symbols and martyrs.

70. Cited in Feldstein, "I Wanted the Whole World to See," 271.

71. For example, in an empirical analysis of the impact of collective memories of significant historical events on Black activism during the civil rights movement that draws on a rare Black public opinion survey conducted in 1966, Fredrick Harris found that knowledge of Till's murder had a greater positive and long-term influence on Black insurgency in both the North and the South than did the Scottsboro trial, the *Brown v. Board of Education* decision, and the Montgomery bus boycott. He argues that "the appropriation of the event by the NAACP and Emmett Till's mother, Mamie Till Bradley, spurred rather than undermined black activism in the South and outside the South by transforming the murder from a symbol of fear to a symbol that represented the need for social change." F. Harris, "It Takes a Tragedy," 26.

72. E. Alexander, "'Can You Be BLACK and Look at This?,'" 87–88.

73. Moten, "Black Mo'nin'," 59, 61–62, 64, emphasis in the original.

74. Feldstein, "I Wanted the Whole World to See," 265.

75. As noted in the previous chapter, Ida B. Wells and later the NAACP used lynching photographs against the intent of the photographers and the white subjects who posed for them, which was to portray and cement white power and Black degradation. Instead, Wells and the NAACP used them as proof that these terrifying acts of violence had occurred, and to shift attention to the lawlessness of the white mob. They succeeded in turning celebrations of racial violence into occasions of national shame. "From the mid-1910s through the 1930s, the NAACP and the black press's concerted efforts to disseminate and publish lynching photographs rendered the South, along with what were perceived as its backward and degenerate punitive practices, the object of a critical national gaze. In doing so, these activists created an alternate form of lynching spectatorship, one that impelled viewers both outside and within the South to bear witness to white injustice and brutality." Wood, *Lynching and Spectacle*, 183.

76. Sontag, *Regarding the Pain of Others*, 8, 25, 91.

77. On the connection between racial violence and spectacle, Wood argues that rather than the violence itself, it was the act's status as a spectacle that accounts for the psychological power of lynching. "The cultural power of lynching—indeed, the cultural power of white supremacy itself—rested on spectacle: the crowds, the rituals and performances, and their sensational representations in narratives, photographs, and films." Wood, *Lynching and Spectacle*, 3. Focusing on the role of spectacle in contemporary Black mobilization, Threadcraft argues that Black death has been central to the creation of Black notions of peoplehood, with problematic consequences for Black women, who suffer from a "spectacular death deficit." Threadcraft, "Spectacular Death, the #metoo Mundane, and Intimate Justice."

78. Makalani, Discussant Comments."

79. Flock, "How Gwendolyn Brooks' Poetry."

80. P. Smith, "Black, Poured Directly into the Wound," 471. The poem is a "golden shovel," a literary form devised by Terrance Hayes in honor of Brooks in which the last word in each line in the new poem is from a line in a Brooks poem. In Smith's poem, the first and last word of each line, in order on the right side and in reverse order on the left, reproduce the full text of "The Last Quatrain." Thanks to Kevin Quashie for pointing me to Brooks's "The Last Quatrain."

81. M. Bradley, "Mamie Bradley's Untold Story." Mamie married her third husband two years after Emmett's death and subsequently changed her name to Till-Mobley. She went on to become a special education teacher in Chicago elementary schools.

82. J. Johnson, "It's Time to Show the Real Horror."

83. Martel, *Unburied Bodies*, 130–31.

84. Rankine, "Condition of Black Life Is One of Mourning." She is right that refusal to forget is a central tenet of Black Lives Matter activists, as is recognizing the fact that Black life is treated as disposable, but they also explicitly avoid some of the dominant scripts of Black grief. See Mullings, "Neoliberal Racism and the Movement for Black Lives"; Woodly, *Reckoning*.

85. Rushdy, "Exquisite Corpse," 75–76. James Byrd was murdered in 1998 in Texas by white supremacists, who dragged his body behind their vehicle thereby dismembering it. The case received national attention, but his family "was uncomfortable with the idea of turning him into a national symbol, and would have preferred to have a quieter service without all the rallying cry."

86. Rankine, "Condition of Black Life Is One of Mourning."

87. Ibid. Similarly, some have suggested turning the anniversary of George Floyd's murder into a National Day of Mourning. McIvor, "May 25 Should Be a Day of Mourning for George Floyd."

88. L. Williams, "Grieving Critically." She argues that counter-eulogies avoid elevating the individual at the expense of the community, inciting violent revenge, and perpetuating uncritical and congratulatory self-praise, the principal flaws of ancient Homeric and Athenian mourning traditions. At the time, commentators praised the Charleston eulogy as Obama's "most fully successful performance as an orator." Fallows, "Obama's Grace."

89. Thompson, "Exoneration of Black Rage," 460.

90. Juhasz, "How Do I (Not) Look?"

91. E. Alexander, "'Can You Be BLACK and Look at This?,'" 90.

92. Ibid., 85.

93. Feldstein, "I Wanted the Whole World to See," 266, 270. In fact, his mother's body garnered almost as much attention as Emmett's, as her attractiveness was repeatedly noted in press coverage of the case. Ibid., 273.

94. Feldstein, "I Wanted the Whole World to See."

95. Reinhardt, "Who Speaks for Margaret Garner?"

96. Feldstein, "I Wanted the Whole World to See," 266, 276. Till-Mobley's public conflict with the NAACP over speaking fees seems to have been as much about needing remuneration to continue as a full-time activist, as about her making appearances and statements that were not choreographed by the organization. The result was that the Black press turned on her and represented her in the same negative terms as the unsympathetic white press. "She became a scapegoat of sorts, a receptacle for anger at the trial's outcome and overlapping anxieties about gender relations and the future of civil rights activism." Ibid., 284. This was hardly the only time the NAACP sidelined a female figure they deemed to be the wrong kind of victim or symbol for failing to adhere to dominant gender and sexual norms. The same year as

Till's murder and funeral, during the Montgomery bus boycott, Claudette Colvin, a teenager, was jailed for refusing to give up her seat months before Rosa Parks's planned protest. Whereas Parks was the secretary of the NAACP, civil rights leaders viewed Colvin "as an inappropriate symbol for a test case." Adler, "Before Rosa Parks."

97. Makalani, "What They Did to My Baby."

98. See, for example, the pioneering account of the divergent responses to rap and hip hop in Rose, *Black Noise*.

99. This link is reflected in the dominance of ocular metaphors in political theory. The word theory itself is derived from the Greek *theoria*, for seeing or the ritual journey to an oracle or religious festival where participation in various rites culminated in viewing sacred images. The task of the political theorist continues to be explicitly associated with enlarged sight, as in Wolin, *Politics and Vision*.

100. Campt, *Listening to Images*, 9. Her book is not about grief, but Campt attributes her attention to "the sonic frequencies of the quotidian practices of black communities" to recalling her father's humming on the day of her mother's funeral "in the face of the unsayability of words. Even now, the memory of my father's quiet hum connects me to feelings of loss I cannot articulate in words, and it provokes in me a simultaneously overwhelming and unspeakable response." Ibid., 4.

101. E. Alexander, "'Can You Be BLACK and Look at This?,'" 83.

102. Moten, "Black Mo'nin'," 72.

103. Baldwin, *Fire Next Time*, 41–42, emphasis added. Thanks to John-Baptiste Oduor for reminding me of this passage.

104. Douglass, *Narrative*, 24.

105. The scene can be viewed, and more importantly heard, at "*12 Years A Slave*: 'Let Me Weep, Solomon'," Searchlight Pictures channel, uploaded October 17, 2013, https://www.youtube.com/watch?v=utBKmU1TJIg. The script is available at the Internet Movie Script Database, accessed October 12, 2022, http://www.imsdb.com/scripts/12-Years-a-Slave.html.

106. Northup, *Twelve Years a Slave*, 82.

107. Cited in Feldstein, "I Wanted the Whole World to See," 271.

108. R. Williams, "Toward a Theorization of Black Maternal Grief," 20.

109. See Holloway, *Passed On*, 162. For an account of Black women's wailing as oriented to mobilizing public mourning, see Celeste, "'What Now?'"

110. See J. Johnson, "It's Time to Show the Real Horror," which applies the concept to the problem of gun violence.

111. See Kafer, *Feminist, Queer, Crip*, 151–52. The essay is based on a presentation Johnson Reagon gave at a conference held at high altitude, and she may suffer from asthma as many African Americans do.

112. McIvor, *Mourning in America*, 21.

113. Nash, "Black Maternal Aesthetics," 552, 554.

114. Honig, *Antigone, Interrupted*, 9, 14.

115. Ibid., 570. I am more skeptical than Nash about the political utility of the Black maternal aesthetics she celebrates, as exemplified by Serena Williams, Beyoncé Knowles, and Michelle Obama. I think it might be subject to the same kind of romanticization she sees in contemporary Black feminist accounts of motherhood that emphasize care and world making while downplaying maternal ambivalence.

116. Quashie, *Sovereignty of Quiet*, 4.

117. Ibid., 23.

118. That Ewing, who was born in 1986 and did not experience the iconic photographs of Till's funeral in real time, would choose to write about him sixty-odd years later shows the continued impact of his story on diverse Black publics. The same year Ewing's poem was first published, Dave Chappelle in his 2018 comedy special *The Bird Revelation*, included an extended discussion of Till's murder, Mamie Till-Mobley's activism, and the fact that Till's accuser finally recanted her testimony as a deathbed confession. And in 2022, *Till* was released, a film about Emmett's murder and his mother's subsequent activism told entirely from Mamie Till-Mobley's perspective. Till's continued resonance today illustrates Elizabeth Alexander's argument that "collective cultural trauma . . . comes to reside in the flesh as forms of memory reactivated and articulated at moments of collective spectatorship." See E. Alexander, "'Can You Be BLACK and Look at This?,'" 80.

119. Ewing, "I Saw Emmett Till This Week at the Grocery Store," in *1919*, 3. The title of the book references a white race riot that occurred that year in Chicago; in its aftermath a report was published on race relations in the city that was Ewing's inspiration for each of the poems in the collection.

120. Ibid.

Conclusion

1. I take the concepts of spectacular and slow death from Shatema Threadcraft and Lauren Berlant, respectively. Threadcraft, "North American Necropolitics and Gender"; Berlant, "Slow Death."

2. Bogage, "Buffalo's East Side Was a Food Desert."

3. The lack of care and concern for Black life was horribly compounded by the 911 operator, who first scolded a manager—who was trying to call for help from within the store while the shooting was taking place—for whispering, before subsequently hanging up. Tan, "911 Call Taker Fired."

4. Woubshet, *Calendar of Loss*, 145.

5. Riggs, "Letter to the Dead," 20.

6. Ibid., 21.

7. Anker and Youmans, "Sovereign Aspirations." They argue that "Trump's campaign transmuted affectively intense experiences of powerlessness into the justification for state violence imagined as sovereign freedom." They note that while Brexit and Trump supporters have not been the most harmed by waning state sovereignty and the growing power of transnational capital, they "feel unable to achieve what they have always been told is their rightful entitlement. The rightful entitlement they desire, Trump knows, is to be like him: a master over self and others, economically and politically dominant, and beholden to no other." Ibid., 13.

8. Kelley, *Freedom Dreams.*

9. On the genres of democratic theory, see Balfour, "Darkwater's Democratic Vision"; Honig, *Democracy and the Foreigner*, 108–9.

10. Stow, "From Upper Canal to Lower Manhattan"; Butler, *Precarious Life.*

11. Levitsky and Ziblatt, *How Democracies Die.*

12. At a minimum, for example, equal political participation would mean that we should cease expecting Black and other nonwhite citizens to be the mules of white democracy, forever toiling, in Sisyphean fashion, to make it live up to its stated egalitarian commitments. It would mean not simply recognizing the essential civic labor and sacrifices on behalf of democracy of Black and other nonwhite activists, but also becoming comfortable with their leadership and political ideas. It would also mean moving past the fetishism of sclerotic constitutionalism as the bulwark of US democracy and being open to transforming current institutions (such as policing, the electoral college, lifetime court appointments) that have become ways to entrench minority rule and racial hierarchy.

13. *Oxford English Dictionary*, "repair," https://www-oed-com.revproxy.brown.edu/view/Entry/162629?rskey=VMKLbR&result=2#eid; "salvage," https://www-oed-com.revproxy.brown.edu/view/Entry/170271?redirectedFrom=salvaging#eid24436108.

14. Du Bois, *Black Reconstruction in America, 67, 151.*

15. Threadcraft, "Feminist Abolition Democracy."

16. Woodly, *Reckoning*, 215.

17. Sharpe, *In the Wake.*

18. McCarthy, "Coming to Terms with Our Past," 751.

19. Du Bois, *Gift of Black Folk.*

20. Balfour, "Living 'in the Red': Time, Debt, and Justice," in Shelby and Terry, *To Shape a New World*, 237.

21. Biss, "White Debt."

22. Kaba, *We Do This 'Til We Free Us*, 3.

BIBLIOGRAPHY

Abrajano, Marisa, and Zoltan Hajnal. *White Backlash: Immigration, Race, and American Politics*. Princeton, NJ: Princeton University Press, 2015.

Adler, Margot. "Before Rosa Parks, There Was Claudette Colvin." *NPR News*, March 15, 2009.

Adorno, Theodor W. "The Meaning of Working through the Past." In *Critical Models: Interventions and Catchwords*, 89–103. New York: Columbia University Press, 2005.

Aitchison, Guy. "Domination and Disobedience: Protest, Coercion and the Limits of an Appeal to Justice." *Perspectives on Politics* 16, no. 3 (2018): 666–79.

Akbar, Amna A. "Toward a Radical Imagination of Law." *New York University Law Review* 93, no. 3 (2018): 405–79.

Alcoff, Linda Martín. *The Future of Whiteness*. Cambridge, UK: Polity, 2015.

Alexander, Elizabeth. "'Can You Be BLACK and Look at This?': Reading the Rodney King Video(s)." *Public Culture* 7, no. 1 (1994): 77–94.

Alexander, Michelle. *The New Jim Crow: Mass Incarceration in the Age of Colorblindness*. New York: New Press, 2010.

Allen, Danielle S. "Ralph Ellison: Democratic Theorist." In *African American Political Thought: A Collected History*, edited by Melvin L. Rogers and Jack Turner, 460–80. University of Chicago Press, 2021.

———. *Talking to Strangers: Anxieties of Citizenship after Brown v. Board of Education*. Chicago: University of Chicago Press, 2004.

Alves, Jaime Amparo, and Débora Maria Silva. "Rebellion in the Brazilian Graveyard: Our Dead Have a Voice!" *LASA Forum* 48, no. 2 (Spring 2017): 31–33.

Anderson, Carol. *White Rage: The Unspoken Truth of Our Racial Divide*. Paperback ed. New York: Bloomsbury, 2017.

Anker, Elisabeth, and William L. Youmans. "Sovereign Aspirations: National Security and Police Power in a Global Era." *Theory and Event* 20, no. 1 (2017): 3–18.

Ansfield, Bench. "The Crisis of Insurance and the Insuring of the Crisis: Riot Reinsurance and Redlining in the Aftermath of the 1960s Uprisings." *Journal of American History* 107, no. 4 (2021): 899–921.

Apel, Dora. "'Hands Up, Don't Shoot': Surrendering to Liberal Illusions." *Theory and Event* 17, no. 3, supplement (2014). muse.jhu.edu/article/559367.

Arendt, Hannah. "Reflections on Little Rock." *Dissent* 6 (1956): 45–56.

———. "A Reply to Critics." *Dissent*, Spring 1959, 179–81.

Aristotle. *The Politics*. Translated by Ernest Baker. Oxford: Oxford University Press, 1948.

Armah, Esther A. "From I Can't Breathe to I Can't Grieve: Black Grief Matters." *Warscapes*, July 19, 2019. www.warscapes.com/column/esther-armah/i-can-t-breathe-i-can-t-grieve-black-grief-matters.

Arora, Maneesh. "How the Coronavirus Pandemic Helped the Floyd Protests Become the Biggest in U.S. History." *Washington Post*, August 5, 2020. https://www.washingtonpost.com/politics/2020/08/05/how-coronavirus-pandemic-helped-floyd-protests-become-biggest-us-history/.

August, Anita. "Shaping Presence: Ida B. Wells' 1892 Testimony of the 'Untold Story' at New York's Lyric Hall." *Peitho* 16, no. 2 (2014): 145–67.

Baldwin, James. *The Fire Next Time*. 1962. New York: Vintage, 1993.

———. "How to Cool It." *Esquire*, July 1968. https://www.esquire.com/news-politics/a23960/james-baldwin-cool-it/.

———. *The Price of the Ticket: Collected Nonfiction, 1948–1985*. New York: St. Martin's/Marek, 1985.

Baldwin, James, Emile Capouya, Lorraine Hansberry, N.A.T. Hentoff, Langston Hughes, and Alfred Kazin. "The Negro in American Culture." *CrossCurrents* 11, no. 3 (1961): 205–24. http://www.jstor.org/stable/24456864.

Balfour, Lawrie. "*Darkwater*'s Democratic Vision." *Political Theory* 38, no. 4 (2010): 537–63.

———. "Ida B. Wells and 'Color Line Justice': Rethinking Reparations in Feminist Terms." *Perspectives on Politics* 13, no. 3 (2015): 680–96.

Ball, Molly. "The Resentment Powering Trump." *Atlantic*, March 15, 2016. www.theatlantic.com/politics/archive/2016/03/the-resentment-powering-trump/473775.

Bay, Mia. *To Tell the Truth Freely: The Life of Ida B. Wells*. New York: Hill and Wang, 2009.

Beckwith, Karen. "Narratives of Defeat: Explaining the Effects of Loss in Social Movements." *Journal of Politics* 77, no. 1 (2015): 2–13.

Bell, Derrick A., Jr. "*Brown v. Board of Education* and the Interest Convergence Dilemma." In *Critical Race Theory: The Key Writings That Formed the Movement*, edited by Neil Gotanda, Kimberlé Crenshaw, Gary Peller, and Kendall Thomas, 20–29. New York: New Press, 1995.

Beltrán, Cristina. "To Understand Trump's Support, We Must Think in Terms of Multiracial Whiteness." *Washington Post*, January 15, 2021. https://www

.washingtonpost.com/opinions/2021/01/15/understand-trumps-support-we-must-think-terms-multiracial-whiteness/.

Benjamin, Ruha. *Viral Justice: How We Grow the World We Want*. Princeton, NJ: Princeton University Press, 2022.

Benjamin, Walter. "Left-Wing Melancholy." In *The Weimar Republic Sourcebook*, edited by Anton Kaes, Martin Jay, and Edward Dimendberg, 304–6. Berkeley: University of California Press, 1994.

Berlant, Lauren. *Cruel Optimism*. Durham, NC: Duke University Press, 2011.

———. "Slow Death (Sovereignty, Obesity, Lateral Agency)." *Critical inquiry* 33, no. 4 (2007): 754–80.

Biss, Eula. "White Debt: Reckoning with What Is Owed—and What Can Never Be Repaid—for Racial Privilege." *New York Times*, December 2, 2015. https://www.nytimes.com/2015/12/06/magazine/white-debt.html.

Bjork-James, Sophie. "Racializing Misogyny: Sexuality and Gender in the New Online White Nationalism." *Feminist Anthropology* 1, no. 2 (2020): 176–83.

Blum, Edward J. "Lynching as Crucifixion: Violence and the Sacred Imagination of W.E.B. Du Bois." In *The Souls of W.E.B. Du Bois: New Essays and Reflections*, edited by Edward J. Blum and Jason R. Young, 188–208. Macon, GA: Mercer University Press, 2009.

Bogage, Jacob. "Buffalo's East Side Was a Food Desert: The Shooting Made Things Worse." *Washington Post*, June 1, 2022. https://www.washingtonpost.com/nation/interactive/2022/buffalo-shooting-tops-food-desert/.

Bradley, Mamie. "Mamie Bradley's Untold Story: As Told to Ethel Payne; Installment VIII." *Chicago Defender*, June 9, 1956, 8.

Bradley, Rizvana. "Close-Up: Fugitivity and the Filmic Imagination; Reinventing Capacity; Black Femininity's Lyrical Surplus and the Cinematic Limits of *12 Years a Slave*." *Black Camera: An International Film Journal* 7, no. 1 (2015): 162–78.

Bradner, Eric. "Huckabee: MLK Would Be 'Appalled' by Black Lives Matter." *CNN*, August 18, 2015. https://www.cnn.com/2015/08/18/politics/mike-huckabee-black-lives-matter-martin-luther-king.

Brooks, Eric. "Nancy Pelosi Roasted for Bizarre Comments on Derek Chauvin Guilty Verdict." *MSN*, April 21, 2021. https://www.msn.com/en-us/news/politics/nancy-pelosi-roasted-for-bizarre-comments-on-derek-chauvin-guilty-verdict/ar-BB1fSiR2.

Browder, Deion. "My Mom Died Trying to Preserve the Legacy of Her Son: Keeping Kids out of Solitary Will Preserve Hers." *USA Today*, April 23, 2019. https://www.usatoday.com/story/opinion/policing/spotlight/2019/04/23/kalief-browder-suicide-solitary-confinement-venida-browder-policing-the-usa/3540366002/.

Brown, Vincent. *The Reaper's Garden: Death and Power in the World of Atlantic Slavery*. Cambridge, MA: Harvard University Press, 2008.

Browne, Simone, and Ben Carrington. "The Obamas and the New Politics of Race." *Qualitative Sociology* 35, no. 2 (2012): 113–21.

Bruce, La Marr Jurelle. *How to Go Mad without Losing Your Mind: Madness and Black Radical Creativity*. Durham, NC: Duke University Press, 2021.

Bump, Philip. "Clinton Voters Express More Economic Distress Than Trump Voters—Including among Whites." *Washington Post*, September 17, 2018. https://www.washingtonpost.com/politics/2018/09/17/democrats-express-more-economic-distress-than-republicans-including-among-whites/.

Butler, Judith. "Between Grief and Grievance, a New Sense of Justice." In *Grief and Grievance: Art and Mourning in America*, edited by Okwui Enwezor, Naomi Beckwith, Massimiliano Gioni, Glenn Ligon, and Mark Nash, 11–15. London: Phaidon, 2020.

———. "Endangered/Endangering: Schematic Racism and White Paranoia." In *Reading Rodney King/Reading Urban Uprising*, edited by Robert Gooding-Williams, 15–22. New York: Routledge, 2013.

———. *Precarious Life: The Powers of Mourning and Violence*. London: Verso, 2004.

Camp, Stephanie M. H. "The Pleasures of Resistance: Enslaved Women and Body Politics in the Plantation South, 1830–1861." *Journal of Southern History* 68, no. 3 (2002): 533–72.

Campi, Ashleigh. "Cultivating Authoritarian Submission: Race and Gender in Conservative Media." *Theory and Event* 24, no. 2 (2021): 456–82.

Campt, Tina M. "Black Visuality and the Practice of Refusal." *Women and Performance: A Journal of Feminist Theory* 29, no. 1 (2019): 79–87.

———. *Listening to Images*. Durham, NC: Duke University Press, 2017.

Cane, Lucy. *Sheldon Wolin and Democracy: Seeing through Loss*. New York: Routledge, 2020.

Capeci, Dominic, and Jack Knight. "Reckoning with Violence: W.E.B. Du Bois and the 1906 Atlanta Race Riot." *Journal of Southern History* 62, no. 4 (1996): 727–66.

Carby, Hazel V. *Race Men*. Cambridge, MA: Harvard University Press, 1998.

———. *Reconstructing Womanhood: The Emergence of the Afro-American Woman Novelist*. New York: Oxford University Press, 1987.

Carnes, Nicholas, and Noam Lupu. "It's Time to Bust the Myth: Most Trump Voters Were Not Working Class." *Washington Post*, June 5, 2017. https://www.washingtonpost.com/news/monkey-cage/wp/2017/06/05/its-time-to-bust-the-myth-most-trump-voters-were-not-working-class/.

Case, Anne, and Angus Deaton. "Rising Morbidity and Mortality in Midlife among White Non-Hispanic Americans in the 21st Century." *Proceedings of the National Academy of Sciences* 112, no. 49 (2015): 15078–83.

Cave, Damien. "Defining Baltimore: #Riot, #Uprising or #Disturbance?" *New York Times*, April 28, 2015. http://www.nytimes.com/live/confrontation-in-baltimore/riot-uprising-or-disturbance/.

Celeste, Manoucheka. "'What Now?': The Wailing Black Woman, Grief, and Difference." *Black Camera* 9, no. 2 (2018): 110–31.

Cheng, Anne Anlin. *The Melancholy of Race: Psychoanalysis, Assimilation, and Hidden Grief*. Oxford: Oxford University Press, 2001.

Chenoweth, Erica, and Jeremy Pressman. "This Summer's Black Lives Matter Protesters Were Overwhelmingly Peaceful, Our Research Finds." *Washington Post*, October 16, 2020. https://www.washingtonpost.com/politics/2020/10/16/this-summers-black-lives-matter-protesters-were-overwhelming-peaceful-our-research-finds/.

Chenoweth, Erica, and Maria J. Stephan. *Why Civil Resistance Works: The Strategic Logic of Nonviolent Conflict*. New York: Columbia University Press, 2011.

Chow, Rey. "Sacrifice, Mimesis, and the Theorizing of Victimhood (a Speculative Essay)." *Representations* 94, no. 1 (2006): 131–49.

Chudy, Jennifer, and Hakeem Jefferson. "Support for Black Lives Matter Surged Last Year: Did It Last?" *New York Times*, May 22, 2021. https://www.nytimes.com/2021/05/22/opinion/blm-movement-protests-support.html.

Cohen, Cathy J. *Democracy Remixed: Black Youth and the Future of American Politics*. Oxford: Oxford University Press, 2010.

Cooper Owens, Deirdre. *Medical Bondage: Race, Gender, and the Origins of American Gynecology*. Athens: University of Georgia Press, 2017.

Coulthard, Glen Sean. *Red Skin, White Masks: Rejecting the Colonial Politics of Recognition*. Minneapolis: University of Minnesota Press, 2014.

Crawley, Ashon. "He Was an Architect: Little Richard and Blackqueer Grief." *NPR*, December 22, 2020. https://www.npr.org/2020/12/22/948963753/little-richard-black-queer-grief-he-was-an-architect.

Crenshaw, Kimberlé, Priscilla Ocen, and Jyoti Nanda. *Black Girls Matter: Pushed Out, Overpoliced, and Underprotected*. New York: African American Policy Forum and Center for Intersectionality and Policy Studies, 2015.

Crenshaw, Kimberlé Williams, and Andrea J. Ritchie (with Rachel Anspach, Rachel Gilmer, and Luke Harris). *Say Her Name: Resisting Police Brutality against Black Women*. New York: African American Policy Forum, July 2015.

Crimp, Douglas. *Melancholia and Moralism: Essays on AIDS and Queer Politics*. Cambridge, MA: MIT Press, 2002.

Daniller, Andrew. "Majorities of Americans See at Least Some Discrimination against Black, Hispanic and Asian People in the U.S." *Pew Research Center*, March 18, 2021. https://www.pewresearch.org/fact-tank/2021/03/18/majorities

-of-americans-see-at-least-some-discrimination-against-black-hispanic-and-asian-people-in-the-u-s/.

Davidson, Cathy N. "Sentimental Novel." In *The Oxford Companion to Women's Writing in the United States*, edited by Cathy Davidson and Linda Wagner-Martin. New York: Oxford University Press, 2005. https://www.oxfordreference.com/view/10.1093/acref/9780195066081.001.0001/acref-9780195066081-e-0720.

Davis, Angela Y. *Abolition Democracy: Beyond Empire, Prisons, and Torture/Interviews with Angela Y. Davis*. New York: Seven Stories, 2005.

Delmas, Candice. *A Duty to Resist: When Disobedience Should Be Uncivil*. Oxford: Oxford University Press, 2018.

DeSante, Christopher D., and Candis Watts Smith. "Less Is More: A Cross-Generational Analysis of the Nature and Role of Racial Attitudes in the Twenty-First Century." *Journal of Politics* 82, no. 3 (2020): 967–80.

Dotson, Kristie. "Accumulating Epistemic Power: A Problem with Epistemology." *Philosophical Topics* 46, no. 1 (2018): 129–54.

———. "Conceptualizing Epistemic Oppression." *Social Epistemology* 28, no. 2 (2014): 115–38.

Douglass, Frederick. *Narrative of the Life of Frederick Douglass, an American Slave. In Frederick Douglass's Autobiographies*. Edited by Henry Louis Gates Jr. New York: Library of America, 1994.

———. "Reminiscences of the Anti-slavery Conflict (as Delivered during the Lecture Season of 1872–1873)." Frederick Douglass Papers, Microfilm Reel 14, p. 4–5. Library of Congress, 1872–73.

———. "What to the Slave Is the Fourth of July." In *The Oxford Frederick Douglass Reader*, edited by William L. Andrews, 108–30. New York: Oxford University Press, 1996.

———. "Why Is the Negro Lynched?" In *The Life and Writings of Frederick Douglass*. Vol. 4, *Reconstruction and After*, edited by Philip S. Foner, 491–523. New York: International, 1955.

Du Bois, W.E.B. *Black Reconstruction in America: An Essay toward a History of the Part Which Black Folk Played in the Attempt to Reconstruct Democracy in America, 1860–1880*. New York: Oxford University Press, 2014.

———. *Darkwater: Voices from within the Veil*. 1920. New York: Oxford University Press, 2014.

———. *Dusk of Dawn: An Essay toward an Autobiography of a Race Concept*. In *W.E.B. Du Bois: Writings*, 549–802. Edited by Nathan I. Huggins. 1st college ed. New York: Library of America, 1986.

———. *The Gift of Black Folk: The Negroes in the Making of America*. New York: Oxford University Press, 2014.

———. *The Souls of Black Folk.* 1903. New York: Oxford University Press, 2007.

———. *W.E.B. Du Bois: Writings.* Edited by Nathan I. Huggins. 1st college ed. New York: Library of America, 1986.

Dumm, Thomas L. "Political Theory for Losers." In *Vocations of Political Theory*, edited by Jason A. Frank and John Tambornino, 145–64. Minneapolis: University of Minnesota Press, 2000.

Easley, Cameron. "American Electorate Continues to Favor Leaving Confederate Relics in Place." *Morning Consult*, July 14, 2021. https://morningconsult.com/2021/07/14/confederate-statues-flag-military-bases-polling/.

Eckhouse, Laurel. "White Riot: Race, Institutions, and the 2016 US Election." *Politics, Groups, and Identities* 8, no. 2 (2018): 216–27.

Ehrich, Tom. "President Obama, Mourner in Chief." *Washington Post*, April 30, 2013. https://www.washingtonpost.com/national/on-faith/president-obama-mourner-in-chief/2013/04/30/3f89e656-b1a5-11e2-9fb1-62de9581c946_story.html.

Eligon, John. "They Push: They Protest; And Many Activists, Privately, Suffer as a Result." *New York Times*, March 26, 2018. https://www.nytimes.com/2018/03/26/us/they-push-they-protest-and-many-activists-privately-suffer-as-a-result.html.

Ewing, Eve. *1919*. Chicago: Haymarket Books, 2019.

Fallows, James. "Obama's Grace." *Atlantic*, June 27, 2015. https://www.theatlantic.com/politics/archive/2015/06/grace/397064/.

Feimster, Crystal. *Southern Horrors: Women and the Politics of Rape and Lynching.* Cambridge, MA: Harvard University Press, 2009.

Feinberg, Ayal, Regina Branton, and Valerie Martinez-Ebers. "Counties That Hosted a 2016 Trump Rally Saw a 226 Percent Increase in Hate Crimes." *Washington Post*, March 22, 2019. https://www.washingtonpost.com/politics/2019/03/22/trumps-rhetoric-does-inspire-more-hate-crimes/.

Feldstein, Ruth. "I Wanted the Whole World to See: Race, Gender, and Constructions of Motherhood in the Death of Emmett Till." In *Not June Cleaver: Women and Gender in Postwar America 1945–1960*, edited by June Meyerowitz, 261–305. Philadelphia: Temple University Press, 1994.

Feller, Madison. "Jacob Blake's Sister Tells the Nation She Doesn't Want Pity, She Wants Change." *Elle*, August 26, 2020. https://www.elle.com/culture/career-politics/a33805628/jacob-blake-sister-family-news-conference-police-shooting/.

Feuer, Alan. "Fears of White People Losing Out Permeate Capitol Rioters' Towns, Study Finds." *New York Times*, April 6, 2021. https://www.nytimes.com/2021/04/06/us/politics/capitol-riot-study.html.

Flock, Elizabeth. "How Gwendolyn Brooks' Poetry Is Connecting Emmett Till with the Violence in Chicago Today." *PBS News Hour*, March 7, 2017. https://www.pbs

.org/newshour/arts/poetry/gwendolyn-brooks-poetry-connecting-emmett-till-violence-chicago-today.

Foreman, Gabrielle. "The Spoken and the Silenced in *Incidents in the Life of a Slave Girl* and *Our Nig*." *Callaloo* 13, no. 2 (1990): 313–24.

Franchot, Jenny. "The Punishment of Esther: Frederick Douglass and the Construction of the Feminine." In *Frederick Douglass: New Literary and Historical Essays*, edited by Eric J. Sundquist, 141–65. Cambridge: Cambridge University Press, 1990.

Francis, Megan Ming. "Can Black Lives Matter inside United States Democracy." *Annals of the American Academy of Political and Social Science* 699, no. 1 (2022): 186–99.

———. *Civil Rights and the Making of the Modern American State*. Cambridge: Cambridge University Press, 2014.

Frank, Jason. *Publius and Political Imagination*. Lanham, MD: Rowman and Littlefield, 2013.

Frank, Jason A., and John Tambornino. *Vocations of Political Theory*. Minneapolis: University of Minnesota Press, 2000.

Gaonkar, Dilip. "Demos Noir: Riots after Riots." In *Nights of the Dispossessed: Riots Unbound*, edited by Natasha Ginwala and Gal Kirn, 29–54. New York: Columbia University Press, 2021.

Garza, Alicia. "A Herstory of the #Blacklivesmatter Movement." *Feminist Wire*, October 7, 2014. www.thefeministwire.com/2014/10/blacklivesmatter-2.

Giddings, Paula. "Missing in Action: Ida B. Wells, the NAACP, and the Historical Record." *Meridians: Feminism, Race, Transnationalism* 1, no. 2 (2001): 1–17.

Gillion, Daniel Q. *The Political Power of Protest: Minority Activism and Shifts in Public Policy*. Cambridge: Cambridge University Press, 2013.

Gilman, Nils. "The Collapse of Racial Liberalism." *American Interest* 13, no. 5 (2018). https://www.the-american-interest.com/2018/03/02/collapse-racial-liberalism/.

Gilmore, Ruth Wilson. *Golden Gulag: Prisons, Surplus, Crisis, and Opposition in Globalizing California*. Berkeley: University of California Press, 2007.

Gines, Kathryn T. *Hannah Arendt and the Negro Question*. Bloomington: Indiana University Press, 2014.

Goldberg, Michelle. "Democracy Grief Is Real: Seeing What Trump Is Doing to America, Many Find It Hard to Fight Off Despair." *New York Times*, December 13, 2019. https://www.nytimes.com/2019/12/13/opinion/sunday/trump-democracy.html.

Goldsby, Jacqueline. *A Spectacular Secret: Lynching in American Life and Literature*. Chicago: University of Chicago Press, 2006.

Gorup, Michael. "The Strange Fruit of the Tree of Liberty: Lynch Law and Popular Sovereignty in the United States." *Perspectives on Politics* 18, no. 3 (2020): 819–34.

Gould, Deborah B. *Moving Politics: Emotion and ACT UP's Fight against AIDS*. Chicago: University of Chicago Press, 2009.

Gregg, Melissa, and Gregory J. Seigworth, eds. *The Affect Theory Reader*. Durham, NC: Duke University Press, 2010.

Hajnal, Zoltan L. *Dangerously Divided: How Race and Class Shape Winning and Losing in American Politics*. Cambridge: Cambridge University Press, 2020.

———. "Who Loses in American Democracy? A Count of Votes Demonstrates the Limited Representation of African Americans." *American Political Science Review* 103, no. 1 (2009): 37–57.

Haley, Sarah. *No Mercy Here: Gender, Punishment, and the Making of Jim Crow Modernity*. Chapel Hill: University of North Carolina Press, 2016.

Hamlin, Françoise N. "Historians and Ethics: Finding Anne Moody." *American Historical Review* 125, no. 2 (2020): 487–97.

Hanchard, Michael. *The Spectre of Race: How Discrimination Haunts Western Democracy*. Princeton, NJ: Princeton University Press, 2018.

Harris, Fredrick C. "It Takes a Tragedy to Arouse Them: Collective Memory and Collective Action during the Civil Rights Movement." *Social Movement Studies* 5, no. 1 (2006): 19–43.

Harris, Johnny, and Binyamin Appelbaum. "Blue States, You're the Problem: Why Do States with Democratic Majorities Fail to Live Up to Their Values?" *New York Times*, November 9, 2021. https://www.nytimes.com/2021/11/09/opinion/democrats-blue-states-legislation.html.

Harris-Perry, Melissa. "Erica Garner Died of a Heart Attack: But It's Racism That's Killing Black Women." *Elle*, January 2, 2018. https://www.elle.com/culture/a14532058/erica-garner-death-black-women-racism/.

Hartman, Saidiya. *Lose Your Mother: A Journey Along the Atlantic Slave Route*. New York: Farrar, Straus and Giroux, 2007.

———. *Scenes of Subjection: Terror, Slavery, and Self-Making in Nineteenth-Century America*. New York: Oxford University Press, 1997.

———. "Venus in Two Acts." *Small Axe* 12, no. 2 (2008): 1–14.

———. *Wayward Lives, Beautiful Experiments: Intimate Histories of Riotous Black Girls, Troublesome Women, and Queer Radicals*. New York: W. W. Norton, 2019.

Havercroft, Jonathan. "Why Is There No Just Riot Theory?" *British Journal of Political Science* 51, no. 3 (2021): 909–23.

Heim, Joe. "Recounting a Day of Rage, Hate, Violence and Death: How a Rally of White Nationalists and Supremacists at the University of Virginia Turned into a 'Tragic, Tragic Weekend.'" *Washington Post*, August. 14, 2017. https://www.washingtonpost.com/graphics/2017/local/charlottesville-timeline/.

Hernandez, Joe. "Darnella Frazier, Who Filmed George Floyd's Murder, Wins an Honorary Pulitzer." *NPR*, June 11, 2021. https://www.npr.org/2021/06/11

/1005601724/darnella-frazier-teen-who-filmed-george-floyds-murder-wins-pulitzer-prize-citati.

Hesse, Barnor. "White Sovereignty (. . .), Black Life Politics: 'The N**** R They Couldn't Kill.'" *South Atlantic Quarterly* 116, no. 3 (2017): 581–604.

Hesse, Barnor, and Juliet Hooker. "Introduction: On Black Political Thought inside Global Black Protest." *South Atlantic Quarterly* 116, no. 3 (2017): 443–56.

Hirsch, Alexander Keller. "Hope, without Guarantees: Mourning, Natality, and the Will to Chance in Book XXIV of the Iliad." *Theory and Event* 18, no. 1 (2015). muse.jhu.edu/article/566092.

Hirsch, Alexander Keller, and David W. McIvor. *The Democratic Arts of Mourning: Political Theory and Loss*. Lanham, MD: Lexington Books, 2019.

Holloway, Karla F. C. *Passed On: African American Mourning Stories; A Memorial*. Durham, NC: Duke University Press, 2002.

Honig, Bonnie. *Antigone, Interrupted*. Cambridge: Cambridge University Press, 2013.

———. *Democracy and the Foreigner*. Princeton, NJ: Princeton University Press, 2001.

———. *A Feminist Theory of Refusal*. Cambridge, MA: Harvard University Press, 2021.

———. *Public Things: Democracy in Disrepair*. New York: Fordham University Press, 2017.

———. *Shell-Shocked: Feminist Criticism after Trump*. New York: Fordham University Press, 2021.

Hooghe, Marc, and Ruth Dassonneville. "Explaining the Trump Vote: The Effect of Racist Resentment and Anti-immigrant Sentiments." *PS: Political Science and Politics* 51, no. 3 (2018): 528–34.

Hooker, Juliet, ed. *Black and Indigenous Resistance in the Americas: From Multiculturalism to Racist Backlash*. Lanham, MD: Lexington Books, 2020.

———. "Black Lives Matter and the Paradoxes of U.S. Black Politics: From Democratic Sacrifice to Democratic Repair." *Political Theory* 44, no. 4 (2016): 448–69.

———. "Black Protest/White Grievance: On the Problem of White Political Imaginations *Not* Shaped by Loss." *South Atlantic Quarterly* 116, no. 3 (2017): 483–504.

———. "'A Black Sister to Massachusetts': Latin America and the Fugitive Democratic Ethos of Frederick Douglass." *American Political Science Review* 109, no. 4 (2015): 690–702.

———. "Hemispheric Comparison in Latin American Anti-imperial Thought." In *The Oxford Handbook of Comparative Political Theory*, edited by Leigh K. Jenco, Murad Idris, and Megan C. Thomas, 415–38. New York: Oxford University Press, 2020.

———. "How Can the Democratic Party Confront Racist Backlash? White Grievance in Hemispheric Perspective." *Polity* 52, no. 3 (2020): 355–69.

———. *Race and the Politics of Solidarity*. New York: Oxford University Press, 2009.

———. *Theorizing Race in the Americas: Douglass, Sarmiento, Du Bois, and Vasconcelos*. New York: Oxford University Press, 2017.

Human Rights Campaign. *Violence against the Transgender Community in 2019*. https://www.hrc.org/resources/violence-against-the-transgender-community-in-2019.

Hutchings, Vincent. "Change or More of the Same? Evaluating Racial Attitudes in the Obama Era." *Public Opinion Quarterly* 73, no. 5 (2009): 917–42.

———. "Race, Punishment, and Public Opinion." *Perspectives on Politics* 13, no. 3 (2015): 757–61.

Icaza Garza, Rosalba, and Xochitl Leyva Solano, eds. *En tiempos de muerte: cuerpos, rebeldias, resistencias*. Buenos Aires: Consejo Latinoamericano de Ciencias Sociales/Cooperativa Editorial Retos/Institute of Social Studies, 2019.

Idia, Tereneh. "The Tree of Life Shooting Devastated All of Pittsburgh: I Can't Help but Ask; Why Aren't Black Lives Mourned This Way?" *Public Source: Stories for a Better Pittsburgh*, November 15, 2018. https://www.publicsource.org/the-tree-of-life-shooting-devastated-all-of-pittsburgh-i-cant-help-but-ask-why-arent-black-lives-mourned-this-way/.

Illing, Sean. "January 6 Should've Moderated the GOP: It Did the Opposite." *Vox*, January 6, 2022. https://www.vox.com/policy-and-politics/22815765/january-6-capitol-insurrection-conservatism-sam-adler-bell.

Ioanide, Paula. *The Emotional Politics of Racism: How Feelings Trump Facts in an Era of Colorblindness*. Stanford, CA: Stanford University Press, 2015.

Irwin, Neil, and Josh Katz. "The Geography of Trumpism." *New York Times*, March 12, 2016. www.nytimes.com/2016/03/13/upshot/the-geography-of-trumpism.html.

Jackson, Sarah J. "Making #Blacklivesmatter in the Shadow of Selma: Collective Memory and Racial Justice Activism in US News." *Communication, Culture and Critique* 14, no. 3 (2021): 385–404.

Jacobs, Harriet A. *Incidents in the Life of a Slave Girl: Written by Herself*. Edited by Lydia Maria Child and Jean Fagan Yellin. Enlarged ed. Cambridge, MA: Harvard University Press, 2009.

Jacobs, Harriet A., John S. Jacobs, Louisa Matilda Jacobs, and Jean Fagan Yellin. *The Harriet Jacobs Family Papers*. Vol. 2. Chapel Hill: University of North Carolina Press, 2008.

Jacobs, John S. "A True Tale of Slavery." In *Incidents in the Life of a Slave Girl: Written by Herself*, 265–92. Edited by Lydia Maria Child and Jean Fagan Yellin. Enlarged ed. Cambridge, MA: Harvard University Press, 2009.

James, Joy. "Abolitionist and Ancestor: The Legacy of Erica Garner." *American Literary History* (2021): e27–39.

———. "The Womb of Western Theory: Trauma, Time Theft, and the Captive Maternal." *Carceral Notebooks* 12, no. 1 (2016): 253–96.

Jardina, Ashley. *White Identity Politics*. Cambridge: Cambridge University Press, 2019.

Johnson, Akilah. "In Alaska Native Villages and across Communities of Color, the Enduring Silence of Grief." *Washington Post*, November 4, 2021. https://www.washingtonpost.com/health/2021/11/04/communities-of-color-loss-grief-gap/.

Johnson, Jeh Charles. "It's Time to Show the Real Horror of Mass Shootings: In Pictures." *Washington Post*, June 1, 2022. https://www.washingtonpost.com/opinions/2022/06/01/uvalde-mass-shootings-graphic-images/.

Johnston, Steven. "Two Cheers for Ferguson's Democratic Citizens." *Theory and Event* 17, no. 3, supplement (2014). muse.jhu.edu/article/559371.

J.T. "'I Lose Too,' Says White Reader." *Freedom: Where One Is Enslaved, All Are in Chains!* 1, no. 10 (October 1951): 1–8.

Juhasz, Alexandra. "How Do I (Not) Look? Live Feed Video and Viral Black Death." *JSTOR Daily*, July 20, 2016. https://daily.jstor.org/how-do-i-not-look/.

Junior, Nyasha, and Jeremy Schipper. *Black Samson: The Untold Story of an American Icon*. New York: Oxford University Press, 2020.

Junn, Jane. "The Trump Majority: White Womanhood and the Making of Female Voters in the US." *Politics, Groups, and Identities* 5, no. 2 (2017): 343–52.

Kaba, Mariame. *We Do This 'Til We Free Us: Abolitionist Organizing and Transforming Justice*. Chicago: Haymarket Books, 2021.

Kafer, Alison. *Feminist, Queer, Crip*. Bloomington: Indiana University Press, 2013.

Kelley, Robin D. G. *Freedom Dreams: The Black Radical Imagination*. Boston: Beacon, 2002.

King, Martin Luther Jr. *Where Do We Go from Here: Chaos or Community?* Boston: Beacon, 2010.

Kirkpatrick, Jennet. *Uncivil Disobedience: Studies in Violence and Democratic Politics*. Princeton, NJ: Princeton University Press, 2008.

Kochhar, Rakesh, and Richard Fry. "Wealth Inequality Has Widened along Racial, Ethnic Lines since End of Great Recession." *Pew Research Center*, December 12, 2014. https://www.pewresearch.org/fact-tank/2014/12/12/racial-wealth-gaps-great-recession/.

Kranish, Michael. "How Tucker Carlson Became the Voice of White Grievance." *New York Times*, July 14, 2021. https://www.washingtonpost.com/politics/tucker-carlson/2021/07/13/398fa720-dd9f-11eb-a501-0e69b5d012e5_story.html.

Kuziemko, Ilyana, and Ebonya Washington. "Why Did the Democrats Lose the South? Bringing New Data to an Old Debate." *American Economic Review* 108, no. 10 (2018): 2830–67.

Lebron, Christopher J. *Color of Our Shame: Race and Justice in Our Time*. Oxford: Oxford University Press, 2013.

———. *The Making of Black Lives Matter: A Brief History of an Idea*. Oxford: Oxford University Press, 2017.

Lemmons, Kasi, dir. *Harriet*. Focus Features, 2019.

LeSure, Ainsley. "The White Mob, (In)Equality before the Law, and Racial Common Sense: A Critical Race Reading of the Negro Question in 'Reflections on Little Rock.'" *Political Theory* 49, no. 1 (2020): 3–27.

Levitsky, Steven, and Daniel Ziblatt. *How Democracies Die*. New York: Crown, 2018.

Lipsitz, George. *The Possessive Investment in Whiteness: How White People Profit from Identity Politics*. Philadelphia: Temple University Press, 2006.

Livingston, Alexander. "Fidelity to Truth: Gandhi and the Genealogy of Civil Disobedience." *Political Theory* 46, no. 4 (2018): 511–36.

Locke, Jill. "Against Nostalgia: The Political Theory of Ida B. Wells." In *American Political Thought: An Alternative View*, edited by Jonathan Keller and Alex Zamalin, 55–71. New York: Routledge, 2017.

———. "Little Rock's Social Question: Reading Arendt on School Desegregation and Social Climbing." *Political Theory* 41, no. 4 (2013): 533–61.

Lopez, German. "Donald Trump's Long History of Racism, from the 1970s to 2020." *Vox*, August 13, 2020. https://www.vox.com/2016/7/25/12270880/donald-trump-racist-racism-history.

Lorde, Audre. *Sister Outsider: Essays and Speeches*. Trumansburg, NY: Crossing, 1984.

Lupino, Ferris. "American Stasis: Conflict, Order, and Leadership in Black Political Thought." PhD diss., Brown University, 2020.

MacKinnon, Catharine A. "Sexuality, Pornography, and Method: Pleasure under Patriarchy." *Ethics* 99, no. 2 (1989): 314–46.

Makalani, Minkah. "Discussant Comments, Panel on Violence, Visuality, and the Racial State of Exception." Western Political Science Association Annual Meeting, Vancouver, Canada, April 13–15, 2017.

———. "What They Did to My Baby: A New Memoir by Trayvon Martin's Parents Lays Bare the Emotional Costs of Watching Your Child's Murder Catalyze a Social Movement." *Slate*, May 23, 2017. https://slate.com/culture/2017/05/rest-in-power-the-enduring-life-of-trayvon-martin-reviewed-by-minkah-makalani.html.

Maly, Michael, Heather Dalmage, and Nancy Michaels. "The End of an Idyllic World: Nostalgia Narratives, Race, and the Construction of White Powerlessness." *Critical Sociology* 39, no. 5 (2013): 757–79.

Mann, Geoff. "Why Does Country Music Sound White? Race and the Voice of Nostalgia." *Ethnic and Racial Studies* 31, no. 1 (2008): 73–100.

Manne, Kate. *Down Girl: The Logic of Misogyny*. New York: Oxford University Press, 2018.

———. "Melancholy Whiteness (or, Shame-Faced in Shadows)." *Philosophy and Phenomenological Research* 96, no. 1 (2018): 233–42.

Marcus, Josh. "Pat Robertson Calls Critical Race Theory an 'Evil' Urging Black People to Take 'Whip Handle' against Whites." *Independent*, June 27, 2021. https://www.independent.co.uk/news/world/americas/pat-robertson-critical-race-theory-b1873399.html.

Mariotti, Shannon. "On the Passing of the First-Born Son: Emerson's 'Focal Distancing,' Du Bois' 'Second Sight,' and Disruptive Particularity." *Political Theory* 37, no. 3 (2009): 351–74.

Martel, James. *Unburied Bodies: Subversive Corpses and the Authority of the Dead.* Amherst, MA: Amherst College Press, 2018.

Martí, José. "A Town Sets a Black Man on Fire." In José Martí, *José Martí: Selected Writings*, trans. Esther Allen, 310–13. New York: Penguin Classics, 2002.

Massanari, Adrienne L., and Shira Chess. "Attack of the 50-Foot Social Justice Warrior: The Discursive Construction of SJW Memes as the Monstrous Feminine." *Feminist Media Studies* 18, no. 4 (2018): 525–42.

Maxwell, Lida, Cristina Beltrán, Shatema Threadcraft, Stephen K. White, Miriam Leonard, and Bonnie Honig. "The 'Agonistic Turn'": Political Theory and the Displacement of Politics in New Contexts." *Contemporary Political Theory* 18, no. 4 (2019): 640–72.

Mbembé, Achille. "Necropolitics." *Public Culture* 15, no. 1 (2003): 11–40.

McAfee, Noëlle. *Democracy and the Political Unconscious.* New York: Columbia University Press, 2008.

McCarthy, Thomas. "Coming to Terms with Our Past, Part II: On the Morality and Politics of Reparations for Slavery." *Political Theory* 32, no. 6 (2004): 750–72.

McIvor, David. "May 25 Should Be a Day of Mourning for George Floyd." *New York Times*, May 21, 2021. https://www.nytimes.com/2021/05/21/opinion/may-25-george-floyd-death.html.

———. *Mourning in America: Race and the Politics of Loss.* Ithaca, NY: Cornell University Press, 2016.

McIvor, David W., Juliet Hooker, Ashley Atkins, Athena Athanasiou, and George Shulman. "Mourning Work: Death and Democracy during a Pandemic." *Contemporary Political Theory* 20, no. 1 (2021): 165–99.

McQueen, Steve, dir. *12 Years a Slave.* Twentieth Century-Fox, 2013.

Menzel, Annie. "'Awful Gladness': The Dual Political Rhetorics of Du Bois's 'Of the Passing of the First-Born.'" *Political Theory* 47, no. 1 (2019): 32–56.

———. "The Political Life of Black Infant Mortality." PhD diss., University of Washington, 2014.

Metzl, Jonathan M. *Dying of Whiteness: How the Politics of Racial Resentment Is Killing America's Heartland.* New York: Basic Books, 2019.

Mills, Charles W. *Black Rights/White Wrongs: The Critique of Racial Liberalism*. New York: Oxford University Press, 2017.

———. *The Racial Contract*. Ithaca, NY: Cornell University Press, 1997.

———. "White Ignorance." In *Race and Epistemologies of Ignorance*, edited by Nancy Tuana and Shannon Sullivan, 13–38. Albany: State University of New York Press, 2007.

Mitchell, Koritha. *Living with Lynching: African American Lynching Plays, Performance, and Citizenship, 1890–1930*. Champaign: University of Illinois Press, 2011.

Monte, Lindsay M., and Daniel J. Perez-Lopez. *Covid-19 Pandemic Hit Black Households Harder Than White Households, Even When Pre-pandemic Socio-economic Disparities Are Taken into Account*. US Census Bureau, July 21, 2021. https://www.census.gov/library/stories/2021/07/how-pandemic-affected-black-and-white-households.html.

Moraga, Cherríe, and Gloria Anzaldúa. *This Bridge Called My Back: Writings by Radical Women of Color*. 2nd ed. New York: Kitchen Table/Women of Color, 1983.

Morrison, Toni. "Unspeakable Things Unspoken: The Afro-American Presence in American Literature." Tanner Lectures on Human Values, University of Michigan, Ann Arbor, October 7, 1988. https://tannerlectures.utah.edu/_resources/documents/a-to-z/m/morrison90.pdf.

Moten, Fred. "Black Mo'nin'." In *Loss: The Politics of Mourning*, edited by David L. Eng and David Kazanjian, 59–76. Berkeley: University of California Press, 2003.

The Movement for Black Lives. "*Vision for Black Lives*." 2020. https://m4bl.org/policy-platforms/.

Mullings, Leith. "Neoliberal Racism and the Movement for Black Lives in the United States." In *Black and Indigenous Resistance in the Americas: From Multiculturalism to Racist Backlash*, edited by Juliet Hooker, 247–92. Lanham, MD: Lexington Books, 2020.

Mutz, Diana C. "Status Threat, Not Economic Hardship, Explains the 2016 Presidential Vote." *Proceedings of the National Academy of Sciences* 115, no. 19 (2018): E4330–39.

Nash, Jennifer C. "Black Maternal Aesthetics." *Theory and Event* 22, no. 3 (2019): 551–75.

———. "The Political Life of Black Motherhood." *Feminist Studies* 44, no. 3 (2018): 699–712.

———. "Unwidowing: Rachel Jeantel, Black Death, and the 'Problem' of Black Intimacy." *Signs: Journal of Women in Culture and Society* 41, no. 4 (2016): 751–74.

National Black Justice Coalition, National Center for Transgender Equality, and the National Gay and Lesbian Task Force. *Injustice at Every Turn: A Look at Black Respondents in the National Transgender Discrimination Survey*. 2019. https://www.hrc.org/resources/violence-against-the-transgender-community-in-2019.

National Partnership for Women and Families. *Black Women's Maternal Health: A Multifaceted Approach to Addressing Persistent and Dire Health Disparities.* April 2018. https://www.nationalpartnership.org/our-work/health/reports/black-womens-maternal-health.html.

Nayak, Suryia. "Occupation of Racial Grief, Loss as a Resource: Learning from 'The Combahee River Collective Black Feminist Statement.'" *Psychological Studies* 64, no. 3 (2019): 1–13.

Nelson, Deborah. *Tough Enough: Arbus, Arendt, Didion, McCarthy, Sontag, Weil.* Chicago: University of Chicago Press, 2017.

Northup, Solomon. *Twelve Years a Slave. Narrative of Solomon Northup, a Citizen of New-York, Kidnapped in Washington City in 1841, and Rescued in 1853, from a Cotton Plantation near the Red River, in Louisiana.* Auburn/Buffalo: Derby and Miller/Derby, Orton and Mulligan, 1853.

Norton, Anne. "The King's New Body." *Theory and Event* 20, no. 1 (2017): 116–26.

Nuamah, Sally A. "The Cost of Participating While Poor and Black: Toward a Theory of Collective Participatory Debt." *Perspectives on Politics* 19, no. 4 (2021): 1115–30.

Nudelman, Franny. "Harriet Jacobs and the Sentimental Politics of Female Suffering." *ELH* 59, no. 4 (1992): 939–64.

Nussbaum, Martha C. *Anger and Forgiveness: Resentment, Generosity, Justice.* New York: Oxford University Press, 2016.

"Official Statement from Samaria Rice, Mother of Tamir Rice, Lisa Simpson, Mother of Richard Risher, and the Collective." March 21, 2021. https://docs.google.com/document/d/1rb4h6d2PjECBz0_ILawSyk7LDEPMjdJpSKSNtwYbhG4/edit.

Ohlheiser, Abby. "Why 'Social Justice Warrior,' a Gamergate Insult, Is Now a Dictionary Entry." *Washington Post,* October 7, 2015. https://www.washingtonpost.com/news/the-intersect/wp/2015/10/07/why-social-justice-warrior-a-gamergate-insult-is-now-a-dictionary-entry/.

Okeowo, Alexis. "Can Stacey Abrams Save American Democracy?" *Vogue,* August 12, 2019. https://www.vogue.com/article/stacey-abrams-american-democracy-vogue-september-2019-issue.

Olson, Joel. *The Abolition of White Democracy.* Minneapolis: University of Minnesota Press, 2004.

Owens, Emily A. *Consent in the Presence of Force: Sexual Violence and Black Women's Survival in Antebellum New Orleans.* Durham, NC: University of North Carolina Press, 2023.

Painter, Nell Irvin. *The History of White People.* New York: W. W. Norton, 2010.

Pape, Robert A., and Keven Ruby. "The Capitol Rioters Aren't Like Other Extremists." *Atlantic,* February 2, 2021. https://www.theatlantic.com/ideas/archive/2021/02/the-capitol-rioters-arent-like-other-extremists/617895/.

Papenfuss, Mary. "Ron Johnson Says He Would Have Been 'Concerned' about Black Capitol Rioters." *Huffpost*, March 12, 2021. https://www.huffpost.com/entry/ron-johnson-capitol-riot-black-lives-matter_n_604c0313c5b636ed337a71ce.

Pasternak, Avia. "Political Rioting: A Moral Assessment." *Philosophy and Public Affairs* 46, no. 4 (2018): 384–418.

Phoenix, Davin L. *The Anger Gap: How Race Shapes Emotion in Politics*. Cambridge: Cambridge University Press, 2019.

Pineda, Erin R. *Seeing Like an Activist: Civil Disobedience and the Civil Rights Movement*. New York: Oxford University Press, 2021.

Pinn, Anthony B. *Why, Lord? Suffering and Evil in Black Theology*. London: Bloomsbury, 1999.

Pitkin, Hanna F. *The Concept of Representation*. Berkeley: University of California Press, 1967.

Price, Melynda. "What Would Mama Do? Save Our Sons and Daughters (SOSAD) and Anti-violence Organizing among Black Mothers of Murdered Children in Detroit." Paper presented at the Center for the Study of Law and Society, University of California–Berkeley Law School, November 6, 2017.

Quashie, Kevin. *The Sovereignty of Quiet: Beyond Resistance in Black Culture*. New Brunswick, NJ: Rutgers University Press, 2012.

Raifman, Julia, Alexandra Skinner, and Aaron Sojourner. *Economic Policy Institute Working Economics Blog*, February 7, 2022. https://www.epi.org/blog/the-unequal-toll-of-covid-19-on-workers/.

Rakia, Raven. "Black Riot." *New Inquiry*, November 14, 2013. https://thenewinquiry.com/black-riot/.

Rankine, Claudia. *Citizen: An American Lyric*. Minneapolis: Graywolf, 2014.

———. "The Condition of Black Life Is One of Mourning." *New York Times*, June 22, 2015. https://www.nytimes.com/2015/06/22/magazine/the-condition-of-black-life-is-one-of-mourning.html.

Reinhardt, Mark. "Who Speaks for Margaret Garner? Slavery, Silence, and the Politics of Ventriloquism." *Critical Inquiry* 29, no. 1 (2002): 81–119.

Riggs, Marlon. "Letter to the Dead." *Breakthrough* 17, no. 1 (Spring 1993): 17–21.

Roberts, Neil. *Freedom as Marronage*. Chicago: University of Chicago Press, 2015.

Robertson, Campbell, and Robert Gebeloff. "How Millions of Women Became the Most Essential Workers in America." *New York Times*, April 18, 2020. https://www.nytimes.com/2020/04/18/us/coronavirus-women-essential-workers.html.

Rodríguez Aguilera, Meztli Yoalli. "Grieving Geographies, Mourning Waters: Life, Death, and Environmental Gendered Racialized Struggles in Mexico." *Feminist Anthropology* 3 (2022): 28–43.

Rogers, Melvin. "Introduction: Disposable Lives." *Theory and Event* 17, no. 3, supplement (2014). muse.jhu.edu/article/559375.

———. "Lynching and the Horrific: From Ida B. Wells to Billie Holiday." In *The Darkened Light of Faith: Race, Democracy, and Freedom in African American Political Thought*. Princeton, NJ: Princeton University Press, forthcoming.

———. "The People, Rhetoric, and Affect: On the Political Force of Du Bois's *The Souls of Black Folk*." *American Political Science Review* 106, no. 1 (2012): 188–203.

Rogers, Melvin L., and Jack Turner. *African American Political Thought: A Collected History*. Chicago: University of Chicago Press, 2021.

Rose, Tricia. *Black Noise: Rap Music and Black Culture in Contemporary America*. Hanover, NH: University Press of New England, 1994.

Rosin, Hanna. "The End of Men." *Atlantic*, July–August 2010. https://www.theatlantic.com/magazine/archive/2010/07/the-end-of-men/308135/.

Rushdy, Ashraf. "Exquisite Corpse." *Transition*, no. 83 (2000): 70–77.

Sampathkumar, Mythili. "Erica Garner Dead: 'I Can't Breathe' Police Brutality Campaigner and Daughter of Eric Garner Dies Aged 27." *Independent*, December 30, 2017. https://www.independent.co.uk/news/world/americas/erica-garner-police-brutality-activist-died-a8134726.html.

Savage, Kirk. *Standing Soldiers, Kneeling Slaves: Race, War, and Monument in Nineteenth-Century America*. Princeton, NJ: Princeton University Press, 1997.

Schaffner, Brian F., Matthew MacWilliams, and Tatishe Nteta. "Understanding White Polarization in the 2016 Vote for President: The Sobering Role of Racism and Sexism." *Political Science Quarterly* 133, no. 1 (2018): 9–34.

Schouten, Fredreka. "'No One with Power Is Listening': Activists Warn Redistricting Moves in the South Threaten Black Political Power." *CNN Politics*, December 9, 2021. https://www.cnn.com/2021/12/08/politics/redistricting-black-political-power/index.html.

Schwartzberg, Melissa, ed. *Protest and Dissent: Nomos LXII*. Vol. 3. New York: New York University Press, 2020.

Setter, Davyd. "Changes in Support for US Black Movements, 1966–2016: From Civil Rights to Black Lives Matter." *Mobilization: An International Quarterly* 26, no. 4 (2021): 475–88.

Sewall, Gilbert T. "The Debasing of Our Civic Currency." *American Spectator*, May 6, 2016. http://spectator.org/the-debasing-of-our-civic-currency.

Sharpe, Christina. *In the Wake: On Blackness and Being*. Durham, NC: Duke University Press, 2016.

Shear, Michael D., Stacey Cowley, and Alan Rappeport. "Biden's Push for Equity in Government Hits Legal and Political Roadblocks." *New York Times*, June 26, 2021. https://www.nytimes.com/2021/06/26/us/politics/biden-racial-equity.html?searchResultPosition=3.

Shear, Michael D., and Maggie Haberman. "Trump Defends Initial Remarks on Charlottesville: Again Blames 'Both Sides.'" *New York Times*, August 15, 2017. https://www.nytimes.com/2017/08/15/us/politics/trump-press-conference-charlottesville.html.

Shelby, Tommie, and Brandon M. Terry. *To Shape a New World: Essays on the Political Philosophy of Martin Luther King, Jr.* Cambridge, MA: Belknap Press of Harvard University Press, 2018.

Shelby, Tommie. *Dark Ghettos: Injustice, Dissent, and Reform*. Cambridge, MA: Harvard University Press, 2016.

Shilliam, Robbie. *Race and the Undeserving Poor: From Abolition to Brexit*. Newcastle upon Tyne: Agenda, 2018.

Shklar, Judith N. *The Faces of Injustice*. New Haven, CT: Yale University Press, 1990.

Simpson, Audra. *Mohawk Interruptus: Political Life across the Borders of Settler States.* Durham, NC: Duke University Press, 2014.

Smith, Christen A. "Facing the Dragon: Black Mothering, Sequelae, and Gendered Necropolitics in the Americas." *Transforming Anthropology* 24, no. 1 (2016): 31–48.

Smith, Patricia. "Black, Poured Directly into the Wound." *Poetry* (February 2017): 471–72.

Smith, William. "Deliberation in an Age of (Un) Civil Resistance." *Journal of Deliberative Democracy* 16, no. 1 (2020): 14–19.

Snorton, C. Riley. *Black on Both Sides: A Racial History of Trans Identity*. Minneapolis: University of Minnesota Press, 2017.

Snorton, C. Riley, and Jin Haritaworn. "Trans Necropolitics: A Transnational Reflection on Violence, Death, and the Trans of Color Afterlife." In *The Transgender Studies Reader 2*, edited by Aizura Aren and Stryker Susan, 66–76. New York: Routledge, 2013.

Snyder, Greta. "'Marking Whiteness' for Cross-Racial Solidarity." *Du Bois Review* 12, no. 2 (Fall 2015): 297–320.

Sokoloff, William W. *Confrontational Citizenship: Reflections on Hatred, Rage, Revolution, and Revolt*. Albany, NY: State University of New York Press, 2017.

Sommer, Doris. *Foundational Fictions: The National Romances of Latin America.* Berkeley: University of California Press, 1991.

Sontag, Susan. *Regarding the Pain of Others*. New York: Picador, 2003.

Southern Poverty Law Center. *Whose Heritage? Public Symbols of the Confederacy.* Montgomery, AL, 2016. https://www.splcenter.org/sites/default/files/com_whose_heritage.pdf.

Spade, Dean. *Normal Life: Administrative Violence, Critical Trans Politics, and the Limits of Law*. Rev. and expanded ed. Durham, NC: Duke University Press, 2015.

Steele, Meili. "Arendt versus Ellison on Little Rock: The Role of Language in Political Judgment." *Constellations* 9, no. 2 (2002): 184–206.

Stern, Julia A. *The Plight of Feeling: Sympathy and Dissent in the Early American Novel.* Chicago: University of Chicago Press, 1997.

Stow, Simon. *American Mourning: Tragedy, Democracy, and the Politics of Public Loss.* Cambridge: Cambridge University Press, 2016.

———. "From Upper Canal to Lower Manhattan: Memorialization and the Politics of Loss." *Perspectives on Politics* 10, no. 3 (2012): 687–700.

Sullivan, Shannon. "White Priority." *Critical Philosophy of Race* 5, no. 2 (2017): 171–82.

Syedullah, Jasmine. "The Kind of Loss Her Freedom Cost: Jacobs' Abolitionist Theory of Contract and Captivity." Paper presented at the Seeing beyond the Veil: Race/ing Key Concepts in Political Theory Conference, Brown University, November 8–9, 2018.

———. "No Place Like Home: Practicing Freedom in the Loopholes of Captivity." In *Paths to Freedom: On the Architectures of Carcerality*, edited by Isabelle Kirkham-Lewitt, 459–84. New York: Columbia University Press, 2020.

Tan, Sandra. "911 Call Taker Fired after Hearing Determines She Mishandled Call during Tops Shooting." *Buffalo News*, June 2, 2022. https://buffalonews.com/news/local/911-call-taker-fired-after-hearing-determines-she-mishandled-call-during-tops-shooting/article_8c8a58ce-e282-11ec-922f-87146267c849.html.

Tate, Claudia. *Domestic Allegories of Political Desire: The Black Heroine's Text at the Turn of the Century*. New York: Oxford University Press, 1992.

Tavernise, Sabrina, Sheera Frenkel, David D. Kirkpatrick, Campbell Robertson, Mark Scheffler and Haley Willis. "'Our President Wants Us Here': The Mob That Stormed the Capitol." *New York Times*, January 9, 2021. https://www.nytimes.com/2021/01/09/us/capitol-rioters.html.

Taylor, Keeanga-Yamahtta. *From #Blacklivesmatter to Black Liberation*. Chicago: Haymarket Books, 2016.

Terry, Brandon M. "Which Way to Memphis? Political Theory, Narrative, and the Politics of Historical Imagination in the Civil Rights Movement." PhD diss., Yale University, 2012.

Tesler, Michael. "The Return of Old-Fashioned Racism to White Americans' Partisan Preferences in the Early Obama Era." *Journal of Politics* 75, no. 1 (2013): 110–23.

Tessman, Lisa. *Burdened Virtues: Virtue Ethics for Liberatory Struggles*. New York: Oxford University Press, 2005.

Thebault, Reis, Andrew Ba Tran, and Vanessa Williams. "The Coronavirus Is Infecting and Killing Black Americans at an Alarmingly High Rate." *Washington Post*, April 7, 2020. https://www.washingtonpost.com/nation/2020/04/07/coronavirus-is-infecting-killing-black-americans-an-alarmingly-high-rate-post-analysis-shows/.

Thomas, Deborah A. *Political Life in the Wake of the Plantation: Sovereignty, Witnessing, Repair*. Durham, NC: Duke University Press, 2019.

Thompson, Debra. "An Exoneration of Black Rage." *South Atlantic Quarterly* 116, no. 3 (2017): 457–81.

Threadcraft, Shatema. "Feminist Abolition Democracy and Toni Morrison's Democratic Ethics of Care." Paper presented at the Third Black Political Thought and History Workshop, Clérac, France, July 3–8, 2022.

———. "Intimate Injustice, Political Obligation, and the Dark Ghetto." *Signs* 39, no. 3 (2014): 735–60.

———. *Intimate Justice: The Black Female Body and the Body Politic*. New York: Oxford University Press, 2016.

———. "North American Necropolitics and Gender: On #Blacklivesmatter and Black Femicide." *South Atlantic Quarterly* 116, no. 3 (2017): 553–79.

———. "Spectacular Death, the #metoo Mundane, and Intimate Justice." Paper presented at the Seeing beyond the Veil: Race-ing Key Concepts in Political Theory Conference, Brown University, November 8–9, 2018.

Tindal, Brenda. "'Its Own Special Attraction': Meditations on Martyrdom and the Iconicity of Civil Rights Widows." In *Configuring America: Iconic Figures, Visuality, and the American Identity*, edited by Klaus Rieser-Wohlfarter, Michael Fuchs, and Michael Phillips, 259–76. Chicago: Intellect Books, 2013.

Tracy, Abigail. "New Photo Suggests Private-Jet Trumpers Proceeded toward Capitol after Rally." *Vanity Fair*, March 24, 2021. https://www.vanityfair.com/news/2021/03/donald-trump-stop-the-steal-rally-memphis-private-jet.

———. "A Private Jet of Rich Trumpers Wanted to 'Stop the Steal'—but They Don't Want You to Read This." *Vanity Fair*, March 18, 2021. https://www.vanityfair.com/news/2021/03/a-private-jet-of-rich-trumpers-wanted-to-stop-the-steal.

Traister, Rebecca. "The Summer of Rage: White Men Are the Minority in the United States, No Wonder They Get Uncomfortable When Their Power Is Challenged." *Cut*, June 29, 2018. https://www.thecut.com/2018/06/summer-of-rage.html.

Tucker, Neely, and Peter Holley. "Dylann Roof's Eerie Tour of American Slavery at Its Beginning, Middle and End," *Washington Post*, July 1, 2015. https://www.washingtonpost.com/news/post-nation/wp/2015/07/01/dylann-roofs-eerie-tour-of-american-slavery-at-its-beginning-middle-and-end/.

Tulis, Jeffrey K., and Nicole Mellow. *Legacies of Losing in American Politics*. Chicago: University of Chicago Press, 2018.

Turner, Sasha. "The Nameless and the Forgotten: Maternal Grief, Sacred Protection, and the Archive of Slavery." *Slavery and Abolition* 38, no. 2 (2017): 232–50.

Tuttle, Ian. "The 'Blood-Stained Banner' in Charleston." *The Corner* (blog), *National Review*, June 18, 2015. https://www.nationalreview.com/corner/blood-stained-banner-charleston-ian-tuttle/.

Tzoreff, Avi-ram. "Carpets, Books, and Jewelry: Why Looting Was Central to the Nakba." *+972 Magazine*, March 24, 2022. https://www.972mag.com/looting-1948-historiography/.

van Den Berghe, Pierre L. *Race and Racism: A Comparative Perspective*. New York: Wiley, 1967.

Varela, Julio Ricardo. "Trump's Anti-immigrant 'Invasion' Rhetoric Was Echoed by the El Paso Shooter for a Reason." *NBC News*, August 5, 2019. https://www.nbcnews.com/think/opinion/trump-s-anti-immigrant-invasion-rhetoric-was-echoed-el-paso-ncna1039286.

von Redecker, Eva. "Ownership's Shadow: Neoauthoritarianism as Defense of Phantom Possession." *Critical Times* 3, no. 1 (2020): 33–67.

Vozzella, Laura, and April Bethea. "'White Lives Matter' Painted on Arthur Ashe Monument in Richmond." *Washington Post*, June 17, 2020. https://www.washingtonpost.com/local/third-confederate-statue-toppled-by-protesters-in-richmond/2020/06/17/9f318446-b054-11ea-8f56-63f38c990077_story.html.

Walker, Hannah, Loren Collingwood, and Tehama Lopez Bunyasi. "White Response to Black Death: A Racialized Theory of White Attitudes towards Gun Control." *Du Bois Review: Social Science Research on Race* 17, no. 1 (2020): 165–88.

Walker, Margaret Urban. "Moral Vulnerability and the Task of Reparations." In *Vulnerability: New Essays in Ethics and Feminist Philosophy*, edited by Catriona Mackenzie, Wendy Rogers and Susan Dodds, 110–33: Oxford: Oxford University Press, 2014.

Wallace, Sophia Jordán, and Chris Zepeda-Millán. *Walls, Cages, and Family Separation: Race and Immigration Policy in the Trump Era*. Cambridge: Cambridge University Press, 2020.

Walt, Vivienne. "How Assa Traoré Became the Face of France's Movement for Racial Justice." *Time*, December 11, 2020. https://time.com/5919814/guardians-of-the-year-2020-assa-traore/.

Warren, Robert Penn. *Who Speaks for the Negro?* New Haven, CT: Yale University Press, 1965.

Wasow, Omar. "Agenda Seeding: How 1960s Black Protests Moved Elites, Public Opinion and Voting." *American Political Science Review* 114, no. 3 (2020): 638–59.

Wells-Barnett, Ida B. *Crusade for Justice: The Autobiography of Ida B. Wells*. Chicago: University of Chicago Press, 1970.

———. *The Light of Truth: Writings of an Anti-lynching Crusader*. Edited by Mia Bay. New York: Penguin Books, 2014.

Williams, Clarence. "Pepper-Sprayed, Arrested, Grieving: The Mother Who Was at the Front Lines of D.C. Anti-police Protests." *Washington Post*, December 20, 2021. https://www.washingtonpost.com/dc-md-va/2021/12/20/karen-hylton-police-protests/.

Williams, Dominic A. "The Death of Erica Garner Teaches Why Violence against the Black Community Still Needs Our Attention." *Blavity*, December 28, 2017. https://blavity.com/the-death-of-erica-garner-teaches-why-violence-against-the-black-community-still-needs-our-attention?category1=community-submitted&category2=news.

Williams, Kidada E. "Writing Victims' Personhoods and People into the History of Lynching." *Journal of the Gilded Age and Progressive Era* 20, no. 1 (2021): 148–56.

Williams, Lucy. "Grieving Critically: Barack Obama and the Counter-eulogy." *Political Research Quarterly* 75, no. 2 (2022): 307–20.

Williams, Rhaisa Kameela. "Toward a Theorization of Black Maternal Grief as Analytic." *Transforming Anthropology* 24, no. 1 (2016): 17–30.

Windell, Maria. *Transamerican Sentimentalism and Nineteenth Century US Literary History*. Oxford: Oxford University Press, 2020.

Wolfe, Patrick. "Settler Colonialism and the Elimination of the Native." *Journal of Genocide Research* 8, no. 4 (2006): 387–409.

Wolfley, Jeanette. "Jim Crow, Indian Style: The Disenfranchisement of Native Americans." *American Indian Law Review* 16, no. 1 (1991): 167–202.

Wolin, Sheldon S. "Fugitive Democracy." *Constellations* 1, no. 1 (1994): 11–25.

———. *Politics and Vision: Continuity and Innovation in Western Political Thought*. Expanded ed. Princeton, NJ: Princeton University Press, 2004.

Wood, Amy Louise. *Lynching and Spectacle: Witnessing Racial Violence in America, 1890–1940*. Durham, NC: University of North Carolina Press, 2011.

Woodly, Deva. *Reckoning: Black Lives Matter and the Democratic Necessity of Social Movements*. New York: Oxford University Press, 2021.

Woodruff, Mandi. "The Income Gap between Blacks and Whites Has Only Gotten Worse since the 1960s." *Business Insider*, August 29, 2013. www.businessinsider.com/the-income-gap-between-blacks-and-whites-2013-8.

Woubshet, Dagmawi. *The Calendar of Loss: Race, Sexuality, and Mourning in the Early Era of AIDS*. Baltimore: Johns Hopkins University Press, 2015.

Yellin, Jean Fagan. *Harriet Jacobs: A Life*. New York: Basic Civitas Books, 2004.

INDEX

A NOTE ON THE TYPE

This book has been composed in Arno, an Old-style serif typeface in the classic Venetian tradition, designed by Robert Slimbach at Adobe.

www.ingramcontent.com/pod-product-compliance
Lightning Source LLC
LaVergne TN
LVHW091028220125
801867LV00008B/335

* 9 7 8 0 6 9 1 2 4 3 0 4 7 *